# GLOBAL INFORMATION
# AND WORLD COMMUNICATION

# Global Information
# and World Communication

## New Frontiers in International Relations

Hamid Mowlana

**SAGE Publications**
London • Thousand Oaks • New Delhi

First edition 1986
Second edition 1997

 SAGE Publications Ltd
6 Bonhill Street
London EC2A 4PU

SAGE Publications Inc.
2455 Teller Road
Thousand Oaks, California 91320

SAGE Publications India Pvt Ltd
32, M-Block Market
Greater Kailash – I
New Delhi 110 048

**British Library Cataloguing in Publication data**

A catalogue record for this book is available from the British Library.

ISBN 0 7619 5256 X
ISBN 0 7619 5257 8 (pbk)

**Library of Congress catalog record available**

Typeset by Mayhew Typesetting, Rhayader, Powys
Printed in Great Britain by Biddles Ltd, Guildford, Surrey

To the memory of my parents,
who first taught me the importance of
communication and its meaning

# Contents

# Preface to the Revised Edition

The view informing this book is that the world society in general and international relations in particular can only be understood through a study of the messages and communication facilities that belong to it. It is also a thesis of this book that the new international relations is more than the political and economic relations among its components. Culture and communication are the fundamental aspects of the process and must be included in the foci of the analysis.

This study, therefore, takes a broader view of the international flow of information than the traditional analysis of mass media messages and communication technologies. It takes an integrative approach to international communication by examining both the human and technological dimensions of global information. In addition to reviewing the works undertaken by communication researchers, it draws considerably on the studies conducted in such areas as economics, political science, sociology, cultural anthropology, and international relations. It is my hope that this enlarged vision will stimulate research in the less conventional areas of international studies and will encourage integration of the diverse aspects of the study of global information flow.

The purpose of the revised edition is to present major areas of international communication in its broadest sense and to explore the vast territories of global information. The revolution in communication and transportation technologies has altered how government, citizens, business, and industry must perform in an international environment. Today international communications is not merely concerned with state actors or transnational corporations. Individual and group flows across national boundaries are equally relevant, especially since the activities involving transborder human flow has grown exponentially since World War II.

Besides the intrinsic growth of international communication as a field of study, drastic world events have also affected its organizational, educational, and practical issues. During the last decade since the publication of the first edition of this volume, we have witnessed the continual upheaval of world politics. Events including the end of the Cold War bi-polar system, the collapse of the Soviet Union and its allied regimes in Eastern Europe, the impact of ethnicity in many parts of the world, and the revival of Islamic movements elsewhere have all challenged basic assumptions and theories of international relations.

For these reasons, it has become necessary to recast the substance and forms of a number of chapters for this edition. In preparing this edition, I have taken into account the many suggestions from teachers and students who have used the book and were kind enough to write to me about its shortcomings and its strengths. Although the same issues and themes are addressed, the sequence of chapters has changed. Additionally, the revised edition is considerably larger than the original. As every teacher of international communication knows from extensive experience in the classroom, it is challenging to begin to formulate such a course. The word "communication" has no universal and unique meaning in its everyday usage. It varies from culture to culture and is defined and perceived differently based on the individuals' experience and understanding of it. The order in which the chapters are arranged is not binding for instructors or general readers, nor does it reflect the priority of issues. Through my own teaching experience, I have found this order to possess special merits, but, like most teachers of international communication, I frequently vary the sequence. The way this book is used as a text will undoubtedly depend on the standards and background of the students.

In short, the continual acceptance and generous reception accorded to the previous four hardcover reprints of this book have encouraged publication of this newly revised edition. The first edition of this book presented an integrated notion of international communication and a new conceptualization of power, thus providing readers with important tools for thinking about issues such as consolidation and mergers in world communication systems, the erosion of state power and national sovereignty. Today, the problems of development and participation, the questions of cultural identity, and the scores of other subjects related to the myths and realities of the "information revolution" have moved to the top of the global agenda. The book anticipated the collapse of the Soviet system and the many political and social debates currently facing Western industrialized nations. Moreover, cutting-edge issues, ranging from the emerging superhighways to human rights, that now resound in a rapidly changing international environment were raised in this volume more than a decade ago.

In the closing decades of the twentieth century the cultural dimensions of world politics have reached their greatest prominence. It now seems more imperative than ever to discuss global issues, not only in explicit economic, geopolitical, and military terms, but equally in the context of cultural communication and information struggle. This revised edition is a step in that direction.

Segments of the following articles have been incorporated in this new edition with the kind permission of the publishers: Hamid Mowlana and Ginger Smith, "Trends in Telecommunications and the Tourism Industry: Coalition, Regionalism, and International Welfare Systems," in J.R. Brent Ritchie and Donald E. Hawkins, Frank Go, Douglas Frechtling, eds,

*World Travel and Tourism Review: Indicators, Trends and Issues*, Vol. 2, (New York: C.A.B. International, 1992), pp. 163–67; Hamid Mowlana, "The Communications Paradox," *The Bulletin of Atomic Scientists*, 51: 4 (July/August 1995), pp. 40–46; Hamid Mowlana and Ginger Smith, "Tourism in a Global Context: The Case of Frequent Traveler Programs," *Journal of Travel Research*, Winter 1993, pp. 20–27.

This space does not permit a description of the help and advice that I received from my many friends and colleagues who looked over and commented on this book throughout the last decade. My greatest debt, however, goes to my graduate assistants Kathleen Lewis-Workman, who kept a close hand on this project from its beginning, and Caroline Hayashi – together they made important and valuable contributions without which this edition would not have been feasible.

I would like to thank my production editor at Sage Publications, Pascale Carrington, and my copy editor, Justin Dyer, for their fine work. Additional thanks go to Sophie Craze for her encouragement and to Amitabh Dabla and Stefanie Leighton for their helpful assistance during the last stages of this project.

# 1

# World Politics in Transition: New Frontiers in International Relations

> Only tribes held together by group feeling can live in the desert.
>
> Ibn Khaldun (1332–1406)
> *The Muqaddimah* (An Introduction to History)

It was Ibn Khaldun, the great Islamic scholar and social philosopher, who centuries ago stressed that the individual human being cannot secure all the things necessary for his livelihood without cooperation with someone else. Thus, in his theory of social organization and in his discussion of cultural identity and intercultural relations, he pointed out that "proper order among men cooperating in such organization" as world society "can exist only when they are governed by justice in the form of restraining influence that keeps them from devouring each other."[1]

The center of Ibn Khaldun's world was man. His own monumental work was a "modest" contribution to the unfinished, and perhaps unfinishable, search to understand human society. Later developments and assumptions, however, colored the vocabulary of texts as well as methods of international and intercultural studies. An emergent field of knowledge in modern history is the study of "international relations." Three decades or so ago it was generally a peripheral subject because it was, in essence, descriptive of diplomatic history. In the last few decades it has become analytical, with new models based on systems, games, bargaining, decision making procedures, and multifarious other methods of approach.[2]

As the complexities of the modern world grew, it became fashionable in the literature to apply a variety of terms to the world stage as a whole, with such phrases as "international community" and "international system." It is, however, doubtful whether the aggregation of states alone possesses these common values and assumptions, which are by definition the essential conditions of the community, and whether or not the working of world society is in some way analogous to that of a mechanical system. The result has been to emphasize the tangible, the formal, and the measurable. Consequently, in the area of international and intercultural communication, the cultural and human components of international and societal relations have been overshadowed by technical, political, and economic aspects of the field. Today the field of international relations is in a stage of self-examination, participants searching for new directions and novel approaches. If the past is indicative, the passing traditional approaches to international relations, as well as some of the contemporary theorizing in the field, will be adequate guides to inquiry.

In the West, especially in the Anglo-Saxon tradition of liberalism, the "idealist" phase of international relations studies began immediately after World War I and was dominant for nearly a decade. It saw Western democratic theory as the cause of peace and forms of dictatorship as the cause of war. These ideas were embodied in the intellectual thinking of Woodrow Wilson, in the origin of the League of Nations, and in the institution of the Permanent Court of International Justice. The "idealist" phase took an historical and legalistic approach to the study of international relations phenomenon.

A second major approach to international relations study and theory found its roots in the works of Karl Marx,[3] and in Lenin's theory of imperialism.[4] It explained political power, the causes of war and conflict, and the entire phenomenon of international relations in terms of underlying economic forces. Its methods of inquiry rested on dialectical materialism and economic determinism. A product of Western philosophy and culture, this approach was, until recently, ironically ignored in the traditional literature of international relations produced in the United States and Britain. This "paradigm," however, remained the major intellectual formulation of international relations in the former Soviet Union and socialist countries, and among some people in less industrialized regions. Some derivations of this theory also became the guiding principles for the Left elsewhere who wished to analyze the phenomenon of international relations in terms of international political economy.

A third major approach to international relations, known popularly as the "realist" tradition, was, in major part, a direct outcome of World War II. Criticizing the idealism and utopianism of the early decades, it attempted to draw a clear line between "aspiration" and "reality." The major contributors were American and European scholars, among them E.H. Carr,[5] Harold Nicolson,[6] Hans J. Morgenthau,[7] and George F. Kennan.[8] Their fundamental proposition was the consideration of power in international relations. Drawing a distinction between domestic and international politics, they viewed nation-states or their decision makers as the most important actors in international relations. International relations was seen as struggle for power. Although new variations of realist as well as radical political economy paradigms have been identified under such terms as neorealism, interdependency, and dependency in an effort to demonstrate the existing complexities of international systems, these new perspectives are still based upon the power-oriented economic and political models.

Whereas the realist tradition has remained the most influential among policy makers and the students of international relations, it has not escaped the harsh criticism of many writers and scholars who were trained under the tutelage of those who shaped it. Mathematical, communication, socio-psychological, linguistic, and other behavioral science models and theories were developed to test or reject some aspects of the realist approach, and to bring about scientific understanding of international relations. The emphasis was on the "is" and not on the "ought." The behavioral movement of the 1950s and 1960s was largely responsible for generating a good number of models and data in the form of events analysis, interaction and information flow, decision-making analysis, game theory and deterrence strategy, and the linkage of domestic policy to international politics.

A recent analysis of international research, however, supports the controversial claim that "the realist paradigm has dominated the field of international relations since the early fifties, and that this paradigm has not been very successful in explaining behavior."[9] It further states "that most scholars in the field share a fundamental view of the world that was promulgated by the realist scholars."[10] If this is the case, it simply means that new basic assumptions or paradigms must be introduced into the study of international relations phenomena. Although there have been some attempts during the last decade to introduce new direction into the field, in terms of issue areas, world order studies, and the like, there seems to be no adequate theoretical or conceptual framework which could replace the dominant paradigm of current scholarship and policy formulation. The research of the last few years has been more successful in showing the inadequacies of the three major approaches just mentioned than creating or presenting a new one that could stand the test of time. Yet it is clear that the economic determinism school of thought, the political power-oriented tradition of the realist phase, and the post-realist and behavioralist approach all have certain commonalities:

1. they share a power-driven notion of international relations which is either political or economic or both;
2. they believe in the notion of nation-state as a "political" state;
3. they make communication and cultural factors subservient to political, economic, and technological superstructures;
4. they tend to classify international relations with natural and biological science; and
5. they tend to measure what is measurable, observable, and tangible.

These fundamental assumptions make it impossible to separate some of the world's most distinguished activities which are not in a simple freeback relationship to politics, work, and production.

It might be profitable, for example, to look at the notion of power as less a problem of governing and more a problem of cooperation, learning, and growth. Here, by applying a more general notion of power, a unified strategy of research can be explained as shown in Figure 1.1. Thus, the dimensions of power in both national and international systems can be viewed in two distinct but integrated, as well as related, categories of tangible and intangible resources available to the actors. The concept of power is defined in Figure 1.1 in terms of control over the particular base values as well as in terms of the flow of interchanges between the main

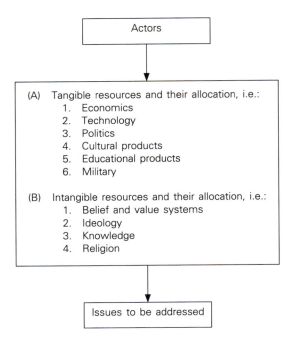

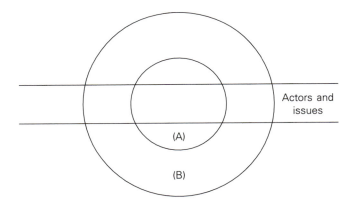

Figure 1.1   *Power unified strategy of research*

sectors of society reflecting the ability to act and to affect something. It is comprised of two dimensions: the access to necessary resources to act, and the ability and will to act. Here, central recognition is given to belief and value systems, or world views, which help determine the nature and parameters of action within and by each system. With such a framework one could specify what kinds of actors possessed what kinds of resources for defining, comprehending, and acting upon certain important issues of the day. Thus, power in national and international systems involves more than just the reallocation of economic, political, and technological values and bases. It involves multidimensional factors with authority, legitimacy, and will playing crucial roles. Only in this context can we hope that the real process of international relations and information flow will be adequately understood.

**International Communication as a Field of Study**

International communication as a field of study grew out of the traditions of international relations theories and policies described earlier. Today's impressive body of highly relevant and methodologically diverse research on international communication was shaped by both the human and the technological activities that took place during the last half century. With the spread of modern technology, especially in the field of communications, the last decade or so has witnessed countless books and articles on such topics as "the age of information," "information society," or "informatic society" – separating them neatly from the old categories of "agrarian society," "industrial society," and "post-industrial society" and assigning them functional paradigms. The trouble is that these categories do not fit the realities of many societies, including some of the ones that have been experimental laboratories for such functions. Cultural components of societies and human psychology are leading to such rapid changes in the process itself that scholars may well be falling behind in their analytical efforts.

A distinction must be made between the process of intercultural and international communication and the description and analysis of that process as a field of study. International and intercultural communication as a field of study is more easily defined than the process itself: a definition might adequately be obtained through a careful examination of the breadth and depth of the literature of the field. Definition of the process of international communication, on the other hand, has been complex and often rather ambiguous, as shown by the state of the field itself.[11] As in the general field of international relations, the central task in this area has been to describe, categorize, analyze, and theorize about the process. Meanwhile, these underlying assumptions about international relations in general and international communication in particular have generated an interesting and challenging debate on the role of communication with regard to cultural identity and intercultural communication.

The field of intercultural communication as an area of research and study, which has been growing during the last several decades and has now become a legitimate area of inquiry, cannot be separated from the broader perspective of international communication outlined in this book. The assumption that intercultural communication under different categories can be studied and analyzed without taking into account the political, economic, and technological boundaries is both naive and unrealistic. Intercultural communication in the modern global context cannot take place in a vacuum as much as the international communication in its narrow and orthodox sense cannot be understood without taking into account the cultural and linguistic context.

## Approaches to International Communication

From our analysis, we can thus conclude that four basic assumptions or approaches have characterized the activities of scholars, governments, media practitioners, and individual citizens in the field of international communication over the last half century. The idealistic-humanistic approach characterizes international communication as a means of bringing nations and peoples together and as a power to assist international organizations in the exercise of their services to the world community. As such, it strives toward increasing understanding among nations and peoples and toward the attainment of world peace. The process of communication here is seen in its most idealistic form.

A second approach, sometimes called political proselytization, sees international communication as propaganda, ideological confrontation, advertising, and the creation of myths and clichés. These are usually one-way communications and they all require central organizing authorities of some kind. They are thus imbued with a certain authoritarian, totalitarian character that makes it possible to manipulate human beings. This approach to international communication has dominated relations between and among states for the last several decades.

A third, increasingly visible approach is to view information in the international context as economic power. Here, its operation is more subtle, the message more subliminal. Overtly respectable international development projects, business ventures, marketing, trade, and technology transfer have characterized this approach and have usually resulted in the domination of weaker, peripheral nations. "Modernization" of less developed countries has in fact resulted in their conversion to Western ways and has made them more amenable to control by Western centers. This process, sometimes referred to as "Westoxification," by encouraging its converts to adopt non-indigenous forms of behaviors could result in a certain schizophrenic paralysis of creative power.

The fourth approach to international communication is to view information as political power. Here, information, in the form of news and data, is treated as a neutral, value-free commodity. A study of international mass media, the wire services, the production of literature, and cinema and television programs reveals a concentration of means in a few countries. When information is conveyed from one country to another, the cultural content of the source is conveyed, and that may not always be in the best interests of the recipient.

These four orientations characterize how states, scholars, and media practitioners have described the increasing capacities of international communication over the last five decades. Needless to say, the division is not mutually exclusive. The four approaches, especially the latter three, are interrelated in varying degrees. For example, student exchange may serve the idealistic-humanistic, political proselytization, or economic power aspects of international communication.

None of these four approaches has escaped criticism. The idealistic-humanistic approach in particular suffers from certain problems. First, it is impossible to achieve the objective transfer of information and values. Every person's knowledge and value system is unique and reflects the accumulated image of all the messages he or she has received. There are no facts, only a changeable value system and images that are malleable and open to socializing influences. As a result, an individual's objectivity is mercurial, unstable, and subjective. Second, whose ideal of international peace and world community are we talking about? Interpretations vary, and unless there is a consensus of an ideal world, it is impossible for the currently dominant ideas to escape the opposing camp's accusations of ideological imperialism. Third, there is a certain inherent defect in equating universal agreement with universal good. Human progress springs from individuals who disagree with the norm, who initiate new lines of thought – creative ideas that are tangential to prevailing opinions. All great truths begin as heresy. When a particular world view or ideological system is proposed as an ideal system, it becomes fossilized as the status quo and resists progressive innovations. This can ultimately result in war, for war is not the extension of dispute, but a refusal to dispute. Fourth, the rational pursuit of human good that idealism demands is an unrealistic expectation from beings whose rational faculty is often overwhelmed by irrationalism and emotion.

If the benign approach of idealism/humanism has been criticized, so too have the three relatively malevolent approaches. International political proselytization has led to a distrust of international media, whose purpose is assumed, sometimes incorrectly, to be manipulative. The "war of ideas" has been charged by ideological rivalry and fueled by intolerance among nations and hatred among peoples. International communication has been guilty of aiding and abetting international tensions, if not intentionally, then at least by not promoting peaceful solutions and not conferring legitimacy on the peacemakers.

In the arena of economic and political power, the last two approaches in this model, information has assumed its place beside petroleum, strategic metals, and uranium as an international resource to be bartered, boycotted, and blackmailed. Megabyte streams of digitalized data have become the source of power in our information-based society. Information means power and its manipulation can have far-reaching effects on economic, social, and political development. For example, broadcasting a television program provides an unparalleled ability to manipulate the collective human psyche. The ability of dominant providers to reach around the world has grown by leaps and bounds. The opportunities of the individual to communicate with others have perhaps increased a hundredfold – if he or she lives in a country rich enough to afford a communications structure, and is rich enough to take advantage of it. But the ability of the truly elite to affect the world has been multiplied a millionfold. Few are wealthy enough to go head-to-head with Ted Turner's Cable News Network (CNN). In short, "global" is not "universal," and "global communication" does not mean "universal communication." More frightening is that the trend toward communications oligarchy is growing.

The call for equal access to information and resources has been replaced by a worldwide movement toward a market economy and capitalism, headed by the United States and the European Union. The disintegration of the Third World as a political force and the collapse of the Soviet Union as a major competitive power in the international system have accelerated the process of the globalization of goods and commodities and, with that, the emergence of a new global information infrastructure.

**International Political Communication**

The diplomatic flow of information has been one of the most traditional forms of international communication. Historically, it can be traced back to the emergence of modern nation-states and the international political system. The traditional style of diplomacy was characterized in the early years by a small group of national elites, using interpersonal forms of communication. But with the advent of modern communication technology and the emergence of nongovernmental actors, a new style of diplomacy arose, one more oriented toward the masses and the public. Researchers have recognized this new flow of information as "political persuasive communication, propaganda," and more recently as "public diplomacy."[12]

One important feature of this new form of communication was the importance placed on public opinion.[13] Technological advancement in communication allowed governments to direct their messages to large national, as well as international, audiences. For example, the development of radio, and more recently television and satellite systems, led to the implementation of international broadcasting. National boundaries were no longer barriers to international political and diplomatic messages. This was only the beginning. Almost all governments around the world set up "information" and "propaganda" agencies, hired public relations firms, and organized regular and systematic "briefing" meetings and lavish diplomatic parties in order to influence their foreign and domestic audiences.

The impact of propaganda during World War I and the development of new techniques in persuasive communication dominated the earlier studies of international political communication. As propaganda and psychological warfare played an important role in World War II, the study of international political communication became a well-established field of inquiry in many universities and institutions around the world. In the post-World War II period, research in this area was greatly influenced by the continuation of the Cold War.[14] The ideological struggle between the United States and the Soviet Union produced yet another round of research. This "war of ideas" was influenced later by several factors, among them the development of sophisticated atomic weaponry, the rise of the new nation-state and the non-aligned movement in the Third World, and the increase of international economic and commercial flow and the resulting exportation of culture. The major focus was now directed towards a "global elite," and the growing number of technocratic intelligentsia, increasing numbers of whom were linked by many common factors transcending national, cultural, or regional differences.

The major strategy of international political communication in the early decades of this century was the blatant use of propaganda. In the years following World War I and continuing to the end of World War II, a new communication strategy was developed. Encouraged by the potential applications of future propaganda, governments enlisted the cooperation of communication and political scientists. The goal was now to develop analytical frameworks. Strategic warfare was now aimed at destroying a country's infrastructural basis as well as the morale of the population for carrying on the war, as was clearly shown during the Persian Gulf War. The more recent strategy, dating back about three decades and continuing until the present, is a structural and sociological strategy. Its purpose is multidimensional – political, economic, and cultural. Now, the process has been well recognized and commented upon by philosophers, sociologists, and scientists alike.

"There is no nonsense so arrant that it cannot be made the creed of the vast majority by adequate governmental action," the British philosopher Bertrand Russell wrote about the nightmarish possibilities of propaganda.[15] In the chilling view of French sociologist Jacques Ellul, this is probably a fait accompli in modern societies.[16] Here, propaganda comes across as a sociological phenomenon rather than as something created by certain people for certain purposes. The aim of propaganda is no longer to change adherence to a doctrine. It does not normally address the individual's intelligence, for intellectual persuasion is long and uncertain, and the transition to action more so. Rather, it tries to make the individual cling irrationally to a process of action because action makes propaganda's effect irreversible. Through the process of rationalization, previous obedience to propaganda obliges future obedience. Thus pre-propaganda, which prepares one for action, becomes active propaganda, after the individual has been converted to action.

Propaganda's internal characteristics are its knowledge of the individual's psychological terrain, and its aim, which seeks not to elevate but to make one subservient. It must express the fundamental currents of modern technological society that humanity's goal in life is happiness, that human nature is naturally good, that history develops in endless progression, and that everything is matter. The collective myth of Science, History, Work, Happiness, Nation, Youth, and Hero is an inter-supporting network, and must be used.

Ellul has listed several categories of propaganda: political and socio-logical, agitation and integration, vertical and horizontal, rational and irrational. On all of these levels, propaganda is a condition in which the existing political, economic, and sociological factors allow an ideology to penetrate individuals or masses. It produces a progressive adaptation to a certain order of things, a certain concept of human relations, which sub-liminally molds individuals and makes them conform to society. This propaganda has profound effects: not only are the propagandees' attitudes and opinions modified, but so are their impulses and mental and emotional structures. It causes psychological crystallization; a refusal to listen to new ideas; an alienated and artificial life of obedience to someone outside oneself; alternate exaltation and depression; and mithridatism, which is a tendency to react to the smallest dose of propaganda.

The sociopolitical effects are similarly deep: once used as a means of spreading ideology externally or fortifying it internally, propaganda then obeys its own laws and becomes autonomous. In this context, ideology not used by propaganda – like humanism – becomes ineffective. The state must become a propagandist because of the need to dispense information, the need for an all-embracing truth, and myths of democratic participation that hide intolerance and minority suppression – ethnocentric attempts to preserve the state's "way of life."

Ellul must be regarded as a Cassandra by British communication scien-tist Colin Cherry, who states that the fear of propaganda is a gross over-estimation of the power of television, radio, and the press. To Cherry, even a harmless statement of one's view is propaganda, and its connotations are not necessarily negative. He goes so far as to state that "propaganda can be a vital factor in human emancipation."[17]

It would be unfair to compare Cherry's view, which makes only a passing mention of propaganda, to the complex and holistic analysis pro-vided by Ellul. However, Ellul seems to stop short of suggesting alterna-tives and solutions, leaving us intelligently unhappy. This is partly justified by Ellul's theological existentialism, which leaves the onus of choice and salvation on the individual. The only escape is individual transcendence.[18]

Yet the importance and crucial significance of international political communication, propaganda, and the new role that the ideological symbols play in international relations have been acknowledged by all the schools of international relations regardless of their political orientation. During the Cold War, Georgi Arbatov, a writer from the former Soviet Union whose work on this subject was mainly linked "with the world division into two socio-political systems" along the line of Marxist-Leninist theory, saw the "war of ideas in contemporary international relations" as "a feature characterizing precisely our epoch," which he said "has no precedent in history because the international relations in the transitional periods (i.e. in the period of transition from one socioeconomic formation to another) of the past had always developed under conditions in which world-wide social systems comparable with those in existence today did not and could not take shape."[19]

In the United States a generation ago, Harold Lasswell advocated the study of the international flow of information in determining the climate of international action.[20] Since part of the manipulative strategy of politics calls for mood control by the use of both communication and noncommunication, Lasswell focused his interest on analysis of the content of elite-to-elite and elite-to-nonelite media of communication in determining the distribution of common moods as well as the distribution of deviations.

During the last two decades, communication models and terminologies have been used in the study of integration at the international level by such scholars as Karl Deutsch, Richard Merritt, and Carl Clark.[21] International relations as a communication process has been discussed by Charles McClelland, Davis Bobrow, and others.[22] Communication models and information flow data have been used by Johan Galtung and his associates in the study of imperialism and world systems.[23] As a result, there has been a shift toward a much more extensive and careful use of communication and information data in international political research.

New theoretical interests have stimulated researchers to use data about communication, mass media, public opinion, and attitude change. There have been attempts to borrow paradigms – mainly those of mediated stimulus, cognitive balance, and cybernetics – from psychology and related fields.[24] Some have gone still further by introducing ideas concerning the role of information in psychiatry and biology and its relation to international relations.[25] An important contribution has been made in the area of communication and foreign policy during the last three decades and the conception of how public opinion and national and international images are formed and held has been significantly changed by such scholars as Herbert Kelman, Kenneth Boulding, Bernard Cohen, Gabriel Almond, and Ralph White.[26]

In general, there seem to be three kinds of communication theory underpinning international relations research: mathematical, sociopsychological, and linguistic. Mathematical theory appears to be a growing field in the United States – the low level mathematical theories coming from empirical and theoretical research done on military strategy and nationalism. For example, Lewis Richardson, Anatol Rappaport, and Thomas Schelling have been as concerned with developing theories of conflict strategy as Karl Deutsch and David Easton have been with politics and international relations.[27] The sociopsychological tradition has had a tremendous influence on politics and mass media research, and the linguistic tradition has led to such areas as symbol analysis and content analysis.[28]

Information flow has been the essential ingredient in the evolution of international political economy, since information and institutional characteristics of any system are interdependent and thus cannot be separated. This information analysis as both a relevant aspect of conceptual models and a substantive area of inquiry in the fields of international political economy and comparative economics has been growing. For example, while Kenneth Boulding and Kenneth Arrow have written on the economics of knowledge and the knowledge of economics, Jan Tinbergen has explored the role of information in the modern international economic order.[29] Joseph Hirshleifer, Fritz Machlup, Egon Neuberger, and William Duffy are among those who have included information flow in their analysis of comparative economic systems as well as the decision-making process.[30] Dallas Smythe and Herbert Schiller are among those political economists who have written extensively on information technology and international communication.[31] Immanuel Wallerstein's world system perspective of political economy has stimulated a number of studies on the role of telecommunications and mass media in the political economy of cultural industry.[32]

## International Strategic Communication

A less explored area in the literature of international relations is the strategic aspect of information flow. Space age technology, to a considerable degree, has changed the traditional strategy and notion of land, sea, and air battlefields. The US government's plans to develop a space-based weapons system that used satellites to identify the former Soviet intercontinental ballistic missiles as they emerged from their silos is a case in point. The Agency (DARPA) at the US Department of Defense was given the mission to identify, create, and develop new technologies that could alter the balance of power between the two superpowers. The "Star Wars" project, as the media labeled it, was supposed to be a deterrent. Robert Cooper, director of DARPA, explained it this way:

> I personally feel that there is a role for military systems in space, a demonstrated role so far, certainly in communications, navigation and surveillance, meteorology. But as far as placing destructive devices in space, it's not clear yet whether it's ever going to be desirable to do that.[33]

Further, during the Cold War the Pentagon completed a strategic master plan to give the United States the capability of winning a protracted nuclear war with the former Soviet Union. According to the press report, "One consequence of this planning has been a commitment of $18 billion to provide a communication system that could endure such protracted nuclear warfare."[34] In short, increasingly accurate missile technology and sophisticated means of communications, coupled with military satellites now in orbit, gave confidence and support to these projected or planned strategies. The Soviet Union, of course, had its own military-oriented space projects that had not yet been publicized.

Indeed, as the collapse of the Soviet Union and the emergence of the so-called "post-Cold War era" demonstrated, these technologies have now become alternative security systems. The ability of the United States and its allies to use modern communication technologies as a major strategic advantage in the Persian Gulf War is indeed a case in point. Yet, the fact remains that non-weapon, sensory communication and computer technology are challenging the strategic balance of power, making the nation-state system less secure and in many ways precipitating a new round in the arms race, especially in such strategic areas as the Persian Gulf.

A monograph discussing the transparency revolution – sensory, communication, and computing – concludes that "effective control of space by one state would lead to planet-wide hegemony."[35] This transparency revolution, which has "created a rudimentary planetary nervous system, fragments of a planetary cybernetic, has militarized yet another natural feature of the planet lying beyond the effective sovereignty of the nation state – the electromagnetic spectrum."[36] In ancient times, Persia's extensive transportation and postal services were the indispensable nerve system in its war with Greece. During the nineteenth century, Britain's control of the underseas cable network was responsible for its naval hegemony in the world. In the twentieth century, the first ocean-spanning satellites enabled the American president to pick up bombing targets in Vietnam in the morning and see photo reconnaissance images of the results in the evening.

The strategic importance of space communication technology has obvious economic dimensions as well. For example,

> INTELSAT provides a system on which about a quarter of the communication traffic either originates or terminates in the United States, a system consisting of billions of dollars worth of satellites manufactured by US firms and a system which provides homes and businesses across America with inexpensive and efficient access to virtually every place on Earth.[37]

At the same time, the globalization of national economies and the fact that a quarter of worldwide economic activities are now involved with international trade and services give further incentives for a country to have a leading edge in communication technology.

The privatization and proliferation of international satellite systems were opposed by many, including Third World countries, because, as was reported by the director of INTELSAT, Richard Colino, in 1986, they were likely to serve only the most lucrative heavier routes of United States–European communication, and doubly harm the Third World.

> A reduction in use of the system by the USA and other North Atlantic countries would correspondingly reduce their investment shares and thus increase the investment shares of the rest of the membership. Consequently, Third World countries would be required to increase their capital contributions as well as pay higher utilization charges if mainstream traffic were lost.[38]

Privatization and commercialization of the communication satellite systems were thus completed by the mid-1990s.

**International Economic Communication**

Information technologies and information-based products and services have become central to the economy as a whole. Today, telecommunications is a vital component of any national economy, and, indeed, of the nations' way of life. Rapid and efficient communication – initially by telegraph, and later by telephone and transportation systems such as railroad – was important in the nineteenth century in the development of national, regional, and imperial powers. As economic markets become more and more internationalized and globalized, many nations' domestic communication systems are important in permitting the domestic-based firms and companies to operate globally and transnationally. It is not surprising, therefore, that many nations are currently exploring the use of telecommunications, and more recently the integrated versions of telecommunications technologies under such terms as National Information Infrastructure (NII) – as in the case of the United States – to overcome some of the most important social, economic, and cultural problems and as a tool to promote the existing national and global economic systems. In the international context, the current US effort to develop the so-called information superhighway under NII has been expanded and developed into the Global Information Infrastructure (GII) by the European Union as well as the Asia-Pacific region and has been endorsed by the International Telecommunications Union (ITU).

Information as a form of wealth and national resource has now brought about new definitions of "property" and considerable modifications of existing antitrust regulations and telecommunications laws as demonstrated in the United States and elsewhere in Europe and many other countries. Multinational and transnational firms now require different types of information and information technology to operate and manipulate markets around the world than those utilized conventionally by domestic firms. Today data banks are all multinational in structure and content: decision models involve many sets of national and regional legal frameworks and communication channels cross international boundaries.

Indeed information and communication technologies now provide an important segment of transnational businesses. As hardware and communications markets continue to develop globally, there is corresponding opportunity to develop software markets. The latter should be thought of in broader terms than merely computer programs for hardware service. They include management systems, data for data banks, and technological know-how. The intermingling of the hardware and software components of communication systems as well as the prominence given to the distribution aspects of communication is well illustrated in a number of major consolidations, mergers, and takeovers in the worldwide communication and information industries. For example, IBM has a huge distribution network through which it sells everything from mainstream computers to business consulting services. Yet the problem is that IBM for years lacked exciting software, thus alienating many potential customers, especially in the personal computer market. It was precisely on this point that IBM stunned its competitors as well as its prey when it made an offer of $3.3 billion in a bid to acquire the Lotus Development Corporation, a large software company. Lotus of course could not re-create IBM's distribution network, but it could create something even better – a computer network. The same phenomenon of software and hardware marriage can be observed when one views the numerous consolidations and mergers between the cable and telephone companies and the television and film industries.

Over the last half a century, much of the modern information and communication technologies such as computers, satellites, space and aviation know-how were developed and used by the military–industrial complex. Today the real pay-off would be the ability to transfer these technologies to new products and services required by society in terms of its domestic and social needs. The world is clearly divided into "have" and "have-not" peoples as the geographically unequal distribution of physical resources becomes further sharpened by a corresponding inequitable distribution of information and knowledge.

Domestic and foreign intellectual property laws – principally the laws covering patents, copyrights and trademarks – are now becoming altered as a result of the development of modern technologies and expansion of global products. To understand the legal and political pressures that new technologies place on the intellectual property systems, we must understand their unique capabilities. The economic stakes of the new technologies are particularly high for the copyright industries – publishing and other industries that rely on the legal protection provided by copyright laws. Information is also a dominant force in our lives, socially, financially, and economically. In the United States and many of the world's industrial and information-oriented societies an enormous amount of information is communicated and commercialized in the form of words through electronic media. In the 1970s, for example, it was estimated that the American population was exposed to about 8.7 trillion words each day through electronic media such as radio, television, newspaper, books, and magazines. This figure has been rising as a result of new computer-related networks at the average rate of 1.2 percent per year. The US government's budget for information technology alone has risen from $9.2 billion in fiscal year 1982 to $15.2 billion in 1986 to an estimated $30 billion in 1996.

The global economy is now truly developing into an information-based economy. Such development and its effects include: the increasing flow of information and information-based products and services among nations; the growing economic importance of information and related products and services within and between nations; the increasing cultural and political significance of information and related products and services; the emergence of new information-based products and services that do not correspond to traditional categories; the increasing difficulty of enforcing intellectual property rights on the international level; and the growing convergence of international intellectual property issues with other international issues. Although the economic implications of modern communication technologies are often discussed within the context of modern urban settings, their impact on rural areas should not be ignored. Economic development in rural areas will not only affect national economic performance, it will also help determine how well a nation fares in an increasingly competitive global economy. Indeed, the economic and social effects of a nation's communication infrastructure are determined not only by its overall technical capabilities but by their availability to the public as a whole and their pattern and directions of use.

The 1993 study by the US Department of Commerce on *Globalization of the Mass Media* acknowledged that modern information technologies are "vehicles through which ideas, images, and information are disbursed across the United States and throughout the world" and are therefore "powerful agent[s] for political and social change." The data, compiled by the US Department of Commerce Bureau for Economic Analysis, indicated that US exports of motion pictures and television programming exceeded inputs by $2.1 billion in 1991. According to data collected by the Motion Pictures Association of America, which uses the firm-based approach rather than the country-based approach, the US motion pictures and television programming industry exported, on a worldwide basis, over $7 billion of motion picture and television programming in 1991. It is estimated that these figures will increase by the end of the 1990s as US cultural industry products continue to expand around the world. The world is being engulfed in a tide of American culture-inspired secularism. For example, in the last 20 years as Latin American countries have adopted free market economic policies, American consumerism has pervaded these countries as never before with much more force than was feared in the 1960s.[39] An even more extreme example of the spread of American consumerism is in Canada, which has struggled with the American culture "invasion" for almost all of its history, without success. In Canada, approximately 95 percent of the films and the revenue generated from those films are American; 66 percent of all the books and 80 percent of magazines are also non-Canadian.[40] The extent of this cultural penetration exists despite a number of protections and subsidies designed to guard and preserve Canadian culture.[41]

Today, electronic communication is defined not only as the traditional, centralized, broadcast media – radio and television – but also by computer networks, fax machines, tape recorders, image recorders, and desktop publishing. Modern communication is developing along two fronts, each creating its own parallel and yet contradictory phenomena. On the one hand, there is the promise of the globalization of personal communications, with its potential to empower individuals. On the other hand, there is the reality of globalization: continuing centralization of mass communications, with fewer players (often international corporations) controlling the choke-points, leaving the overwhelming majority of the world's people increasingly marginalized on the periphery. The increasing concentration of the world's communication and information systems in the hands of a few leads to the domination of the world's networks by a handful of powerful conglomerates which become the lords of the global village and constitute vast communication empires that totally eliminate national boundaries. It is important to note that the increasing concentration of wealth in the hands of a few is hurting not only developing nations but developed countries as well. The impact of growing competition on the incomes of Americans is a "winner-take-all" economy which is widening the gap between rich and poor and concentrating incomes and wealth in fewer hands.[42] Another important aspect of the shrinking global village and the dense concentration of wealth and poverty is the question of human rights, which include collective and individual rights as well as public and private rights.

Nevertheless, the newest communication technologies can be molded into their users' images. Rather than replacing indigenous communications and culture, they can exist side by side with them. The same local information that was not economical to broadcast to an entire country suddenly becomes valuable and pertinent when the medium of dissemination is a computer bulletin board. These new communication technologies can encourage increased participation and equality. By creating an alternative to the temporarily dominant mass media channels, these forms of communication offer the promise of preserving indigenous culture in a new form, rather than simply replacing it with an inappropriate new Western paradigm. Of course, such progress is limited. While it may be far cheaper to run an electronic bulletin board with a $2,000 computer rather than to run a multimillion-dollar broadcast network, $2,000 is still more than a year's pay for most people. Moreover, many of the necessary electronic infrastructures for decentralized communications, such as telephone lines, are centered in the richest handful of nations. But at least there is hope – and that is something that no one could have said a decade ago.

## Intercultural Communication and Conflict

One characteristic of our age is that small nations, more than ever, are now challenging the world political and economic structures. The experience in Vietnam and the Islamic revolution in Iran during the 1970s were only two dramatic examples of both political and ideological conflict between the superpowers on the one hand and smaller countries on the other. The post-Cold War surge in so-called "ethnic conflict" is the continuation of a trend that began in the 1960s. The end of the Cold War contributed to the long-term trend of state conflict by increasing the number of nation-states experiencing such a power transition. It can be argued that because the great powers have a high stake in international system maintenance, and because they must maintain a posture to satisfy their domestic political, military, and economic elites, they have little interest under the existing

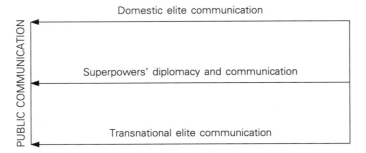

Figure 1.2    *Inter-elite communication and the public*

international system to make any revolutionary and fundamental changes in the international communication structure as we now know it.

Thus the present international communication and information flow may be described as the E phenomenon (see Figure 1.2). Here, information flow and communication usually occur horizontally among and between the elite structure in three distinct and somewhat international levels: (1) domestic elite communication, socialization, and policy debate; (2) great powers' elite diplomacy and "cooperation," "detente," or acquiescence; and (3) international and transnational elites, socialization, and activities.

This somewhat global intra-elite communication and information flow tends to take a vertical and downward direction to the public. This is not to say, by any means, that there is no intra-elite competition, but simply to indicate that the growing conservative and system-maintenance orientation of these three levels of elite activities in international communication and international relations tend to generate a highly similar vertical line of messages, which seem to grow more in the direction of a global vertical line if we view the present international system as a whole. There are, of course, certain exceptions to this on a specific functional level, but generally this has been a major characteristic of international relations since the mid-1960s.

Until the fall of the Soviet Union, competition and conflict between the superpowers took different forms and contents. Since a war between the major powers would have meant global destruction, and because of the development of sophisticated atomic weapons a total victory was no longer possible for either power, two important poles of international military, diplomatic, technological, and intellectual communications emerged, each trying to maintain, protect, and, if possible, advance its dominance over the global society by controlling and manipulating information and symbols. Access to domestic and international communication channels became the major goal for advancing the perceptions of military, economic, and cultural superiority. In short, communications hardware and software became instruments in globalizing the Cold War and "detente" systems, often with correlation of the middle-level powers or even the small powers, who either had no front or unity of their own independent from the superpowers, or were in such a state of flux that they tended to ally themselves with one camp or the other on a number of issues and fronts. In such a system of international relations, agenda setting is the main source of power. In the last two decades, as a result of nationalism, revolution, ethnicity, and religio-political movements around the world, the monopoly of the great powers' agenda setting systems has been constantly challenged and in some cases even reduced.

Because the control over the means of international communication is expensive and subject to economies of scale, there is little room for smaller countries to inject themselves into the increasing global communications markets. Today, the world's seven richest nations – the United States, Britain, Canada, France, Germany, Italy, and Japan – control not only the bulk of the world's wealth, but also the bulk of its future. But even within these rich countries there is concentration of wealth, and smaller countries such as France and Canada fear that their own cultures will be overtaken by the American cult of commercialism. In the global society, those who hold mastery of information and ready capital, rather than military might, dictate the course of the world. This so-called globalization of the mass media combined with the globalization of the economy has resulted in the production and the distribution of television, video, and other cultural industry products that have led not only to the homogeneity of the products but also to the reproduction of violent programs across national boundaries just because they are simply inexpensive and have the ability to cross cultural barriers.

We have entered a period of challenging and chaotic digital transformation. The result will be a redefinition of international politics in terms of communication and cultural activities. The unpredictability of international events and the insecurity of the major powers, are no longer necessarily masters of their own fates, are included in this unsettling reality, as are the erosion of the legitimacy of the nation-state system and the increasing demands for change from smaller nations and groups. It is neither an "end of ideology," as American sociologist Daniel Bell predicted some year ago, nor the "end of history" that one conservative commentator, Francis Fukuyama, more recently noted. Simply put, history clearly is open; quests for new ideologies and a new world order have begun.

The agenda setting of the day – what to table and what to think about – becomes more important than what position one must take about the issues that are confronting the world community. The conflict is just as much about the priority and primacy of the issues as about the nature of the issues themselves. Thus control over information flow and communication must accompany access to material and natural resources. It is only under a powerful communication and information system that one can determine the parameters of international security debates. In short, conceptualization of world, regional, and national problems is the basis for political, economic, and military mobilization.

## Notes

1. Ibn Khaldun, *The Mugaddimah: An Introduction to History*, translated from Arabic by Franz Rosenthal (London: Routledge and Kegan Paul, 1967), pp. x, 97.
2. For a sample of works in the field of international relations see: E.H. Carr, *International Relations Between the Two World Wars, 1919–1939* (New York: Harper and Row, 1966); Inis L. Claude, *Power and International Relations* (New York: Random House, 1962); Ernest B. Haas, *Beyond the Nation State* (Standford, CA: Standford University Press, 1968); John W. Burton, *International Relations: A General Theory* (Cambridge: Cambridge University Press, 1965); and his *Conflict and Communication* (London: Macmillan, 1969); Stanley Hoffman, *Contemporary Theory in International Politics* (Englewood Cliffs, NJ: Prentice Hall, 1960); K.J. Holsti, *International Politics: A Framework of Analysis* (Englewood Cliffs, NJ: Prentice Hall, 1977); Morton A. Kaplan, *Systems and Process in International Politics* (New York: Wiley, 1957); James Rosenau and Sidney Verba, eds, *The International System* (Princeton, NJ: Princeton University Press, 1961); Joyce Kolko and Gabriel Kolko, *The Limits of Powers* (New York: Harper and Row, 1972); Charles A. McClelland, *Theory and the International System* (New York: Macmillan, 1966); Hans J. Morgenthau, *Politics Among Nations* (New York: Knopf, 1973); Anatol Rappaport, *Strategy and Conscience* (New York: Schocken Books, 1964); Richard N. Rosecrance, *Actions and Reactions in World Politics* (Boston: Little, Brown, 1963); J. David Singer, ed., *Quantitative International Politics* (New York: Free Press, 1968); Glen H. Snyder and Paul Diesing, *Conflict Among Nations: Bargaining, Decision-Making, and System Structure in International Crisis* (Princeton, NJ: Princeton University Press, 1977); Kenneth N. Waltz, *A Theory of International Politics* (Reading, MA: Addison-Wesley, 1979); and Dina A. Zinnes, *Contemporary Research in International Relations: A Perspective and a Critical Appraisal* (New York: Free Press, 1976).
3. Karl Marx, *Capital*, 3 volumes (Moscow: Foreign Language Publishing House, 1959).
4. V.I. Lenin, *Imperialism: The Highest Stage of Capitalism* (New York: International Publishers Company, 1939).
5. E.H. Carr, *The Twenty Years' Crisis, 1919–1939: An Introduction to the Study of International Relations* (New York: Harper and Row, 1939).
6. Harold Nicolson, *Diplomacy* (London: Oxford University Press, 1939).
7. Hans J. Morgenthau, *Scientific Man vs. Power Politics* (Chicago: University of Chicago Press, 1946) and his *Politics Among Nations* (New York: Knopf, 1948).
8. George F. Kennan, *American Diplomacy* (New York: Mentor, 1952).
9. John A. Vasquez, *The Power of Power Politics* (New Brunswick, NJ: Rutgers University Press, 1983), p. xi.
10. Ibid., p. xii.
11. Hamid Mowlana, "The Communication Dimension of International Studies in the United States: A Quantitative Assessment," *International Journal of Communication Research* (University of Cologne), 1: 1 (Winter, 1974), pp. 3–22; also Hamid Mowlana, "Trends in Research on International Communication in the United States," *Gazette*, XIX: 2 (1973), pp. 79–90.
12. For example, Richard L. Merritt, ed., *Communication in International Politics* (Urbana, IL: University of Illinois Press, 1972); W. Phillips Davison, *International Political Communication* (New York: Praeger, 1965); and Glen H. Fisher, *Public Diplomacy and the Behavioral Sciences* (Bloomington, IN: University of Indiana Press, 1972).
13. See Walter Lippman, *Public Opinion* (New York: Free Press, 1922); Daniel Katz, Dorwin Cartwright, Samuel Eldersveld, and Alfred McClung Lee, eds, *Public Opinion and Propaganda* (New York: Holt, Rinehart and Winston, 1954); and Bernard Berelson and Morris Janowitz, eds, *Public Opinion and Communication* (Glencoe, IL: Free Press, 1950).
14. Harold D. Lasswell, Daniel Lerner, and Hans Speier, eds, *Propaganda and Communication in World History*, Vol. III, *A Pluralizing World in Formation* (Honolulu: University of Hawaii Press, 1980); George N. Gordon and Irving A. Falk, *The War of Ideas* (New York: Hastings House, 1973); Georgi Arbatov, *The War of Ideas in Contemporary*

*International Relations* (Moscow: Progress Publishers, 1973); and Ralph K. White, "Images in the Context of International Conflict: Soviet Perceptions of the U.S. and USSR," in Herbert C. Kelman, ed., *International Behavior: A Socio-Psychological Analysis* (New York: Holt, Rinehart and Winston, 1965), pp. 238–76.

15. Bertrand Russell, *Unpopular Essays* (London: Penguin Books, 1950).

16. Jacques Ellul, *Propaganda: The Formation of Men's Attitudes* (New York: Alfred A. Knopf, 1965).

17. Colin Cherry, *World Communication: Threat or Promise?* (London: John Wiley-Interscience, 1971), p. 121.

18. Ellul, *Propaganda*, p. 257.

19. Arbatov, *The War of Ideas*, pp. 33–34.

20. Harold D. Lasswell, "The Climate of International Action," in Kelman, ed., *International Behavior*, pp. 337–353.

21. See Karl W. Deutsch, *Political Community and the North Atlantic Area* and his *International Political Communities: An Anthology* (Garden City, NY: Doubleday, 1966); Richard L. Merritt, *The Growth of American Community: 1735–1775* (New Haven, CT: Yale University Press, 1964); Carl Clark and Richard L. Merritt, "European Community and Intra-European Communications: The Evidence of Mail Flows," International Studies Association Conference, Atlanta, Georgia, March 18–31, 1984.

22. Charles A. McClelland, *Theory and the International System* (New York: Macmillan, 1966); Davis Bobrow, "Transfer of Meaning Across National Boundaries," in Merritt, ed., *Communication in International Politics*, pp. 33–62.

23. Johan Galtung, "A Structural Theory of Imperialism," *Journal of Peace Research*, 8: 2 (1971), pp. 81–118.

24. Karl W. Deutsch, *The Nerves of Government: Models of Political Communication and Control* (New York: Free Press, 1963); and Bobrow, "Transfer of Meaning Across National Boundaries," pp. 33–62.

25. Howard Rome, "Psychiatry and Foreign Affairs," and Bryant Wedge, "Training for Psychiatry in International Relations," *American Journal of Psychiatry*, 125 (1968); and Ralph Pettman, *Human Behavior and World Politics* (New York: St Martin's Press, 1975).

26. Kelman, *International Behavior*; Kenneth Boulding, *The Image* (Ann Arbor, MI: University of Michigan Press, 1965); Bernard Cohen, *The Press and Foreign Policy* (Princeton, NJ: Princeton University Press, 1963); Gabriel Almond, *The American People and Foreign Policy* (New York: Macmillan, 1961); Ralph K. White, *Nobody Wanted War* (New York: Doubleday Anchor Books, 1970).

27. Lewis Richardson, *Arms and Insecurity* (Chicago: University of Chicago Press, 1960); Anatol Rappaport, *Fights, Games, and Debates* (Ann Arbor, MI: University of Michigan Press, 1960); Thomas Schelling, *The Strategy of Conflict* (New York: Macmillan, 1963); Karl W. Deutsch, *Nationalism and Social Communication* (Cambridge, MA: MIT Press, 1953); and David Easton, *A Framework for Political Analysis* (Englewood Cliffs, NJ: Prentice Hall, 1965).

28. Harold Lasswell, Nathan Leites and Harold Dwight, *Language of Politics* (Cambridge: MA: MIT Press, 1949), and Lasswell's *Comparative Study of Symbols* (Stanford, CA: Stanford University Press, 1952), as well as his *World Politics and Personal Insecurity* (New York: World Publishing, 1935).

29. Kenneth Boulding, "The Economics of Knowledge and the Knowledge of Economics," *American Economic Review*, 56 (May 1966), p. 5; K.J. Arrow, "Limited Knowledge and Economic Analysis," *American Economic Review*, 64 (March 1974), pp. 1–10; Jan Tinbergen, *Shaping the World Economy* (New York: Twentieth Century Fund, 1962), and his *Toward a New World Economy* (Rotterdam: Rotterdam University Press, 1972); Richard I. Savage and Karl W. Deutsch, "A Statistical Model of the Gross Analysis of Transaction Flows," *Econometrica*, 28: 3 (July 1960), pp. 551–572; D.M. Lamberton, ed., *Economics of Information and Knowledge* (Harmondsworth: Penguin Books, 1971); George Stegler, "The Economics of Information," *Journal of Political Economy*, 69 (June 1961), pp. 52–65.

30. Joseph Hirshleifer, "Where Are We in the Theory of Information?" *American Economic Review*, 63 (May 1973), pp. 31–39; Egon Neuberger and William Duffy, *Comparative*

*Economic Systems: A Decision-Making Approach* (Boston: Allyn and Bacon, Inc., 1976); and Fritz Machlup, *The Production and Distribution of Knowledge* (Princeton, NJ: Princeton University Press, 1972).

31. Dallas Smythe, *Dependency Road: Communication, Capitalism, Consciousness, and Canada* (Norwood, NJ: Ablex Publishing Corporation, 1981); Herbert U. Schiller, *Who Knows: Information in the Age of the Fortune 500* (Norwood, NJ: Ablex Publishing Corporation, 1981).

32. Immanuel Wallerstein, *The Modern World-System*, Vols I and II (New York: Academic Press, 1974, 1980); Herbert I. Schiller, *Communication and Cultural Domination* (White Plains, NY: International Arts and Sciences Press, 1976).

33. Quoted in Michael Schrage, "The Sword of Science," *The Washington Post Magazine*, October 9, 1983, p. 22.

34. Robert Scheer, "Nuclear 'Win' Strategy Developed for Reagan," *The Miami Herald*, August 15, 1982.

35. Daniel Deudney, "Whole Earth Security: A Geopolitics of Peace," *Worldwatch Paper 55* (Washington, DC: Worldwatch Institute, July 1983), p. 13.

36. Ibid., p. 20.

37. Statement of Richard R. Colino, director general-designate, International Telecommunications Satellite Organization (INTELSAT), before the Subcommittee on Arms Control, Oceans, International Operations and Environment, Senate Foreign Relations Committee, October 19, 1983, p. 3.

38. Ibid., p. 15.

39. "From Language to Literature, a New Guiding Lite," *The Washington Post*, September 5, 1995, Sec. A1.

40. Ibid.

41. Ibid.

42. *The Washington Post*, November 12, 1995, Sec. A, pp. 1, 14.

# 2
# International Flow of Information: A Framework of Analysis

Research and writing on the international flow of information have had an astonishing growth in the field of international communication during the last two decades. Among the factors responsible for the increased study and research in the international flow of information are:

1. the development of modern information and communication technologies, and their use and impact on the nature, volume, and content of information and communication;
2. the increased awareness of nation-states, institutions, groups and individuals in the importance of information flow, the existing imbalances, and their consequences and impact on the national and international decision-making processes as well as on the individual and private lives of people around the world;
3. the increasing number of international and transnational actors in almost all aspects of the international flow of information with political, social, and economic ramifications, particularly in respect to such areas as trade, marketing, education, and culture;
4. the growing interest in comparative cross-cultural as well as public opinion and image studies, accompanied by the sharpening of our research and investigatory tools and improved means of collecting, sorting, retrieving, and sharing data;
5. and more specifically, the debate generated and articulated over the New International Economic Order and the New World Information/ Communication Order in the 1970s, particularly the UNESCO declarations and activities on information flow and communication policies and the ensuing discussions over the relationship between the economic and communication aspects of the world's resources.

As the supply of information is increasing at an extraordinary rate, both internationally and domestically, information and equal access to it are seen as vehicles for reducing dependency in economic, political, and cultural relations. In a broad sense, the study of the international flow of information is another approach to the study of international relations. Consequently, it should not only include the flow of information and messages through technological channels and the conventional media, but it must take into account the totality and the diversity of both channels and

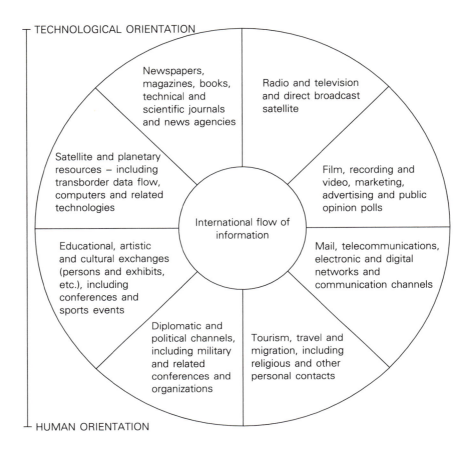

Figure 2.1   *Channels and types of international flow of information. The technological orientation and human orientation should be thought of as being complementary, interrelated, and adaptive*

messages transferring information across national boundaries. This would include the study of messages flowing through channels that are oriented toward human movements as well as scientific and artistic pursuits.

Therefore, a more realistic and comprehensive analysis of the international flow of information should include the examination of a variety of economic, political, and cultural activities, as shown in Figure 2.1.

However, no study has been performed that includes or integrates all of these dimensions toward a more rigorous analysis of the international flow of information. Historically, the study of the international flow was undertaken to examine the international political, as well as news, aspects of flow, moving in the last three decades to include technological, cultural, and economic aspects. In light of this, we should broaden our concept of the international flow of information beyond the narrow scope of the mass media and the growing technological channels to include and integrate all the fundamental areas of information flow.

The task is, of course, not an easy one, and the prospects for its total accomplishment may not be that promising at present. The primary emphasis must be placed on an introduction to the activities focused on the phenomenon of the international flow of information, with the hope that the enlarged vision will stimulate research in the less conventional areas and will encourage integration of the diverse aspects of the study of information flow.

**What is Information?**

The divergent opinions about information can be related to different conceptions of the phenomenon. In medieval Latin, *informatio* had the sense of image, instruction, and formation, while in classic French the word *information* was used in the singular term *une information* to mean processing and collecting facts in legal investigation. In its common and everyday usage, information is associated with a human situation, with a communication medium, with something that can be added and accumulated, with something factual, valuable, useful, useless, or with knowledge. Thus it is said that information is good, and more information is better, that information is power, information is lost; that a book, a letter, a newspaper, or a conference contains information.

The term "information" is used in this study in its semantic and pragmatic context and not on the syntactic level alone, which is commonly used in the statistical and mathematical theory of information. Information is defined here as a patterned distribution or patterned relationship between events, objects, and signs. It is about something other than the "things" and signs themselves. Furthermore, it involves activators (i.e., creators, users) and it is not limited to a structural property such as the diversity of material things and processes. The question whether information is material or ideal has been discussed elsewhere; suffice it to say that this question is related to the "nature of information" and has been elaborated by others in the realm of philosophy and epistemology.[1]

The purpose here is to synthesize the relevant research already undertaken by different institutions and organizations in all aspects of the international flow of information – both in its human and technological dimensions. However, attempts have been made to draw the attention of the reader to the existing research and literature in such diverse areas of the international flow of information as tourism, international conferences and exchanges of scientific information, and the flow of educational, political, and economic materials and personnel across national boundaries.

The study will reflect the current situation with regard to the international flow of information. A further goal of the study is to analyze political, cultural, economic, technological, legal, and professional practices affecting the international flow of information. It will identify, in particular, the nature of obstacles involved during the different stages of production and dissemination.

International flow of information is defined here as the movement of messages across national boundaries among two or more national and cultural systems. A definition of international flow of information should combine both a national and international dimension. It is a term used to describe a field of inquiry and research that consists of the transfer of messages in the form of information and data through individuals, groups, governments, and technologies, as well as the study of the institutions responsible for promoting and inhibiting such messages among nations, peoples, and cultures. It entails an analysis of the channels and institutions of communication, but, more importantly, it involves examination of the mutually shared meanings which make communication possible. Therefore, the examination of the international flow of information should include both the content, volume, and direction of information as well as the economic, political, cultural, legal and technological factors responsible for its initiation and diffusion.

To date, the efforts in studying international flow of information have been far from systematic. The diversity of sectors (public, private, and academic) interested in flow and the myriad reasons and purposes motivating study have precluded meaningful coordination. This same barrier to coordination, however, is a powerful justification for combining efforts to produce a maximum amount of quality data. The recent efforts to encourage and facilitate research cooperation in this area are significant in that they show recognition of the need to coordinate research with the hope of building a body of knowledge in this vital and demanding area.

There have been several major barriers to coordination of research effort in flow studies. First, the arenas or sectors in which flow studies are sponsored are highly diverse. Studies are undertaken in education, private industry, government, and even in international arenas. Each sector has specific motivations for the study of flow and these motivations may be different from those of other sectors. Additionally, those interested in flow in any one sector may be unaware of the interests and efforts of those in other sectors.

Second, the diversity of the types of international information flow has been a factor in the somewhat fragmented nature of flow studies. Studies have concentrated on such widely different topics as the flow of broadcast news, the structure of news agencies, distribution of educational material, transborder and planetary data, and also in such specialized areas as tourism, international law, and international education. At first glance the topics may seem unrelated, but if considered within the larger framework of information flow, the interrelationships become apparent. Such relationships and convergence could have significant impact on the assumptions, conduct, and conclusions of further research.

Third, even within specific topic areas of flow, there has been little coordination of research on the variables involved in the entire process.

Consequently, in any given area, examination of one variable may exclude other important variables. For example, few studies have ever considered both the intra- and extra-media variables in the flow of news, although the interrelationship of these two sets of variables may seem obvious.

The fourth barrier to cooperation is the polarity of the two dimensions of flow – human and technological – which has, in part, precluded coordination of research between them. The modern and technical aspects of communication have received predominant attention at the expense of the human dimension. In short, technological variables, at times, have dominated research efforts where cultural and social variables, which should be considered concurrently, have been neglected. Human and social utilities have not been given as much attention as the technological and economic utilities, nor have they been integrated to show a more realistic picture of the international flow of information.

Finally, the absence of a clear and comprehensive definition of the phenomena of flow has made it difficult to identify scholars whose works are applicable. Often, researchers may not recognize they are orchestrating "flow studies" because boundaries in the form of definition of component parts, aspects, and processes have not been set.

### Perspectives on the Study of Flow

The study of the international flow of information, like any other area of inquiry in social science and policy studies, has been the object of debate of a scholarly and professional nature for its epistemological orientation. It is not the purpose of this study to discuss in any thorough manner the criticisms leveled at the "objective/subjective dimension" of the conduct of inquiry; this type of question has generated an interesting debate within the international communication community and several essays have appeared covering precisely this question. Nevertheless, it is important to underline that the literature on international flow of information also exhibits different epistemological and methodological approaches, ranging from "positivism/antipositivism," "determinism/voluntarism," and "nomothetic/idiographic," to the assumptive frameworks about the nature of society, ranging from "status quo/radical change," "consensus/domination," "solidarity/emancipation," and "actuality/potentiality."[2] Given the nature and sociology of international flow of information research over the past two decades, however, the consensus is that the previously hegemonic positivist/empiricist research has been supplemented by a good deal of critical theory and critical analysis of all kinds. Consequently, the approaches to the conduct of inquiry in this field have become comparatively more diverse, multidimensional and, indeed, varied.

Under these varied epistemological orientations, several important perspectives have been developed examining the international flow of information. It must be noted that none of these perspectives to be discussed is necessarily identified with a particular epistemological point of view; rather, the careful scrutiny of the literature shows that a given perspective might be shared by different philosophical schools of thought but may differ as to methods of investigation and analysis.

International communication in general and information flow in particular, like other branches of social science, acquire their legitimacy and consistency largely from the perspectives and methods of inquiry used by those who study the subject. Following are the major perspectives covering the broad area of the international flow of information. It should be noted that the perspectives identified here are by no means mutually exclusive, but may overlap in the attempt to be exhaustive.[3]

1. *International relations and systems perspective.* A number of information flow studies are designed to test some aspect of international relations theories and phenomena. Within this category we may find the studies dealing with theories of imperialism, integration, conflict and cooperation, and the general hypotheses aiming at image and perception among nations. For example, international flow of news has been analyzed in the discussion of imperialism and center–periphery dimensions of international relations, as has the flow of telecommunications data, such as the mail and telephone, in testing the level of regional and international integration.

2. *Communication and development perspective.* This approach undertakes the study of international information flow from the perspective of developmental policies and theories – national and international – examining both a nation's internal and external communication systems and its political, economic, social, and cultural development in a national, regional, and international context. This category also includes studies on the balance and imbalance of information flow, the direction and pattern of flow, and at times relates them to such factors as ideology, ethnocentricity, commercialism, or proximity. Here the emphasis has been to study the content, volume, and frequencies of communication in general and the message in particular. This has been a growing perspective since the 1960s.

3. *Institutional and commercial perspective.* A large group of flow studies examines international actors and the impact of political and persuasive messages on the behavior of individuals and nations. This perspective includes propaganda and policy studies for a variety of purposes such as conflict management, domination, and commercial promotion, as well as stereotyping or image manipulation and control. Additionally, research regarding the effectiveness of the role of actors and institutions – governmental and nongovernmental – and its importance and impact on the international flow of information are included in this perspective. The major emphasis is on content analysis, audience analysis, readership survey, and public opinion poll. This perspective, which flourished during the 1940s and the 1950s, continues to influence many flow studies at present.

4. *Political economy and structural perspective.* This perspective approaches the study of international information flow from the aspect of national and international communication structures, as well as the political economy of information. Such research would be concerned with the elements of and factors influencing the process of international flow, including gatekeepers and gate producers, as well as examining the technological and human dimensions and formal and informal institutional structures of both production and distribution aspects of the process of international information flow. This has been a growing line of inquiry since the 1970s.

5. *Technical and legal perspective.* This approach is a combination of the very new and the very old in that these aspects, which have been concerns of scholars for decades, are rapidly revolutionizing the international information system. Studies in this area include the technology as well as the techniques of international information gathering and processing, national and international regulations and standards of information industries as well as of flow, and the resulting issues; and the technical aspects of transferring data, information, and messages across national boundaries or from point to point. Studies have increased in recent years as a result of the rapid development of satellites and computers, the growing power and importance of transnational organizations, and the greater attention of regional and international organizations to the complex problems of technology, information, and services.

**Problems of Measurement**

Most studies on information flow have consisted simply of the measurement of repetitive events, wherein the researchers have been concerned at the outset with statistical analyses of messages rather than the individual message itself. Quantitative measurement of information flow has been made either as volume or frequency per unit time, as proportion of some total volume or messages, or as a proportion of the time or facilities involved in dealing with messages. Other dimensions of volume might include the speed at which messages are transmitted as well as the fidelity with which their format and content are preserved in the transmission process. They could also include media units as well as the number of both senders and recipients of communication.

Taking the process of information flow to the international communication level, we should be interested in the simplest ratio of output to intake of communication among countries and peoples. This would imply that we should measure not only how much and what kind of information a country or an organization or system is transmitting, but also how much and what kind of information – both quantitatively and qualitatively – it is receiving from other countries and systems.[4]

When hard data are available, the intake–output ratio can tell us a good deal about the two-way flow of information. For example, the number of US foreign correspondence around the world fell from 563 in 1969 to 435 in 1975,[5] while the number of foreign correspondents representing other countries in the United States had increased from about 200 in 1954 to 835 in 1975.[6]

The ratio of intraboundary processes in a given country to cross-boundary processes among several countries, originating or terminating in that same country, would be another basic operational measure. Local to nonlocal news or mail, nonlocal to foreign news or mail, and domestic versus foreign news or mail are examples of measurement ratios in this category. Inside–outside ratios of information flows can explain the "national" and "international" dimensions of such activities as science, education, and student exchanges, and the directions in which they might be changing.

It must be noted that these measurements are quantitative in nature; qualitative measurements are more difficult in the context of the inter-national flow of information. Although several attempts have been made in this direction, the result has been far from satisfactory due to its methodo-logical and cultural diversity.

Until recently, the studies on the flow of information were concerned primarily with the examination of channels and content, leaving either end of the process – the source and the destination – untouched. There are now some serious efforts to examine the source of the process, to discover the new actors, and to analyze the gate producers as well as the message producers. Similar attempts are being made to study precisely who makes what use of which kind of information, and how the information is finally delivered and absorbed by the audience. For example, there is growing research awareness that the global diffusion of news and information involves factors beyond those that are usually inferred from its distribution. Because of these, and due to the lack of systematic research, the present state of knowledge in the international flow of information is so fragmented that no full-scale investigation has shown the possible effects of international information systems on international policies, politics, and economics.

## A Framework for the Study of Flow

Elsewhere, I have emphasized a need for a shift in emphasis in the analysis of communication systems from an exclusive concern with the source and content of messages to analysis of the message distribution process.[7] Control of the distribution process is the most important index of the way in which power is distributed in a communication system, which may be the global community, a country, or some smaller political unit. The flow of information in the international system, when the above distinction is made, may then be represented in rudimentary terms as in Figure 2.2.

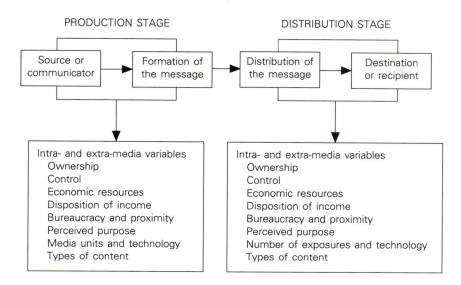

PRODUCTION STAGE        DISTRIBUTION STAGE

Figure 2.2 *The two stages of information flow*

The growth of communication technology, the expanding national and international market, and the creation of institutional policies and regulations all have made the distribution stage the most important sequence in the chains of communication systems. Emphasis upon the distribution stage affords an immediate advantage in analyzing the message-sending activities of national actors. Unless a nation has control over the entire distribution process, its messages may be ineffectual. Certainly, the most ingeniously designed message, if it goes nowhere, will have no effect.

A further elaboration of the process of information distribution in the international system is provided in Figure 2.3, wherein a technology axis is added to the communication axis. Figure 2.3, representing the international flow of information, now properly depicts the pivotal role played by communication technology in the international communication process. Between the formation and distribution of messages stands the means of distribution – communication technology – itself divisible into two components. These components are the communication hardware, which is the actual physical carrier of messages (such as satellites, broadcasting and receiving equipment, and microwave relay stations), and the communication software, which is, in the broadest sense, the know-how and means to utilize the hardware (such as program production, content, manpower skills, and education).

The distinction between the two components of communication technology – hardware and software – to which Figure 2.3 draws attention is an important one, but one that is frequently ignored. Even when the importance of control over the technology is recognized, it is often assumed

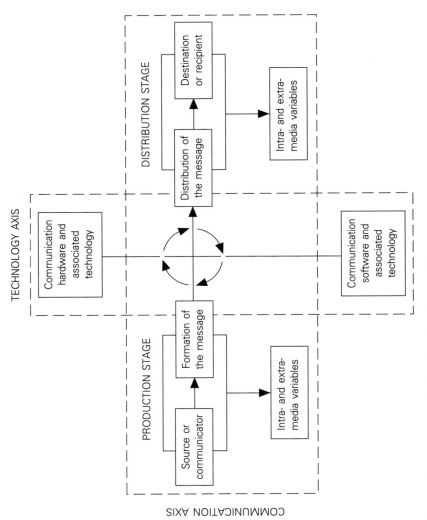

Figure 2.3   *International flow of information model*

that ownership of the actual physical components of the system is sufficient to provide control over it. But just as the ability to form messages affords no guarantee in itself that those messages will be disseminated, neither is control of communication hardware alone sufficient to assure the distribution of one's intended message. Absolute sovereignty in the formation and distribution of messages is assured only when a nation controls both the hardware channels through which the messages are sent and the necessary know-how to program its messages for effective distribution.

Thus, the entire process of international flow of information can be illustrated by looking at the quadrants created by the communication and technology axes. The implications of this model become clear when the diagram is seen as representing the components of control and autonomy in a communication system, and when intra-media and extra-media variables are added to the stages of production and distribution separately.[8] In the absence of a single actor controlling all four components, effective control of a system will fall to the possessors of certain of the components before others. For example, a country may have the most sophisticated television broadcasting apparatus imaginable and the technical know-how to disseminate messages through it, but unless this country is also producing its own messages in terms of programs, contents, marketing, and research and development (the lower right and left portions of the communication–technology cycle), its dependency on the outsider system increases. In terms of flow studies and investigation, clearer national, regional, international, and global pictures will emerge if a given process of flow is examined in terms of each quadrant against the variables indicated.

**Factors in the Flow**

A few examples can illustrate the utility of this framework of analysis employing the variables that are listed under both production and distribution stages of information (Figure 2.2). The variables, once elaborated and further developed to fit the specific criteria of a given type of information flow and communication system, can account for political, economic, cultural, and technical factors in impeding or facilitating the flow of information. These variables can also be used to compile data for comparative and international analysis of different communication systems.[9]

*Ownership.*　In the search for non-culture-bound concepts and operational definitions, each stage of production (or formation) and distribution of a communication and information system can be divided into three broad areas of public, private, and mixed sectors, with further suitable categories for data gathering.

*Control.*　In the production and distribution stages of a given international flow, the aspect of control is by far one of the most significant variables in its complexity and measurement. Control over the system can take many forms; it comes from outside the structure of a given communication or media system as well as being exerted from within. Some controls are actual (i.e., formal, legal, technical), others are perceived (i.e., informal and based on unwritten but understood rules and regulations that can be understood only within the cultural and ideological orientation of the system under investigation). Thus, the variable of control can be further subdivided into four distinct categories: (1) *Internal actual controls.* These are specific rules and regulations such as education, professional qualification, internal rules, and hierarchy created and institutionalized formally by the system itself, to which members in a communication system subject themselves. (2) *Internal perceived control.* Social control within a communication system, peer-group pressure, perceived gatekeeping functions, and unwritten but understood rules of the internal conditions of the system are examples of perceived control. These are the "rules of the game," and consist of all the arrangements that regulate the way members of the system behave within the perceived institutional boundaries of the unit in which they work. (3) *External actual control.* Direct censorship, licensing, and any other external legal, professional, governmental, or institutional factors form this category. Further subcategories can be established here to divide external actual control into such areas as constitutional, legal, economic, social, and political sectors. (4) *External perceived control.* In every society we have such systems as culture, personality, social structure, and economic and political elites. Each of these constitutes a major set of variables in the process of demands entering a communication system. Not all demands and influencing factors have their major locus inside the institutional system of communication. Important factors in determining the outcome of both the production and distribution stages of a communication system stem from constraints and unwritten rules of the environment. Predisposition and wants of readers and audiences and participants, reactions to perceived political and cultural preferences and idiosyncrasies, and pressures exercised by elites and organizations in the society are examples of this type of control. Strong arguments have been made to include culture as an important factor – and in the opinion of some writers as the ultimate factor – influencing the relationship between objective and subjective social indicators.

*Economic resources.* Primarily an index of the information system's dependence upon capital and income, this variable is at times inversely proportional to the size of a given communication system or a mass media system as a whole. It has been shown that "such politico-economic factors as size of population, GNP and international data can explain between one and two thirds of variations in international political news."[10] For example, in the case of mass media, such categories as sales, advertising, public subsidy, private subsidy, and licensing can be described here to accommodate the variety of income sources in different systems and media under study.

*Disposition of income.* Fiscal policies and priorities as they affect the ways in which income and capital are spent and invested are influencing factors in both the production and distribution stages of the message. The fierce competition among the communication systems and the high cost of technology and labor make it almost imperative to invest in the continuing improvement of the product. For example, as applied to telecommunications and the media systems, this variable can be subdivided into such areas as facilities, profits, and others. The facilities category here could refer to all technical and personal matters in a given system with further subdivisions such as technical, personnel, or administrative. In the technical subcategory, we can gather data on machinery and hardware, and the personnel category can account for salaries in creative work (writers, artists, editors, etc.), while the administrative and production categories include such areas as labor, managerial, and administrative personnel.

*Bureaucracy and proximity.* A bureaucracy of a communication system can be defined as a hierarchy of nonhereditary positions subject to the authority of the executive. In organizations in which dependence upon the government is rather extensive, a study of the bureaucracy is required for proper evaluation of the degree of autonomy or even reliability of message-gathering and distribution levels of the institution. The network of the organization of the communication system as a whole, its subsidiaries, its sister organizations, its organizational chart and the concentration of ownership, the capacity of the system to adopt itself to internal and external environments, and such items as job mobility, the degree of turnover, promotional policies, and the movement of information in the system itself – in short, the infrastructure of bureaucracy – are important elements to ensure efficient and timely output in the formation and distribution of messages.

*Perceived purpose.* In different countries and in different political economies, a newspaper, a broadcasting system, or any information and communication system as a whole may define and perceive its role and purpose in different ways. Here we are concerned with the perceived purpose of a communication and information system as a large unit in both the production and distribution stages.

*Media units and technology.* This variable deals with the technology of the media. By media units we mean the number of media and technologies in the system under analysis and comparison. For example, units per medium in the production stage of a press system stands for such things as the number of newspapers and publications, and, in the case of broadcasting, for the number of radio and television stations. Further subdivision can be created. For example, in the production stages of the message this is indicated by redundancy. Here the researcher can gather data on such aspects of the media system as uniformity and group reading and readership and audience data. In short, in the distribution stage this variable should indicate the number of exposures to the message as well as the circulation of the content and the recipients of the message.

*Types of content.*   This last category is an obvious variable and has been the most widely used category in the flow studies. In fact, content analysis has been the most popular method in determining the process of information flow by the students of mass communication. The suggestion here is that any further subcategories of this variable must be broad enough to provide some guidelines for cross-national comparison. The tendency in the past has been to start from specific categories with a definite cultural bias. For example, what may be considered "entertainment" in one system can be "educational" and/or cultural and "informational" in another.

The framework of analysis proposed here is a modest attempt to examine all kinds of international flow of information – both human and technological – and it is designed to direct the attention of the researcher to some of the most critical factors in international and comparative studies. It is realized that the type of taxonomic research schema discussed here poses some restrictions on the user and necessitates the exploration of a rather exhaustive set of categories. However, our understanding of the nature and the process of information flow will be incomplete if we continue with the general and heuristic notions of the past and consider those factors that are easily available and statistically measurable.

The proposed framework of analysis demands different types of data, some of which may be readily available, while a substantial portion may require various research techniques to obtain. However, the sociocultural, economic, political, and technological categories of variables suggested in the framework can be summarized under four kinds of data. The first are aggregative data – the kind of statistical data on ownership, number of media, budget, and economics of production and distribution. The second type are sample survey data giving the researcher evidence on aspects of control and such factors as audience analysis and readership. The third type of data stems from a careful content analysis describing the message. Finally there are the cultural data that cultural anthropologists and other scholars can uncover, and which can be a major tool for closing the gaps in the aggregate and survey data.

Recognizing the delineation of three major types of potential actors in the process of international flow of information (Figure 2.4), each section of this study has been organized around the following themes:

1. Types of international flow of information.
2. Actors in the international flow of information.
3. Factors influencing the flow.
4. Directions and patterns of the flow.

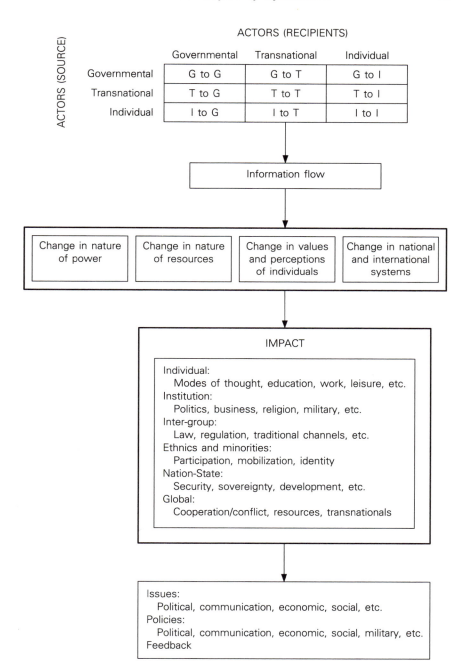

Figure 2.4  *Types and impacts of international flow of information*

5. Impact and effects of the flow.
6. Assumptions and theories underlying flow research and the flow itself.
7. Content of the flow.
8. Case studies and research contributions.

It is also important to emphasize that some of the graphics and tables presented in this study are not intended to provide an overview or synthesis of a global nature. Data of this kind and scope are simply not available. Rather, country and regional illustrations are presented (based on the best and latest data available) in an attempt to show a selective mapping, which endeavors to approach some of the key topics from different angles and perspectives in a manner that might assist the reader in a more comprehensive and interrelated assessment. To that end, various other sources external to the study have been drawn upon also, where they may help to illuminate and clarify the discussion of major themes.

## Notes

1. See Norbert Wiener, *Cybernetics, or Control and Communication in the Animal and the Machine*, new edn (Cambridge, MA: MIT Press, 1961), and his *The Human Use of Human Beings: Cybernetics and Society* (New York: Avon Books, 1967); Colin Cherry, *On Human Communication* (Cambridge, MA: MIT Press, 1961); Karl W. Deutsch, *The Nerves of Government: Models of Political Communication and Control* (New York: Free Press, 1963); and Peter Paul Kirschenmann, *Information and Reflection: On Some Problems of Cybernetics and How Contemporary Dialectical Materialism Copes With Them* (Dordrecht: D. Reidel Publishing Company, 1970).

2. Karl Erik Rosengren, "Communication Research: One Paradigm, or Four?," *Journal of Communication*, 33: 3 (Summer 1983), pp. 186–187. Also published in E.M. Rogers and F. Balle, eds, *Mass Communication Research in the United States and Europe* (Norwood, NJ: Ablex Publishing Corporation, 1983).

3. Research and bibliographical references for these perspectives are provided in the following chapters. For studies dealing with international flow of news see Hamid Mowlana, ed., *International Flow of News: An Annotated Bibliography* (Paris: UNESCO, 1983).

4. Karl W. Deutsch, "Shifts in the Balance of Communication Flows: A Problem of Measurement in International Relations," *Public Opinion Quarterly*, XX: 1 (Spring 1956), p. 146.

5. Ralph Kliesch, "A Vanishing Species: The American Newsmen Abroad," *Overseas Press Club Directory* (New York: Overseas Press Club of America, 1975), p. 17.

6. Hamid Mowlana, "Who Covers America?," *Journal of Communication*, 25: 3 (Summer 1975), pp. 86–91. According to Karl W. Deutsch, "All foreign newspapers and news agencies together maintained in 1954 only about two hundred regular full-time correspondence in the United States." "Shifts in the Balance," p. 147.

7. Hamid Mowlana, "A Paradigm for Source Analysis in Events Data Research: Mass Media and the Problems of Validity," *International Interactions*, 2: 1 (1975), pp. 33–44; and Hamid Mowlana, "A Paradigm for Comparative Mass Media Analysis," in Heinz-Dietrich Fischer and John C. Merrill, eds, *International and Intercultural Communication* (New York: Hastings House, 1976), pp. 471–484.

8. Hamid Mowlana, "Political and Social Implications of Communication Satellite Applications in Developed and Developing Countries," in Joseph N. Pelton and Marcellus S.

Snow, eds, *Economic and Policy Problems in Satellite Communications* (New York: Praeger, 1977), pp. 124–142; also in Brent D. Ruben, ed., *Communication Yearbook*, Vol. 1 (New Brunswick, NJ: Transaction Books, 1977), pp. 427–438

9. Control and other variables have been elaborated in Hamid Mowlana, "A Paradigm for Source Analysis."

10. Rosengren, "Communication Research," p. 11.

# 3

# News and Views: Designing the World's Symbolic Environment

There has been a nearly geometric progression in the study of news flow across national boundaries during the 1970s, the 1980s, and the early 1990s.[1] In the 25 years since the first appearance of my bibliography on international communication, major changes have occurred in the field. At the end of the 1960s there were only a handful of studies dealing with the actual flow of international news. Research in the broad category of the international flow of information totaled no more than 318 publications between 1850 and 1969.[2] Whereas the early studies dealt with a single communication system or a single country, the recent trend is toward comparative studies of geographical, regional, and international systems.[3]

For the purpose of this study, current research and studies on international flow of news, including bibliographical collections by UNESCO, were analyzed. Over 440 different materials dealing with the flow of news were examined which also included computer listings of sources in the US Library of Congress, various papers presented at international and regional conferences, and books and journal articles covering the period from 1973 through the early part of 1993. Additionally, a few earlier studies were included due to their methodological, geographical, and topical contributions. Of the total works examined for this report, 221 were published in 84 different journals, 80 are unpublished materials presented at conferences and meetings, 110 are books, and 36 studies published as monographs or occasional papers. A good number of these studies were dated 1978, the year of the UNESCO Twentieth General Conference in Paris at which the Declaration of Mass Media was adopted.

Looking at the distribution of studies regionally, the regions that were most often the focus of research and analysis were Asia, Latin America, and North America. This was due in part to the work of several institutions involved in communication studies, mainly the Asian Mass Communication Research and Information Center in Singapore, the Latin American Institution for Transnational Studies in Mexico City, and the East–West Communication Institute in Honolulu, Hawaii. For the first time in the history of international communication, a substantial number of these studies were carried out by the "Third World" scholars. Whereas the previous studies concerning the flow of news were conducted by North American and European individuals and institutions, the great bulk of inquiries at present are associated with the scholars from Latin America,

Asia, and the Middle East. This promises to be the beginning of a major breakthrough in international communication, for if it continues, it will help to correct the imbalance in communication research.

**Emerging Issues**

The primary sources of information on the pattern of international news flow are content analyses of mass media and sample surveys, which provide data on the amount of foreign news and the circulation of domestic news outside national boundaries based on the characteristics of the units sampled. Until recently, data of this type were available for only a few industrialized nations, and generalizations about patterns of distribution of news were therefore based on very limited information. The situation has changed considerably during the last three decades, especially since the New World Information/Communication Order became a major item of debate in UNESCO and other international, regional, and national forums. Since then, large numbers of surveys, reports, and articles have been published in both the developed and the developing countries and are increasingly being used in discussions and analyses of international communication issues.

Unfortunately, the increase in data availability has not been accompanied by an adequate improvement in theoretical, methodological, or even statistical quality. In many cases, the growing interest in the subject has simply led to the proliferation of crude estimates of news distribution and dissemination for various regions and countries around the world based on data sources that may be "the best available" but are simply not good enough. A comprehensive review of these problems is beyond the scope of this chapter, but some indication of their importance can be obtained by considering the following major sources of problems.

First, for obvious reasons, the definition of news used in many studies falls short of a comprehensive and universally accepted definition. In fact, there is doubt whether there can be a definition of what constitutes news which will be acceptable to all.

Second, even if the news concept is "properly" defined, it may be difficult to measure in practice. Very different problems arise at the two ends of the communication process – the source and the destination; the process of news diffusion is a complex one. For example, the simple measurement of news originating in a given international or national news agency, or the simple measurement of the content of news in a given newspaper or magazine, might not be an accurate description of the flow of news in a country, a system, and/or among the population or decision makers at large. Assuming that the social structure of a given system or country acts to impede or facilitate the rate of news diffusion, then the study of norms, social status, and patterns of reading or listening or information seeking becomes imperative. Additionally, it is imperative that the hierarchy of the political, social, economic, and cultural systems influencing the decision and behavior of individual recipients and groups be studied as well. Clearly, in addition to power elites, a score of other social, cultural, and economic forces serve as gatekeepers in controlling the flow of news in all stages of formation, production, distribution, and diffusion.

Related to this is the problem of accuracy in estimating the distribution of news among the population from the observed distribution in sample surveys or content analyses. The accuracy of sample estimates depends on a number of factors relating to the size of the sample and its representativeness. Many available news flow studies are derived from samples that are statistically inadequate in these respects, with the result that sample estimates are both biased and have a substantial variance.

Third, there is the problem of quantity versus quality in news reporting and dissemination. Unless some criteria are defined to design a study to investigate the nature and quality of what is being reported and distributed, the studies of flow of international news will be measured only on quantity and volume levels, with less or no attention paid to the qualitative and relevant nature of what is being measured. Of course, this is a difficult task indeed and requires a totally different method of analysis and measurement. These limitations present a familiar dilemma in empirical and critical analysis.

Most often the definitions of news fail to make an important distinction – that between news and reported news. The tendency seems to be to talk of news as a finished product: thus the old cliché that news "is the account of an event, not the event itself," and that "what the reporter writes is news."

Furthermore, there are limitations within the concepts employed in the measurement of flow of news. A classic example is the concept of gatekeeping. We know that in any flow process an item does not move through a channel by itself, but is moved directly or indirectly by an individual, an institution, and a set of social, political, economic, and cultural factors. Therefore, gatekeeping analyses of the flow of world news are directed toward those forces which initiate the flow. However, before we examine the factors affecting the gatekeeper's function, fundamental questions arise: Who are the gatemakers or gate producers? What are the characteristics and nature of the news channels? What are the roles of individuals, institutions, nation-states, and technologies in producing and creating news communication channels in the first place? The traditional gatekeeping studies have not addressed themselves to these basic questions.

Since the concept of gatekeeping was taken from the work of Kurt Lewin in psychology, the tradition of communication research in the past employed the concept to test social norms and social controls in media channels without asking the basic structural questions to determine the political, economic, cultural, and technological forces creating the gates themselves. After all, Lewin was a psychologist interested in small group interactions and not a political economist analyzing the structural changes of the system. It is interesting to note that Lewin's concept as applied in communication research has been a dominant factor for so long without its limitations being challenged.

## Current Lines of Inquiry

As research on the international flow of news has expanded during the last 20 years with most dramatic growth at the beginning of the 1980s, it has been accompanied by several new lines of inquiry which can be grouped according to two main categories: (1) studies dealing with the actual flow and content of news, and (2) studies concerning factors determining the flow of news.

The first category – actual flow and content of news – can be divided into four distinct lines of investigation. The first line of investigation examines the flow and content of news from one country to another, or, in a comparative way, it examines the direction and the amount of flow in a region or at the international level. Many of the early studies of news flow by scholars in the United States, and many of the studies currently being undertaken in other parts of the world, are of this kind.[4] In the early days, this line of inquiry dealt with the flow of news between the East and the West, shifting to the North–South examination after the New World Information/Communication debate became the focus of analysis. The primary purposes of this tradition have been to assess the balances and imbalances in the flow of news, the different categories and the nature of news content, and the emphasis given to the coverage of various events.

The second line of analysis is characterized by many studies on the role of "center–periphery" and "dominance–dependency" in news flow studies. It has formed a core of analysis for many European and Latin American scholars, and is used as a framework for many other flow researchers. Foundations for these types of dependency studies have developed separately in the United States, in the Scandinavian countries, and in the Middle East. For example, one researcher has explicitly linked communication and culture concepts in his analysis of the "structure of imperialism."[5]

A third line of inquiry focuses on the meaning and the qualitative nature of news by examining the images and perceptions contained in the content.[6] The UNESCO "Foreign Images" content study, for example, is in this tradition and offers important insights into the flow of news.

The final approach, which has been used through a major cross-section of scholars studying foreign policy and international systems, is commonly called "events–interaction analysis." The aim of this method is to interpret the "interaction" of nations or actors as reflected by the analysis of "events" or news data. In many of these analyses *The New York Times* and *The Times* of London have been used as the sources of data, and their pattern of international news reporting has been the basis of "cooperation and conflict" analysis.[7]

Almost all of the research in the above four lines of inquiry is conducted in the traditional style of content analysis of news: what is printed or broadcast, what is carried by the news agencies, who is supplying the news, what countries are reported, and the pattern thereof.

The second category of studies – factors determining the news flow – is of two lines of investigation: studies dealing with the media factors influencing the flow of news,[8] and those examining extra-media factors determining the content and news flow.[9] These two lines of inquiry, concentrating on structure, political economy, cultural, social, and ideological factors, have grown tremendously during the last 15 years. Many studies have tried to research the flow of news in such areas as "news bias," "accuracy," and time as a factor in flow research. Others have concentrated on the structural analysis of institutions, actors, and bureaucracies involved in the production and distribution of news. Examples of such studies are numerous and include the role of transnational actors in the flow of news, the location and movement of foreign correspondents around the world, and the cultural, ideological, legal, and technological factors determining the flow of news and its content. Although some content analysis techniques have been employed in these studies, the researchers have used multiple sources of data of an aggregate nature and survey analysis.

Studies investigating in the direction of news flow have hypothesized three distinct patterns. First is the "center–periphery" pattern exemplified in the work of Johan Galtung in his analysis of the structural theory of imperialism. Here the world is divided into two parts: the "center," or dominant communities, and the "periphery," or dependent areas (see Figure 3.1). Galtung relates these theoretical constructs to communication and cultural interaction and points to vertical interaction as the major factor in the inequality of nations, a division reinforced by "feudal networks of international communication" dominated by nations in the "center."

Galtung's hypothesis can be summarized in four statements characterizing international news:

1. There is a preponderance of "center" news events reported in the world press systems.
2. There is a much larger discrepancy in the news exchange ratios of "center" and "periphery" nations than in the exchange ratios of "center" nations.
3. "Center" news occupies a larger proportion of the foreign news content in the media of "periphery" nations than the "periphery" news occupies in the "center" nations.
4. There is relatively little or no flow of news among "periphery" nations, especially across colonial-based bloc borders.[10]

Several research efforts have been undertaken to test Galtung's "center–periphery" hypothesis, concluding that the pattern is indeed a feudal

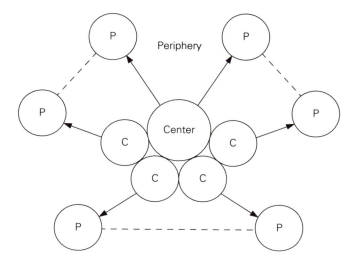

Figure 3.1    *Center–periphery flow*

one. The "periphery" nations, however, while contributing to diplomatic entropy, have not moved significantly toward class confrontation patterns.[11] Robert Buijtenhuijs and René Baesjou concluded from their study of two African newspapers that, contrary to Galtung's assertion, there is a news flow across bloc borders in Africa; however, they reaffirmed the dominance of "center" news agencies in the news of the two African countries served by the newspapers examined.[12] Further affirmation of Galtung's hypothesis is the content analysis study of Australian mass media performed by Bruce McKenzie and Derek Overton in 1981, where it was concluded that the pattern of international news flow to and from Australia largely remained colonial with traditional news sources prevailing.[13]

The second pattern is based on the hypothesis that news flow is vertical from developed countries (North) to developing countries (South), with supplemental horizontal flows within the North and within the South, although flow within the latter is substantially lesser in volume (see Figure 3.2). While there exists a good deal of news flow from South to North, it tends to be significantly less in volume in comparison with the flow from North to South. Further, within the North–South pattern, a direction termed "round flow" can be identified, in which news gathered in the South by Northern correspondents is transmitted to the North for processing and editing before its eventual return to the media in the South.

Several researchers have targeted North–South flow patterns, among them Reyes Matta, whose 1975 study of Latin American newspapers revealed that the flow from the North dominated foreign news in Latin America, although its proportion was somewhat less than had been shown by a 1960 study conducted by CIESPAL.[14] A 1974 study had concluded

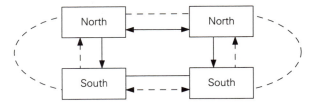

Figure 3.2    *North–South flow*

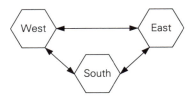

Figure 3.3    *Triangular flow*

that news from Latin America and Africa was poorly represented in Australian newspapers, although Shelton A. Gunaratne's 1979 study of the two major Australian dailies showed a marked difference in their coverages of Third World news, one with decreasing coverage of development news and the other with an increase of such coverage.[15] However, the study of news flow in nine Arab Nations as late as 1978 demonstrated the dominant presence of South–North flow within that region.[16]

Frank Kaplan's study of the US media noted an insufficiency in the amount, scope, and type of news disseminated, particularly in the coverage of the developing world.[17] The major news agencies of the developed world (AP, UPI, AFP, Reuters) cover the news that they perceive as interesting to their home publics. In the case of the US newspapers, this interest was correlated with wealth, elitism, and the political potency of the readers.[18]

The third pattern is a triangular flow that divides the North into East and West, connecting each to the South (see Figure 3.3). In one of the most geographically comprehensive studies, George Gerbner and George Marvanyi concluded that in foreign news, East and West first cover their respective geopolitical areas as well as East–West relations, whereas Third World media in general devote the greatest proportion of foreign news coverage to the North – meaning both the East and the West. Additionally, Gerbner and Marvanyi found that Western Europe was the most frequently reported region around the globe, and that the socialist nations received little coverage in the Western press. Two-thirds of the content in the US press system, for example, concerned Western Europe, South Asia, the Far East, North America, and the Middle East. The Soviet press covered Eastern Europe the most, and North America second. Eastern Europe ranked their own region and Western Europe high as far as coverage, and reported on the Soviet Union relatively less than the other press systems. In the Third World press, the Soviet Union received the greatest coverage – an exception to low coverage it received from other press systems in the study. The authors suggested that "the process of reciprocal information may be out of joint."[19]

More recently, a study by Robert L. Stevenson and Richard R. Cole concluded that "regional proximity is clearly the dominant characteristic of foreign news" and that Western Europe and North America were the most visible areas in the world media while Eastern Europe and developing regions received the least visibility.[20]

## News Agencies and News Exchange

A major aspect of the international flow of news is the functioning of wire services or news agencies, which received little attention from researchers in communication until the 1960s, as a result, perhaps, of the relative invisibility of their functioning. In the late 1960s and especially during the 1970s, however, research on the news agencies and their role in the international flow of information experienced a tremendous growth in the writings of communication scholars. Studies based on the ownership and the organization of the "big four" agencies – Agence France Press (France), Associated Press (USA), Reuters (UK), and United Press International (USA) – had also experienced significant growth by this time. These studies represented the majority of the research in the preceding decade.

At the end of the 1970s and the beginning of the 1980s, the euphoria of the initial flourish of research was calmed, and scholars began to be more involved in detailed quantitative studies and less analytical essays. Consequently, the scope of the new agencies' research was broadened and the scenario now tends to be focused on three main actors in the field: (1) world agencies (the "big four") and the multinational enterprises collecting and disseminating news all over the world; (2) national agencies undertaking the circulation of news inside a country and domestic news abroad; and (3) regional agencies and their arrangements for cooperation in information exchange to increase the role of the Third World in the international flow of news.

Studies on news agencies indicate little or no change in the total production of the "big four" agencies since the late 1970s. Compared with major transnational news agencies, the amount of news distributed by national or regional news agencies is still low, though there is evidence that the quantity of news input–output of national and some regional agencies is steadily increasing.

The most significant alternative to the transnational news agencies has been the News Pool of the non-aligned nation's news agencies. This News Pool was established at the New Delhi Conference of Information

Ministers and representatives of the news agencies of the non-aligned nations in 1976. From the beginning the Pool was seen as an arrangement for exchange of news between non-aligned countries that was unavailable from the Western transnational news agencies.

The Pool's policy is to handle and treat news as a valuable resource for development and public welfare, instead of just as a commodity. The entertainment aspect of news is de-emphasized in favor of information that editors believe to be valuable for the liberation and development of the people. Background is strongly emphasized, so that news items can be understood in context.

In Western journalistic terms, the Pool looks more like a "features syndicate" than a "news agency," which it claims to be, but the terminology used to describe the Pool is immaterial. What the Pool's advocates find most important is that the reports prepared by the Pool originate in the non-aligned countries themselves, and therefore represent those countries as they are seen by their own people, rather than by outsiders, who are typically on the scene only in times of crisis.

The Non-Aligned News Pool, therefore, has not really entered directly into competition with the Western agencies, since it does not attempt to supply fast, spot news. What is important is that the over one hundred countries that now participate in the Pool's news exchange system have a channel through which they can express themselves in their own way.[21]

The extent of media dependency on the world agencies has been documented in several academic and professional studies over the past 30 years. This dependency takes a variety of forms, the most visible being the quantitative extent to which media around the world depend on world agencies, not only for general world news, but for news of their own geopolitical regions as well.

As early as the 1960s, an analysis of coverage of three international crises in four Norwegian newspapers showed that 87 percent of the analyzed news items came from the "big four" agencies.[22] A content analysis of the most important papers in India, Kenya, Lebanon, Japan, and Norway, in monthly periods of 1961 and 1968, showed that at least half of the international news items were from the same four news agencies.[23] Over a decade later, an analysis of the Third World news coverage of 14 Asian newspapers in 1977 concluded that more than three-quarters of all nonlocal Third World news came from the big world agencies.[24] One year later, in 1978, a study of reciprocal coverage of the United States and Canada showed that the world agencies accounted for over 70 percent of US news in Canadian newspapers.[25] A similar pattern was discerned in Latin America, where Fernando Reyes Matta's analysis of 16 dailies in 14 Latin American countries found that 80 percent of foreign news came from the "big four" news agencies.[26]

The major agencies not only supply conventional news and features but also broadcast television material to their clients as well. For example, UPI and Reuters, through their involvement in UPITN and VISNEWS, provide international news film for television. Thus the potential total dependency of some countries on print and film from these agencies is even higher. Although there are few empirical data to document worldwide dependency of this nature, a study by Peter Golding and Phillip Elliot analyzing Nigerian broadcast media in 1977 showed that the combined input of Reuters, AP, AFP, and VISNEWS as sources of foreign stories amounted to 85 percent of total foreign news.[27]

However, in this area, the following two studies are more interesting in terms both of the sampling and of the somewhat contradictory conclusions. The first study, conducted by Wilbur Schramm and Erwin L. Atwood, traces the flow of Third World news from its origin to the items reprinted by newspapers and then to the readers themselves. In the study, which was conducted in December 1977 but published in 1981, Schramm and Atwood have analyzed news content of 19 Asian daily newspapers in eight different languages, four international news agencies (AP, UPI, Reuters, and Agence France Presse), and the New China News Agency wire services delivered to Asian clients. The major conclusion of this study is that the circulation of news in the Third World cannot be understood entirely in terms of the international news agencies, that international news agencies are probably doing a better job quantitatively than qualitatively, and that the quality and quantity of news in the Third World are very much related to each country's own national agencies.[28]

Three weaknesses in this study make the conclusion tentative. The first is that the readership survey in the Schramm–Atwood study is limited to only one newspaper – in the Philippines. The second weakness is that in many of the Third World countries, due to limited resources as well as the lack of telecommunications infrastructure, the governments are very much involved in the process of news flow into and out of the country. Schramm and Atwood's conclusion does not account for this fact. The third point is the very definition of news and the utility of applying Western news values to judge the flow and content of news in Asian newspapers. The authors, aware of this last weakness, suggest that such a detailed analysis of content be undertaken jointly by Asian and Western journalists, admitting the difficulties observed in qualitative measurement.

The second study, by G. Cleveland Wilhoit and David Weaver, published in 1983 updating their 1979 study, examines foreign news coverage and two US wire services, tracing the flow of foreign news from these two wires into a random sample of 11 small dailies in Indiana. The major focus of this study is comparative. The baseline wire service data compiled in the authors' earlier study is compared to similar samples gathered two years later. This study replicates the earlier content analysis that was based on a coding protocol developed by the UNESCO/International Association for Media and Communication Research research group. Separate measures of conflict news, developed in a doctoral research seminar, and an intensive study of newspaper use of wire news add important new dimension to this work, according to the authors.[29]

The study concludes that

> the frequency of coverage of major world hemispheres of geo-political-economic
> similarity – in this case, North and South divisions of more or less developed
> nations – appears to shift from year to year, with relative parity of coverage
> likely over the long term. News from "official" sources of government and
> military dominates news from all world areas.

The authors observe that

> one begins with a relatively rich mixture of news . . . even including news that
> may be classified as development coverage . . . and ends with a very scanty,
> violence- and conflict-laced portrayal of the world in smaller newspapers. . . . The
> tendency of wire services to give more frequent coverage to news of conflict in
> developing nations was enhanced by the even greater proportionate use of such
> dispatches by the newspapers.[30]

Thus their findings suggest an intensifying focus on Third World violent
conflict. Their concluding remarks take on the news values where the
Schramm–Atwood study left off:

> Regardless of the reasons for the differential treatment of less developed and
> more developing countries as one moves down the news "funnel," the results
> reported here strongly emphasize the need to reassess basic news values if US
> newspaper readers in small-to-medium-size communities are to get a picture of
> the world that is less incomplete and distorted.[31]

National agencies have been studied and considered an important
intermediary factor in the control and distribution of news, supplementing
the recognized function of the "big four."[32] In spite of their acknowledged
role as significant actors, few data have been collected, just as very little
research has been done in the importance of regional agencies as an
alternative mode for sharing information among regions and countries of
developing areas. Nevertheless, it is apparent that national and regional
agencies will be subjects of future research since such inquiry is necessary to
measure the effect and impact of news agencies at those levels on the
content and direction of international news flow.

The studies that have been conducted on the national news agencies
between the mid-1950s and the late 1970s show three basic results: (1) their
remarkable dependence on world news agencies for foreign news; (2) their
direct and integral role in the dissemination of local news within a country;
and (3) their increasing participation in the output of "Third World news"
by the world news agencies.

National agencies have their own qualitative and quantitative selection
practices in domestic markets, and it is through the national agencies that
the world news services are distributed to the media. A study of the
Canadian national agency (Canadian Press) showed that the influence
exerted by world agencies was not as great as Canadian Press's influence in
setting the international discussion agenda of its customers. Further,
although the world news agencies dominate the world inputs, they have no
direct control over the selective or quantitative gatekeeping practices

employed by national agencies to fashion the world picture. According to this study, world agencies do not dominate world image-making because selective and quantitative control is firmly in the hands of national news agencies.[33]

At the end of the 1970s and the beginning of the 1980s, more attention was given to the study of the national news agencies. Most of the research undertaken at this point deals with organization and ownership systems. There are three types of ownership systems within the existing national news agencies: (1) government owned and subsidized, representing about 43 percent of the total national news agencies in the world; (2) media or cooperatively owned, accounting for 31 percent of the total; and (3) mixed enterprises (government and media owned); comprising 27 percent. According to statistics, governments have shared in about 73 percent of the total national news agencies around the world.

Few systematic studies are available on the flow of news by regional agencies. Apart from the papers prepared for the International Commission for the Study of Communication Problems (MacBride Report) on the subject in the late 1970s, the works published by Oliver Boyd-Barrett and Gertrude Robinson in the early 1980s, and a few monographs issued by the Friedrich-Ebert-Stiftung on television news exchange in 1979 and 1981, there are no major writings on regional news agencies.[34] Most publications in this area tend to be descriptive in nature and include workshop reports, resolutions, and recommendations. Boyd-Barrett's work treats regional agencies in the context of international news agencies, their forms of organization and their positions in their respective countries, and their role in agenda setting and gatekeeping functions. Robinson's analysis examines news flow from its theoretical and methodological aspects, with particular attention paid to Canada, the United States, and the former Yugoslavia. She argues for the value of an organizational, systems-level perspective in gatekeeping studies and for the value of an institutional systems perspective in understanding international news flow.

An important development in the area of regional news agencies and news exchange occurred between 1979 and 1983 in two areas: the first was the actual development of regional news agencies and the second was improved technical and professional cooperation between and among the various news and broadcasting associations and unions in Asia, Africa, and Latin America. Such arrangements were made according to geographical, economic, political, and even religious bases. They included improving cooperation between Arab and Asian television news services, new projects by the Asian Pacific Broadcasting Union for the exchange of television news in various regions in Asia, and inauguration of the Asian-Pacific News Network (ANN) by the Organization of Asian News Agencies (OANA) for the distribution of news from Tokyo, Manila, Jakarta, New Delhi, and Moscow. Inter Press Service, which was founded in 1964 by a group of Latin American and European journalists and represents a specifically Third World perspective, has established several cooperative arrangements from its bases in Rome and Panama, including an exchange of material with a US-based Interlink Press Service, which uses IPS information for distribution in the United States.[35]

Other important efforts have been the establishment of the Caribbean news agency CANA, the Pan African News Agency (PANA), the Latin American Regional Agency (LATIN), and the very recent creation of an OPEC news agency in Vienna by its member nations.

Although several studies have targeted the content aspect of international news, few have focused specifically on it, and those that have generally present qualitative rather than quantitative assessments of content. The studies on this aspect of news flow attempt to show the imperfections of current world news flows and demonstrate five shortcomings of world news.

The first is that international news is "Western-centric" since the sources of news, even in most of the Third World, are Western news agencies and wire services. The second point, as illustrated by several studies, is that the Third World coverage that does exist focuses on negative or "bad" news – catastrophes, violence, and corruption – rather than "developmental" news or education information. Further, the research conducted by Stevenson and Cole[36] revealed that negative news is not only predominant in Western media, but in the Third World media as well, a conclusion also drawn by Ume-Nwagbo in his 1982 study of African newspapers.[37] Third, international news tends to be shallow and oversimplified in that it concentrates on political leanings of governments rather than accurate and comprehensive coverage of conflicts affecting nations and people. Fourth, international news covers elites rather than the masses. And finally, the research shows that the emphasis of international news is on events rather than on factors leading to and causing events.

Another tier of research studies to be discussed here is image studies. These works are usually done in conjunction with content analyses that attempt to analyze the type of images portrayed in the flow of news and editorial material through newspapers, magazines, and in some cases radio and television. They also pay implicit and explicit attention to the probable impact and effect of the quality and quantity of flow on national and international images.

One of the studies relating the flow of news to national and international images was the joint IAMCR/UNESCO project. This project was premised on the assumed importance of the news media in determining public images of, and attitudes toward, "foreign" nations and peoples. Although this unique international comparative research project was able to provide an updated inventory of international news presentation, it was less successful in measuring the images portrayed in international news reporting. The project examined news presentation in both the press and broadcast media and included national media systems from all regions of the world. The quantitative data were gathered by 13 participating teams using a formal coding instrument designed to measure rough volume and present the overall structure of international news reporting. The news itself and a straight forward-frequency count were the units of analysis. The results showed the dominance of political news in international news reporting and the prominence of regionalism.[38]

While some studies analyze the non-advertising content of the media as the source of their data, others concentrate on specific editorial content such as "editorial page" material, which refers to the editorials that take a position or stand on behalf of the medium under examination or on behalf of a given individual, institution, or country. Still others concentrate on such special contents as "comics," "letters to the editor," sports, or financial and economic items.

For example, a study designed by Peter M. Clark and myself, examining specific editorial material in the press, demonstrated how the world view of a nation's political elite – in this case Iran's pre-revolutionary political elite and their view of Western Europe – can in turn determine their own self-image. Our contention was that a study of policy articulation and images through the media can provide a valuable framework for understanding national development. The study was conducted four years before the Iranian revolution and was carried out on the basis of the observation that policy articulation under the Shah occurred through a limited number of communication channels – one of which was the national newspaper *Kayhan*. Editorials and policy statements were divided into two time periods – pre- and post-OPEC oil price escalation – and then keyed to 18 selected variables, ranging from power to revolution and culture, regarding Iran's perception of five countries in Western Europe and of Iranian–European relations. By comparing the dominant perceptions and images of both time periods, we hoped to show how changes in perceptions and policy objectives correlate with a changing self-image reflected in the media. The most important trend in the two periods under consideration (1970 and 1974) was Iran's admiration of technological expertise and its downplay of cultural, religious, and nationalistic elements at home. The study concluded that the political elites of the time viewed "the importance of technology as inherently good because it can be naturalized into the developmental scheme in a way that ideological and political institutions cannot."[39]

Contrasting and checking such images against the background of news and symbols generated by the mosque, the bazaar, and other traditional channels of communication in Iran, in another analysis in 1974 – five years prior to the Iranian revolution – I concluded that religious and theological discourse still may be used to foster revolution in Iran and force unpopular government out of power.[40] Indeed, in contrast to the conventional big media channels such as newspapers and television, through a combination of traditional channels of news and modern small media – such as tape recorders and cassettes – the Iranian masses obtained their information and accomplished the 1978–9 Iranian revolution.[41]

Ever since the Iranian revolution, a considerable number of articles, essays, and in some cases empirical data have appeared, examining the flow of news and images across national boundaries and the role played by the media in the subsequent US–Iranian conflict. Thus far, evidence has been gathered in the following areas: the crucial role played by the transnational media in the process of legitimization; the weakness of the media in interpreting the events in light of cultural and religious factors;[42] the importance of prior patterns of information in understanding the current development of the world; the importance of geopolitical and economic interests in dissemination of news and information; the role of international telecommunication in conflict and crisis reporting; and the commercial and political nature of the media.[43] Furthermore, research on the flow of information about the Iranian revolution and other international and national crises demonstrates that a distinction must be made between the volume and effectiveness of information flow, since information can flow at a high volume and at the same time suffer reduction in quality through physical and cultural distortion.[44]

The study of the content and images contained in newspapers, magazines, and news agency files is far from being systematic. While the earlier studies dealt with political and ideological coverage of news and editorials, the relationship between content and the ideological orientation of the audience and the editors, and the proportionate allocation of space dedicated to different subjects and the images held by national and international political leaders,[45] the current trend is toward the study of specific issues and the images of particular segments of the population, such as the portrayal of minorities and women in the media.

One category of content studies that holds particular promise for future research endeavors is concerned with the much debated issue of cultural identity. It is also the least scrutinized thus far of the kinds of studies examined for this volume. Unlike studies of news or editorial page material, those that fall into this category are not preoccupied with the political underpinnings contained in the content of news and editorials. Rather, they analytically explore non-news material that is more culture-bound and that, therefore, can provide evidence of the distinction between cultures and of the need to retain the uniqueness of separate cultures in a particular atmosphere.

An example is a study of Japanese and US graphics as a reflection of a newspaper's social role, conducted by James R. Beniger and Eleanor Westney. A comparison between the uses and style of the graphics of *The New York Times* and *Asahi Shimbun* led the authors to conclude that organizational, cultural, and social factors are responsible for the difference between them. For instance, the social role of *The New York Times* as a reporter versus *Asahi*'s traditional role as educator is aptly displayed in the visual and contextual differences in the graphics of each. *The New York Times*'s graphics tend to be of a statistical nature and are relegated to the economics and business sections. To the contrary, *Asahi* responds to the Japanese people's familiarity with the visual conveyance of meaning and to their relatively sophisticated eye with a graphic style that contains flowing lines and less formalized construction.[46]

Reasons why there are so few studies dealing with specific content of newspapers and magazines in contrast with general overall studies of non-advertising material of the press and wire services is a matter of conjecture. In electronic and audio-visual media, especially those which reach large proportions of the audience such as television and radio, there appear to be two divergent strains of research – one dealing with "news" and the other with "cultural" or "entertainment" programming. Perhaps this is the result of the myopic assumptions of some researchers; print media are recognized as the dominant news sources while other media are seen as having more important cultural implications. Thus empirical studies concerned with what is termed "non-news" do not abound in the study of newspapers and magazines.

**The Direction of Flow**

There are approximately 38,000 magazines published around the world. Newsmagazines as a group have the largest international distribution and American newsmagazines, in particular, enjoy the largest international circulation. Consequently, a great bulk of writings and studies done on the flow, content, and operations of magazines have dealt with primarily American periodicals that have worldwide circulation and are transnational in nature.

*Reader's Digest*, as the magazine with the highest worldwide circulation (27 million copies a month in 18 different languages),[47] is discussed by several authors, including Armand Mattelart, who reports that the local content of this magazine in the less developed countries is only between 10 and 20 percent while in the more developed countries the local content can reach as high as 50 percent.[48] *National Geographic* also has enjoyed a fair amount of attention from the media scholars, among them Tom Buckley and Herbert Schiller.[49] Both authors conclude that the coverage of this magazine is one of concealment and omission. The magazine is conservative, "pro-status quo," and "militaristic." It is claimed that it appeals to Middle America and its illusions, but does not help to gain a true understanding of the Third World. *Time* and *Newsweek* operations, as well as their editorial policy *vis-à-vis* their international editions, have also been the subject of several analytical studies.[50] Since 1973, *Time* has engaged in a limited decentralization of its content in Europe but maintains vertical control in the United States. *Newsweek*'s international edition, on the other hand, can have content that differs up to 50 percent from its American edition.[51]

Specialized business, political, and economic magazines such as *The Economist* and *Business Week* are extremely important to the international flow of information, especially among the decision makers and elites.[52] Although there are some early descriptive studies of their activities internationally, no systematic or comprehensive studies are available on their contents, operations, and utilization beyond the traditional readership survey and readers' interest. Another thriving international magazine market comprises the "entertainment," "consumer," and popular science magazines. Recent writings on the influx of foreign, especially US, magazines in Japan and Mexico, indicate a growing demand for editorial and financial control over imported publications.[53] For example, Japanese publishers may not only press for greater financial control of the imported US popular science magazines, but insist that only 50 percent of the content of such magazines be of original US copy.[54] Similarly, a study of the Mexican edition of *Cosmopolitan* shows relatively more traditional coverage compatible with local cultures and tastes.[55]

While most studies have examined American magazines, a few have looked at other magazines with international distribution. One such article, by Karen F. Dajani, discusses *Howa*, a magazine for Arab women.[56] *Howa* has an international market in the Middle East and an approximate circulation of 200,000. The magazine focuses on problems of working women and homemakers. Efforts are made to preserve *Howa*'s cultural identity: Westernization is avoided. Studies also show a good deal of concentration of newly published ethnic magazines in such metropolitan centers as London, Paris, New York, and Washington. These magazines, often published by immigrant or exiled groups, focus on political, social, and economic affairs – some with a wide regional or international circulation.

In an expanding worldwide market not only are the industrialized countries of the North searching for readership and joint ventures in the South among the less industrialized regions of the world, but they are also engaged in fierce competition among themselves in Europe and North America. The 1990s have seen major mergers and consolidations taking place within the mass media. Particularly in the press and television industries these mergers and consolidations have successfully joined the mass media in the hands of a few multinational firms and corporations.

Additionally, several studies have examined the state of the domestic magazine industries in various countries such as Italy, Germany, and the Philippines. In many cases, the domestics are heavily influenced by their American counterparts and in some cases are affiliated with them.[57]

Research into the content and coverage of magazines with regional and international circulation is spotty and, at times, scarce.[58] Such content analyses have ranged from examining the image of Latin America and the Soviet Union in 10 US magazines in the 1960s to the coverage of Asia by leading US newsmagazines in the early 1970s and similar studies dealing with Africa in the early 1980s. In the rapidly changing environment of the market, readership, and international affairs the findings of these studies tend to be partial, tentative, and inconclusive. However, a few general observations can be made: the tone of most of these magazines often tends to be patronizing; the emphasis is frequently on negative elements such as conflict and violence; there is a general neglect of domestic development in various countries unless it has some implications for the foreign policy of the country in which the magazine is published; and international coverage tends to focus on political/governmental topics and crisis/trivia stories.

One of the most intriguing studies of content is C.B. Pratt's analysis of the differences between images projected of Africa by US "news" (*Time, Newsweek, U.S. News and World Report*) and "opinion" (*The Nation, The New Republic, National Review*) magazines. However, Pratt's study shows more similarities than differences between the two categories of publications and even between "opinion" magazines on different ends of the political spectrum. The "opinion" magazines have a slightly higher number of stories on Africa than do "news" magazines, but both are under 4 percent of the total editorial space. All the magazines portrayed Africa as "politically gullible, naive and immature but also as a continent whose course of action is precariously dependent on the Big Powers." The image of the conflict-ridden continent is clear: while coverage of geography and topology is virtually ignored, coverage of coups, public executions, and of countries in trouble spots was highlighted.[59]

In another study of coverage of foreign affairs by American "elite and mass periodicals," Robert L. Bledsoe and his colleagues reported that Europe receives the most coverage, although Asia was important in the early 1970s. South America is virtually ignored and emphasis is on trouble spots rather than overview stories. They conclude that there is a "general orientation toward political events and actors to the virtual exclusion of more fundamental problems."[60] Other studies show how in the cases of consumer and general magazines, advertising and editorial content work on each other to form a mutually reinforcing cycle. Thus magazine contents are affected by editorial economic decisions.

Research on concentration of media ownership is currently in a period of confusion and transition. The introduction of new technologies and the smooth integration of the media industries have made the old "clear-cut" formulas of encouraging diversity in the press, broadcasting, and film obsolete or contradictory. Media industries face a multitude of great new opportunities for investment and great economic risks and they are going against the old forms of regulatory compromise that were often more of a form of protecting media interests than an incentive to diversify. Most importantly, the traditional consensus among researchers and policy groups in liberal democracies, which were usually concerned with and focused on improving and fine-tuning the existing mechanisms for avoiding the worst abuses of media concentration, has broken down. For researchers today there are a variety of positions, but in place of the unstable consensus there are emerging two very different and conflicting approaches to the issue of concentration of economic power in media. The first group advocates letting the free market and technology decide, while the second group calls for a greater need for more democratic social structure. Both groups may be committed to diversity in the media, but they differ greatly in what is meant by diversity and how it is to be achieved.[61]

Four major conclusions can be drawn from the research on the direction of international news flow. The first is that the majority of international news flows from the "center," the "North," or the "West" by way of their dominant news agencies; that is, the flow is vertical from the developed to the developing nations. Second, proximity – physical, psychocultural, and political – is a major factor in determining news coverage in that indigenous media tend to select items regarding their own geographical region. A third conclusion is that Western Europe and the United States receive the greater amount of coverage in the media while the former socialist countries and Third World receive the least. Finally, although horizontal flows do exist within the developing as well as the developed world, this type of flow constitutes a substantially smaller portion of the overall coverage than does vertical flow or "round" flow.

In summary, it is difficult to depict adequately the current state of research on content in international news, since most authors, although presenting assumptions on this aspect, have not undertaken comprehensive research in this area. Another major problem is disagreement and conflicting results as evidenced in studies conducted by Schramm, Stevenson and Cole, Al Hester, Wilhoit and Weaver, and several others. However, one conclusion is manifest in nearly all of the studies: although there has been some improvement over the quantity of international news, largely provided by recently established agencies as well as national and regional efforts, the quality of international flow of news remains poor, with intensifying focus on Third World violent conflict and crisis as one moves down the news "funnel." Conflicting news values are indeed crucial factors contributing to the way the world and its problems are portrayed in the media. Thus qualitative evaluation remains a definite weakness in the current research on the content of news flow.

The review of the literature clearly shows a large gap in our knowledge about the flow of international news. For example, we know more about the quantity and quality of the "Third World" coverage by the "West" but less about the "Third World" coverage of the "West" – and still less about the flow of news between and among the less industrialized or "Third World" countries around the world.

Additionally, one of the aspects of news imbalance is the uneven distribution of communication resources, and, at least in one instance, the foreign correspondence. My 1975 survey showed a total of 865 foreign correspondents reporting foreign news media in the United States. Wide variance was noted in stationing of correspondents – none from Black Africa, 23 from Israel, 1 from Pakistan, 23 from Taiwan. Western Europe accounted for more than half of the correspondents, with few from Latin America, the Middle East, or Asia. There was a total absence of foreign correspondents from several countries.[62] However, my 1981 update shows that there were 1,262 foreign correspondents covering the United States – an increase of over 45 percent in six years. Twelve new countries have joined the list, all of which are Third World members. On a regional level, there are still no reporters from Black Africa.[63] What bearing does this increase in correspondents have on the flow of news? It seems clear that a flow and content analysis of those countries increasing their correspondents or installing them in the United States for the first time might tell us something about the volume and quality of international news reporting. In short, to measure the actual two-day flow we need more of the intake–output ratio, a research strategy that is often neglected.

There are several factors that have been found to influence the global flow of news. One of the most frequently examined factors in news gathering and dissemination, and one that is influential on an individual, organizational, regional, and global level, is economics. Economics affects the quality, quantity, availability, and distribution of news in a number of ways. Among these are the number of foreign correspondents, the ability of regions to establish their own infrastructures for news gathering and transmission, the ability to produce news media that can compete successfully with transnational media in advertising, news quality, and journalist compensation; telecommunication tariffs, and the ability of the masses to purchase the news product.[64]

Political factors have an effect on both news content and the actual flow of news.[65] The political climate of a state clearly affects the international news value of events associated with that state as well as having other direct effects such as censorship, controlling the entry and exit of journalists, and controlling the importation and marketing of news products. Additionally, official and unofficial perceptions of news value, and of the function and role of news and information within a given political system, and between systems, directly influence the content and flow of news within that system.

One of the most complicated factors influencing the global flow of news is sociocultural differences.[66] Here cultural, religious, and traditional beliefs that differ significantly from one region or country to another create serious barriers to a smooth flow of news and information. Language, translation difficulties, and ethnic biases are perhaps the most common sources of such problems.

One of the most obvious factors affecting the content and flow of news internationally is the development of technology and the infrastructure associated with it.[67] In developing areas where infrastructural development is primitive, rare, or nonexistent, it is difficult to gather and disseminate news in a timely fashion. The solution has been news importation, which has stirred concern over the issues involved in the economic, political, and sociocultural factors of global news flow.

Associated with the above factors are others referred to as "extra-media" factors, such as literacy level, population, and trade.[68] Among these would be included physical, cultural, and psychological proximity that affects the group's view of the outside world. These factors, intertwined with the broader economic, political, and cultural elements, directly affect the content and dissemination of news in any given area, and can enhance the global flow of news as well as impede it.

Research regarding the possible effects – positive and negative – of the international flow of news has concentrated on such issues as content, stereotypes, cultural domination, and expectations. News stereotyping and its effect on the audience have been studied in Africa, Latin America, Asia, and the Middle East. A good number of writers and researchers view the Northern-dominated (meaning both East and West) flow as distorting information on cultural, political, and economic progress in the developing world. Others carrying this a step further conclude that such domination has led to a massive consumer culture eroding national identity and sovereignty in different parts of the world. Still, a few analyses observe the dysfunctioning processes of such imbalances on international conflict, national discontent, and the New International Economic Order. Similarly, several studies conclude that the news media reinforce the status quo, which is a division of the world between high- and low-status nations, and present the world as more conflict-laden than it really is, to emphasize the use of force rather than peaceful solutions. Yet, there are those analyses which caution that the world news media are incapable of assembling an accurate, complete, and current picture of objective reality in every corner of the globe, and that news should be considered only one source of information and not a physical map of the world.

## Notes

1. Hamid Mowlana, ed., *International Flow of News: An Annotated Bibliography* (Paris: UNESCO, 1983).

2. Hamid Mowlana, *International Communication: A Selected Bibliography* (Dobuque, IA: Kendall/Hunt Publishing Company, 1971). See also Hamid Mowlana, "Trends in Research on International Communication in the United States," *Gazette* XIX: 2 (1973), pp. 79–90, and my more extensive review, "The Communication Dimension of International Studies in the United States: A Quantitative Assessment," *International Journal of Communication Research* (University of Cologne), 1: 1 (Winter 1974), pp. 3–22. For earlier bibliographical publication in international communication see Harold Lasswell, Ralph Casey, and Bruce L. Smith, *Propaganda and Promotional Activities: An Annotated Bibliography* (Minneapolis, MN: University of Minnesota Press, 1953).

3. Alexander Szalai's study (with Margaret Croke and Associates) *The United Nations and the News Media* (New York: United Nations Institute for Training and Research [UNITAR], 1972), is the most extensive international comparative study in the field under scrutiny. Prominent in the entire field has been UNESCO's effort to encourage and sponsor comparative research during the last twenty years. See UNESCO's publications, *Reports and Papers on Mass Communication*, especially nos 65, 69, 70, 74, 75, 76, 77, 79, 81, 83, 85, 87, 90, and 92.

4. See: Jacques Kayser, *One Week's News: Comparative Study of 17 Major Dailies for a Seven Day Period* (Paris: UNESCO, 1953); Wilbur Schramm, *One Day in the World's Press* (Stanford, CA: Stanford University Press, 1960); International Press Institute, *The Flow of News* (Zurich: International Press Institute, 1963); George Gerbner and George Marvanyi, "The Many Worlds of the World's Press," *Journal of Communication*, 27: 1 (Winter 1977), pp. 52–66; Al Hester, "Five Years of Foreign News on U.S. Television Evening Newscasts," *Gazette*, 24: 1 (1978), pp. 86–95; Robert L. Stevenson and Richard Cole, "Foreign News in Selected Countries," *Research Reports*, International Communication Agency, US Govern-

ment, Washington, DC (July 1980); and Wilbur Schramm and Erwin L. Atwood, *Circulation of News in the Third World: A Study of Asia* (Hong Kong: Chinese University Press, 1981).

5. Johan Galtung, "A Structural Theory of Imperialism," *Journal of Peace Research*, 8: 2 (1971), pp. 81–118; Johan Galtung and Mari H. Ruge, "The Structure of Foreign News: The Presentation of the Congo, Cuba and Cyprus in Four Norwegian Newspapers," *Journal of Peace Research*, 2 (1965), pp. 64–91; Rafael Roncagliolo, "Flow of News and Freedom of the Press," *The Democratic Journalist*, March 1979, pp. 7–11; Fernando Reyes Matta, "The Information Bedazzlement of Latin America," *Development Dialogue*, 2 (1976), pp. 29–42; and Herbert I. Schiller, "Freedom from the 'Free Flow,'" *Journal of Communication*, 24: 1 (Winter 1974), pp. 110–117.

6. Peter M. Clark and Hamid Mowlana, "Iran's Perception of Western Europe: A Study in National and Foreign Policy Articulation," *International Interactions*, 4: 2 (1978), pp. 99–123; International Association for Mass Communication Research/UNESCO, "The World of the News: The News of the World," Final Report of the "Foreign Images" study undertaken by IAMCR for UNESCO (London/Paris, 1980); Edward Said, *Covering Islam: How the Media and the Experts Determine How We See the Rest of the World* (New York: Pantheon, 1981; James D. Halloran and Virginia Nightingale, "Young TV Viewers and Their Images of Foreigners: A Summary and Interpretation of a Four Nation Study," Centre for Mass Communication Research, University of Leicester, 1983; UNESCO, *Mass Media: The Image, Role and Social Condition of Women*, Reports and Papers on Mass Communication, No. 84, Paris, 1979; and C.B. Pratt, "The Reportage and Image of Africa in Six U.S. News and Opinion Magazines: A Comparative Study," *Gazette*, 26: 1 (1980), pp. 31–45. These are examples of the studies using news stories and editorials as the base of data. Studies dealing with perceptions and images using survey research and other sources are not considered in this study.

7. For examples of this method see Charles A. McClelland, "Answers to Common Questions About the World News Index and International Event Analysis," Los Angeles, University of Southern California, July 1976; Philip M. Burgess and Raymond W. Lawton, *Indicators of International Behavior: An Assessment of Events Data Research*, (International Studies Series) (Beverly Hills, CA: Sage Publications, 1972); Hamid Mowlana, "A Paradigm for Source Analysis in Events Data Research: Mass Media and the Problems of Validity," *International Interactions*, 2: 1 (Summer 1975), pp. 33–44; and Robert Burrowes, Gary D. Hoggard, Russell J. Long, Hamid Mowlana, Sophia Peterson, Warren R. Phillips, and Alvin Richman, "Events–Interaction Analysis: Selected Bibliography of Recent Research," American Political Science Association Annual Meeting, Chicago, September 1971.

8. For illustrations see UNESCO's series, *Reports and Papers on Mass Communication: News Dependence*, No. 93 (1980); *Transnational Communication and Mass Cultural Industries*, No. 92 (1982); *Mass Media: Codes of Ethics and Councils*, No. 86 (1979); *News Values and Principles of Cross-Cultural Communication*, No. 85 (1979). See also Jim Richstad and Michael H. Anderson, eds, *Crisis in the International News: Policies and Prospects* (New York: Columbia University Press, 1981); Oliver Boyd-Barrett, *The International News Agencies* (Beverly Hills, CA: Sage Publications, 1980); Friedrich-Ebert-Stiftung, *Mass Media Manual: Television News in a North–South Perspective* (Bonn, 1981); and Thomas Szecsko, *Recent Studies (on Radio and Television) 1976–77* (Budapest: Mass Communication Research Centre, 1978).

9. For a discussion of extra-media data in flow of international news see Karl Erik Rosengren, "International News: Methods, Data and Theory," *Journal of Peace Research*, 11: 2 (1974), pp. 145–156; and Hamid Mowlana, "A Paradigm for Comparative Mass Media Analysis," in Heinz-Dietrich Fischer and John C. Merrill, eds, *International and Intercultural Communication* (New York: Hastings House, 1976), pp. 474–484. My paradigm integrates the extra-media variables with intra-media variables as well as making a distinction between production and distribution of the message in the flow. Rosengren directly challenges the approach by Galtung and offers the extra-media approach as an alternative. For a follow-up and a specification of Rosengren's extra-media data notion see his "Bias in News: Methods

and Concepts," in Cleveland Wilhoit, ed., *Mass Communication Review Yearbook I* (Beverly Hills, CA: Sage Publications, 1980), pp. 249–264.

10. Galtung, "A Structural Theory of Imperialism."

11. Herb Addo, "Structural Bases of International Communication," *Peace, Science, Society*, 23 (1974), pp. 81–100.

12. Robert Buijtenhuijs and René Baesjou, "Center and Periphery in Two African Newspapers: Testing Some Hypothesis on Cultural Dominance," *Kroniek Van Africa*, 33: 3 (1974), pp. 243–271.

13. Bruce McKenzie and Derek Overton, "International News Via Tasmanian/Australian News Media Outlets: An Analysis of Sources, Flow Biases, Weaknesses and Consequences," paper for the ANZAAS Congress, Brisbane, Australia, May 1981. See also Jim Richstad and Tony Mnaemeka, "Information Regions: Context for International News Flow Research," paper prepared for Association for Education in Journalism Convention, Boston, MA. August 1980.

14. Reyes Matta, "The Information Bedazzlement of Latin America."

15. Shelton A. Gunaratne, "Reporting the Third World in the 1970s: A Longitudinal Content Analysis of Two Australian Dailies," *Gazette*, 29 (1982), pp. 15–29.

16. Gehan Rachty, "Foreign News in Nine Arab Countries," *Communication and Development Review*, 2: 2 (Summer 1978), pp. 23–25.

17. Frank Kaplan, "The Plight of Foreign News in the U.S. Mass Media," *Gazette*, 25: 4 (1979), pp. 233–243.

18. Andrew K. Semmel, "The Elite Press, the Global System, and Foreign News Attention," *International Interactions*, 3: 4 (1977), pp. 317–328.

19. Gerbner and Marvanyi, "The Many Worlds of the World's Press."

20. Robert L. Stevenson and Richard R. Cole, "Foreign News and the 'New World Information Order' Debate," Foreign News in Selected Countries, Part II, International Communication Agency, US Government, July 1980.

21. D.R. Mankekar and J.S. Yadava, "News Agencies Pool of Non-Aligned Countries," *Communication Research Trends: A Quarterly Information Service from the Center for the Study of Communication and Culture*, 10: 4, (1982) pp. 12–13.

22. Galtung and Ruge, "The Structure of Foreign News."

23. Barbara A. Salamore, "Reporting of External Behaviors in the World's Press: A Comparison of Regional Sources," paper presented at the Annual Meeting of the International Studies Association, Washington, DC, February 1975.

24. Wilbur Schramm, "International News Wires and Third World News in Asia: A Preliminary Report," Center of Communication Studies, Chinese University of Hong Kong, 1978.

25. Vernon M. Sparkes, "The Flow of News Between Canada and the United States," *Gazette*, 55: 2 (1978), pp. 260–268.

26. Fernando Reyes Matta, "El Encandilamiento Informativo de América Latina," *La Circulation de Noticias en América Latina* (Mexico: Federación Latinoamericana de Periodistas, 1978), pp. 115–139.

27. See Peter Golding and Phillip Elliot, *Making the News* (London: Longman, 1979).

28. Schramm and Atwood, *Circulation of News in the Third World*.

29. G. Cleveland Wilhoit and David Weaver, " Foreign News Coverage in Two U.S. Wire Services: An Update," *Journal of Communication*, 33: 2 (Spring 1983), pp. 132–147.

30. Wilhoit and Weaver, "Foreign News Coverage in Major U.S. Wire Services and Small Daily Newspapers," paper read at the International Association for Mass Communication Research, 13th Scientific Conference, Paris, September 1982, p. 16.

31. Wilhoit and Weaver, "Foreign News Coverage in Two U.S. Wire Services: An Update," p. 147. For their earlier study see "Foreign News Coverage in Two U.S. Wire Services," *Journal of Communication*, 31: 2 (Spring 1981), pp. 55–63.

32. See monographs I, II, and III on news agencies published by the International Commission for the Study of Communication Problems, Paris, UNESCO, 1979–80; also Boyd-Barrett, *The International News Agencies*; and Sophia Peterson, "International News

Selection by the Elite Press: A Case Study," *Public Opinion Quarterly*, 45: 2 (1981), pp. 143–163. Also Gertrude Joch Robinson, *News Agencies and World News in Canada and the United States and Yugoslavia: Methods and Data* (Fribourg: University Press of Fribourg, 1981).

33. Robinson, *News Agencies and World News in Canada, the United States and Yugoslavia*, pp. 206–210.

34. Ibid. See also references to monographs published by the International Commission for the Study of Communication Problems, *Many Voices, One World* (Paris: UNESCO, 1980), pp. 297–298; Boyd-Barrett, *The International News Agencies*; and Friedrich-Ebert-Stiftung, *Report of the URTNA Study Mission 1979 for the Feasibility for TV News Exchange in the URTNA Region* (Bonn: Friedrich-Ebert-Stiftung, 1979); and Friedrich-Ebert-Stiftung, *Mass Media Manual*. For references to other regions of the world see Mowlana, ed., *International Flow of News*.

35. Cees J. Hamelink, *Cultural Autonomy in Global Communications* (White Plains, NY: Longman, 1983), pp. 72–78.

36. Stevenson and Cole, "Foreign News and the 'New World Information Order' Debate."

37. Ebele N. Ume-Nwagbo, "Foreign News Flow in Africa: A Content Analytical Study on a Regional Basis," *Gazette*, 29 (1982), pp. 41–56.

38. For a summary of this report see Annabelle Sreberny-Mohammadi, "The World of the News: The News of the World," in *New Structures of International Communication?: The Role of Research*, Main Papers from the IAMCR Caracas Conference (1980): Leicester, International Association for Mass Communication Research, 1982, pp. 183–193; for the complete version see IAMCR/UNESCO, "The World of News: The News of the World."

39. Clark and Mowlana, "Iran's Perception of Western Europe: A Study in National and Foreign Policy Articulation," p. 123.

40. Hamid Mowlana, "Mass Communication, Elites and National Systems in the Middle East," in *Der Anteil der Massenmedien bei der Herausbildung des Bewusstseins in der sich wandelnden Welt* (Proceedings of the International Association for Mass Communication Scientific Conference), Leipzig, September 1974, Karl-Marx-Universität, pp. 55–71.

41. Hamid Mowlana, "Technology versus Tradition: Communication in the Iranian Revolution," *Journal of Communication*, 29: 3 (Summer 1979), pp. 107–112. The study of the Iranian revolution and the flow of news and political messages between the West and Iran prior to the revolution underlined the importance of an appreciation of the total communication system in a given culture. In this article I discuss the conflict between the official culture of the government that I believed was dominated by the Western media systems, and the traditional culture of the masses rooted in the Iranian national and religious traditions.

42. Said, *Covering Islam*. Also see William C. Adams, ed., *Television Coverage of the Middle East* (Norwood, NJ: Ablex Publishing Corporation, 1981).

43. Hamid Mowlana, "The Role of the Media in the U.S.–Iranian Conflict," in A. Arnow and W. Dissanayakea, eds, *The Role of News Media in National and International Conflict* (Boulder, CO: Westview Press, 1984), pp. 71–99.

44. Hamid Mowlana, "Communication for Political Change: The Iranian Revolution," in George Gerbner and Marsha Siefert, eds, *World Communications: A Handbook* (White Plains, NY: Longman, 1984).

45. For example of these earlier studies see: W.W. Waymack, "Editorial Pages in Wartime. Their Technique and Ideology," *Journalism Quarterly* (March 1942), pp. 34–38; J. Zvi Namenwirth and Richard C. Bibbee, "National Distinctions: Mass and Prestige Editorials in American and British Newspapers," paper presented at the International Studies Association meeting, New York, March 16, 1973; Wayne Wolfe, "Images of the U.S. in Latin American Press," *Journalism Quarterly*, 41 (1964), pp. 75–79; C.A. Oliphant, "The Image of the United States as Projected by the Peking Review," *Journalism Quarterly*, 41 (1964), pp. 460–469; and Ithiel de Sola Pool, *The Prestige Papers: A Study of Their Editorials* (Stanford, CA: Stanford University Press, 1952). See Godwin C. Chu and Leonard Chu, "Parties in Conflict: Letters to the Editors of the People's Daily," *Journal of Communication* (Autumn, 1981), pp. 90–96.

46. James R. Beninger and Eleanor Westney, "Japanese and U.S. Media: Graphics as a Reflection of Newspapers' Social Role," *Journal of Communication*, 31: 2 (Spring 1981), p. 27;

see also Alan Shuttleworth, "People and Culture," in Peter Dauson, Rolfe Mayersohn, and Edward Shils, eds, *Literary Taste, Culture and Mass Communication*, Vol. 14 (Teaneck, NJ: Somerest House, 1980), p. 153.

47. The *Reader's Digest* 1995 circulation figure was obtained from its headquarters in New York City, November 1995.

48. Armand Mattelart, *Multinational Corporations and the Control of Culture* (Brighton: Harvester Press, 1979), p. 221.

49. Herbert I. Schiller, *The Mind Managers* (Boston, MA: Beacon Press, 1973), pp. 86–94; and Tom Buckley, "With the *National Geographic* on its Endless, Cloudless, Voyage," *New York Times Magazine*, 1970, p. 13.

50. L. John Martin, "American Newsmagazines and the European Scene," *Gazette*, 2: 6 (1960), p. 209.

51. Mattelart, *Multinational Corporations*, pp. 213–220.

52. In connection with newsmagazines see Henryka Schabowska and Ulf Himmelstrand, *Africa Reports on the Nigerian Crisis: News, Attitudes and Background Information* (Scandinavian Institute of African Studies), (Uppsala: Holmes and Meier, 1979). See also Derry Eynon, "U.S. Business Periodicals for Overseas Readers," *Journalism Quarterly*, 48 (Autumn 1971), p. 548.

53. Anna Lucia Zornosa, "Collaboration and Modernization: Case Study of Transnational Magazine," paper presented at the Workshop on Sex-Roles in the Mass Media, International Association for Mass Communication Research Conference, Paris, September 1982.

54. "U.S. Science Magazines Become Popular in Japan," *Business Week*, June 28, 1982, p. 44.

55. Zornosa, "Collaboration and Modernization," p. 6.

56. Karen Finlon Dajani, "Magazine for Arab Women: *Howa*," *Journalism Quarterly*, 59: 1 (Spring 1982), p. 117.

57. J.H. Schacht, "Italian Weekly Magazines Bloom Wildly but Need Pruning," *Journalism Quarterly*, 47: 1 (Spring 1970), p. 140.

58. See John R. Whitaker, *The Image of Latin America in U.S. Magazines* (New York Magazine Publishers Association, 1960); Sharif al Mujahid, "Coverage of Pakistan in Three U.S. Newsmagazines," *Journalism Quarterly*, 47: 1 (1970), pp. 126–130, 156; John Lent and Shanti Rao, "A Content Analysis of National Media Coverage of Asian News and Information," *Gazette*, 1: 25 (1979), pp. 16–22; Daniel J. Leab, "Canned Crisis: U.S. Magazines, Quemoy and the Matsus," *Journalism Quarterly*, 44: 2 (Summer 1967), p. 341; Anita M. Dasbach, "U.S.–Soviet Magazine Propaganda: *America Illustrated* and *USSR*," *Journalism Quarterly*, 43: 1 (Spring 1966), pp. 73–84; and Eugene J. Rosi, "How 50 Periodicals and the *Times* Interpreted the Test Ban Controversy," *Journalism Quarterly*, 41: 3 (Autumn 1964), p. 547.

59. Pratt, "The Reportage and Images of Africa in Six U.S. News and Opinion Magazines," p. 35.

60. Robert L. Bledsoe, Robert Handberg, William S. Maddox, David R. Lennox, and Dennis A. Long, "Foreign Affairs Coverage in Elite and Mass Periodicals," *Journalism Quarterly*, 59: 3 (1982), pp. 471–474.

61. Robert A. White (Issue Editor), "Perspectives in Communication Research: What Kind of Media Diversity? Let the Free Market and Technology Decide," *Communication Research Trends: A Quarterly Information Service from the Center for the Study of Communication and Culture*, 4: 1 (1983), p. 7.

62. Hamid Mowlana, "Who Covers America?," *Journal of Communication*, 25: 3 (Summer 1975), pp. 86–91.

63. Hamid Mowlana, "Who Covers America: An Update," School of International Service, American University, Washington, DC, 1983.

64. For economic factors affecting the flow of news see sections on Asia, Latin America and Africa in Mowlana, ed., *International Flow of News: An Annotated Bibliography*, pp. 104–202, and 251–306.

65. Political factors have been discussed in a number of works, among them Anthony

Smith's *The Geopolitics of Information: How Western Culture Dominates the World* (New York: Oxford University Press, 1980).

66. For illustration of sociocultural factors see Edward Said, *Orientalism* (New York: Vintage Books. 1989), and his *Covering Islam*.

67. For examples see "Structural Issues in Global Communications," A Report Based Upon a Meeting at Leeds Castle, Kent, England, 1982, The Tobin Foundation, Washington, DC, 1982; Edward W. Ploman, "The International Flow of Information: Legal Aspects," in Friedrich-Ebert-Stiftung, *Mass Media Annual* (Bonn: Friedrich-Ebert-Stiftung, 1981); see also such technical reports as ITU, INTELSAT, etc.

68. Karl E. Rosengren, "International News: Methods, Data and Theory," *Journal of Peace Research*, 11: 2 (1974), pp. 145–156; and his "Bias in News: Methods and Concepts."

# 4

# Broadcasting the World: National and International Images

An important part of the international flow of information occurs through the technology and methods of broadcasting. In this respect, three areas of inquiry occupy a major position in international communication: television, international radio broadcasting, and the most recent technology and phenomenon in international relations, the Internet.

## Perspectives in Television Flow

The early studies on the international flow of information were concerned with print media and news agencies, but it was not long before television was singled out from the diversity of media by national planners as well as communication scholars as a primary area of importance. The rapid technological advances of this medium contributed to its growth and the degree of interest generated. For example, in 1950 only five countries had regular television service, but by the late 1970s, there were 400 million television receivers in 138 countries.[1] Additionally, it is estimated that the number of television sets worldwide has increased at least 60 percent in the last two decades.

The character of international television flows may be viewed from two historical perspectives. The first is a review of the progression of scholarly research and inquiry conducted in the field, represented by the early empirical work of Kaarle Nordenstreng and Tapio Varis in a 1974 report prepared for UNESCO, which provided the first empirical documentation of worldwide flows of television programming.[2] Through data compiled via questionnaires administered in over 50 countries covering topics such as general content and percentages of imported versus domestic programming, Nordenstreng and Varis were able to identify two predominant trends in global television programming: one-way flow from big exporters to the rest of the world and the predominance of entertainment programming. On the basis of average hours of television programming exported per year, the leading producers and distributors at that time were the United States (150,000 hours per year), the United Kingdom and France (both 20,000 hours per year), and the Federal Republic of Germany (6,000 hours per year).[3]

Nordenstreng and Varis were aware that the scope of their study was limited to clarifying actual general patterns of international flows of all kinds of television programming. This narrow scope permitted omission of relevant issues such as ownership, historical analysis of flows, and in-depth investigation of the cultural, economic, and political implications of one-way global television traffic. In spite of these limitations, their findings served as a springboard for a flurry of discussion and highlighted the urgency for further research in this area.

A second historical approach to reviewing global television flows is to examine the growth of television as it interfaces with the production and distribution of news within a nation. A number of studies have been conducted to examine the significance of television news and other programmed material. Among these studies are those of Elihu Katz,[4] Russell W. Neuman,[5] and John Robinson,[6] who have treated such subjects as Third World television programming, patterns of recall among television news viewers, and the larger question of comprehension. There have also been more specific studies dealing with images, impressions, and stereotypes in the content of news programs. Such studies as those by William C. Adams, Haluk Sahin, Dennis K. Davis and John Robinson and others,[7] when treated cumulatively, portray the "world of TV news" as a self-contained, coherent area, with its own internal logic and dynamics, which tend to form social reality in specific ways.

Studies of television coverage of international affairs by American networks show that, with the exception of the Middle East and Vietnam, news coverage of the Third World is, at best, sparse. Most of the studies dealing with television news are crisis-oriented and deal mainly with television coverage of the Third World. This is not only because the United States as a major power is involved in many of these world events, but also because television has become a major source of news and information for large segments of the American public, and data on television news are readily available in indices and abstracts.

The crucial question in analysis of the media in international affairs is not only speculative and normative (what the media *can* or *should* do) but also functional (how the media currently operate under certain structural conditions and in response to particular environmental factors). Some studies do address themselves to the structural conditions of television news, but most of the analyses undertaken address the whole question of news flow and news coverage by examining the pattern of the television coverage of certain international issues.

Some studies in the United States are of particular interest here. One deals with television coverage of the Middle East and analyzes some of the most intensely reported news stories of the past two decades: the Iranian hostage crisis, the Soviet involvement in Afghanistan, and Anwar Sadat's trip to Jerusalem.[8] The other contains 13 issue-oriented and wide-ranging studies of television coverage of such topics as terrorism, the Third World, Vietnam, and Latin America.[9] The focus of these studies is the role of Western television coverage in the developing countries. For example, Adams examines controversies of television coverage of international affairs in terms of thoroughness versus superficiality, US versus global vantage, left versus right, and Hobbesian versus Panglossian (liberal model versus "new class" leftist views).[10] James F. Larson presents an overview of international affairs coverage on US evening network news from 1972 to 1979, showing the sparsity of the coverage and supporting the conclusion of others that "many portions of the globe scarcely existed as far as viewers of US network TV news were concerned."[11] Unfortunately, there is little coverage of Europe and such issues as the arms race and disarmament, and none of Eastern socialist countries, let alone the forgotten continent of Africa.

One of the studies conducted by Peter Dahlgren suggests that three motifs – social disorder, flawed development, and primitivism – have pervaded Third World coverage by television networks in the United States. He reports the following:[12]

- According to the cumulative imagery that emerges from network news reports, disorder looms eternal in the Third World.
- This violence is a very particular kind; it is overt, blatant, and often irrational.
- The West stands for rationality: science over magic, purpose over activity, man over nature.
- Corruption in the Third World takes on more of a systematic quality and a similar treatment characterizes human rights violations.
- Idealization of the primitive is implicit in much of the reporting, becoming relatively explicit only occasionally. When reports highlight manifestations of primitivism, they can be grouped under one of two sub-motifs: exoticism or barbarism.
- Reports of the Third World, like the other stories on TV news, offer the viewer a form of truth, the literal truth of facticity.

Studies in the United Kingdom, Sweden, and several other Western countries over the past decade or so show that the world of television news, in its depiction of domestic and internal development, tends to address the needs and interests of the social classes and economic and political elites. Dahlgren notes this observation and adds that "though TV news' proximity to the political economic processes of the international arena are more remote compared to the domestic arena, its way of seeing reveals a hegemonic approach in characterizing social and political realities between countries."[13]

Attention has also been given to the political/economic processes of international television news and programs. However, two factors have contributed to the expansion of the flow of television news in regions such as Asia-Pacific. Firstly, there has been considerable improvements and expansion of terrestrial communication networks covering the region as a whole, capable of carrying television signals and secondly, the low cost of satellite tariffs, which has been reduced from the maximum of $2,000 for the initial 10 minutes in 1980 to a maximum of $185 for the same time period in 1996.

There has also been a growing tendency toward the expansion of commercial television in several Western European countries, particularly in the United Kingdom and Germany. On the other hand, because of internal political change and communication policies adopted in some of the Third World countries, such as Iran and Nicaragua, commercial television and importation of foreign materials have been restricted in favor of public service and national developmental objectives.

## Impact and Effects of Television Flows

At the global level, television flow can be seen as the offspring of previously existing broadcasting and film flows. Not surprisingly, the patterns of introduction and development of television in many nations are similar to those in the United States, where the infrastructure and resources of broadcasting and film were already in place to nurture the growth of television. This process is traced by Everett M. Rogers and Livia Antola in their study on television flows in Latin America. In this instance, Mexico plays a crucial role both as a regional producer of television programs and as a gatekeeper for American programs being distributed throughout Latin America, having gained its advantage in the late 1950s when dubbing in Cuba was no longer possible. Because Mexico possessed dubbing capability and a suitable infrastructure resulting from its film industry, its potential market and proximity to the United States provided the additional necessary ingredients for the development of a television industry. A trend was established that foreign television programming is broadcast within Latin America only after Mexico has first purchased it.[14] More recently, dubbing studios have opened in Brazil and Peru and those nations, along with Argentina and Venezuela, now compete with Mexico in television programming in Latin America. Despite such competition, Mexico maintains its key position as a gatekeeper in television flow in Latin America.

As described by Rogers and Antola, it is enlightening to follow the process by which foreign television programs are transferred to Latin America. US television producers exhibit pilot programs at an annual two-week screening session in Los Angeles in May, attended by those purchasing programming for Latin American TV. When there are enough interested buyers for the American networks to cover costs and make a profit, the programs are sent to Mexico for dubbing and distributed from there to those Latin American networks that have agreed to buy them.[15]

Within other regions of the world, major producing nations are beginning to function in a gatekeeping role similar to that of Mexico. Lebanon, Egypt and Iran are important television centers in the Middle East, as is Japan for the Far East.

The most comprehensive summaries of international television flows are found in the original work of Nordenstreng and Varis[16] and a venture to map international television flow with a new methodology by the London-based International Institute of Communication (reported periodically in *Intermedia* magazine). On the basis of their work, and on additional literature reviewed, it can be said that little has changed in the past two decades in the geographical distribution of studies on television flow. The bulk of information is derived from research conducted in the United States and Western Europe on television flows in and out of those regions. While the number of studies done on television flows in Latin America has increased, there is still a lamentable lack of material dealing with Eastern Europe, the Middle East, Africa, and Asia (excluding Japan and the People's Republic of China). Canada, with its special concerns for broadcast spillovers from the United States, has taken greater strides toward making its voice heard by conducting its own research and attempting to clarify its communication policies.

In order to obtain a more precise view of both direction and content of international television flow, a number of research projects have been undertaken at regional and national levels. Additional studies, such as Graham P. Chapman's 1981 study on international television flows in Western Europe, have focused on tracking changes in the flow over time or on supplementing the knowledge obtained by the Nordenstreng and Varis report.[17] Based on his review of seven channels in Sweden, Italy, Finland, and the United Kingdom, Chapman concludes that there seems to be little departure from the flow patterns described by Nordenstreng and Varis, but he provides even greater detail on the content and viewing patterns, such as the percentage of broadcast time allocated to imported programs catalogued by the day and time of broadcast and records of monthly variations. Foreign programming was found to be concentrated at peak viewing hours on Mondays and on weekends. Particularly in Sweden, there is more foreign programming in the winter than in the summer. The United States is the primary programming supplier for Great Britain and Italy, although the latter also receives programs from Great Britain and France. Sweden and Finland rely primarily on European sources for imported programming. While the imported programs are mainly for entertainment purposes, the content of domestic programming is far more diversified.

Interfacing with the work of Chapman, Jeffrey Johnson's research focusing specifically on Swedish television flows during 1977 reveals an average of 58 hours per week of domestic programming and 33 hours of imported programs. Of the 44 countries whose programs appear on Swedish television, those responsible for more than one hour a week were Great Britain, the United States, Finland, France, West Germany, Italy, Norway, and Denmark. Through careful recording of the subject matter of imported television shows, Johnson discovered most television drama and documentaries came from British sources, most television movies were

American, light performances were produced by both the United States and the United Kingdom, and programs addressing ethical issues were British, American, West German, Finnish, and French in origin.[18]

George Gerbner's findings on television violence carry serious implications for policy makers:

> Violence on television is an integral part of a system of global marketing, and it dominates an increasing share of the world's screens. It inhibits other dramatic approaches to conflict, depressed independent television production, deprives viewers of more popular choices, victimizes some and emboldens others, heightens general intimidation, and invites repressive postures that exploit the widespread insecurities it itself generates.[19]

The problem, as seen by Gerbner, is that in the United States these questions of television and violence have not been placed on the agenda of public discourse.[20] Gerbner's analysis of international data shows that violence dominates US film and television exports. Two hundred and fifty US programs that were exported to ten countries were compared to 111 programs shown in the United States during the same year. "Violence was the main theme of 40 percent of home-shown and 49 percent of exported programs. Crime/action series comprised 17 percent of home-shown and 46 percent of exported programs."[21]

A distinct richness emerges from research efforts of this nature as detailed accounts of the direction of television flows are incorporated with content analysis. Yet even with this added insight, there remain myriad questions to be addressed by decision makers and researchers. As the research leads to interesting conclusions about the international flow and expanding television activities provoke greater curiosity, the need for continued and more consistent research efforts becomes evident. Just one day of television viewing over five channels in Japan provided 323 programs for categorization and study.

The potential for dramatic swings in television scheduling and the increasing complexity involved in monitoring television flows suggest the difficulties faced by researchers attempting to reconstruct accurate and timely descriptions of global television flows.[22] Additionally, increased awareness on the part of local and national decision makers, such as in Latin America, is progressively bringing about a restructuring of television programming. Rogers and Antola confirm a general trend in Latin America of producing more and importing less; initial steps in this direction are being taken by the longtime industry leader, Mexico, and followed by Venezuela, Brazil, and Argentina.[23]

Among the most stimulating publications are Tomo Martelanc's study on international broadcasting and the series of Cultural Cooperation studies and experiences of "Three Weeks of Television: An International Comparative Study" sponsored by UNESCO.[24] The growth in the intensity of debate over the New World Information/Communication Order, UNESCO's efforts to encourage and stimulate cooperative multinational research projects, and preliminary (although not comprehensive) findings of research reports such as the one cited here have provided sufficient stimulus for many national leaders to seriously reexamine past trends in the television policy-making process, and to look for appropriate alternatives.

Governments and national institutions frequently are the primary actors in television program production, distribution, and exchange because a majority of nations have government-owned and -operated broadcasting facilities. However, the degree to which public systems are combined with commercial enterprises varies considerably among the different nations of the world.

In a commercial environment, single organizations evolving over time and groups of organizations adjusting to the environment have expanded through horizontal and vertical integration, as well as diversification of their portfolios, to remain competitive actors in television flow. Pursuing the ramifications of this process in various industrial sectors, Charles Fombrun and W. Graham Astley discover that previously unrelated organizations dealing in entertainment and information are uniting through a series of acquisitions and joint ventures.[25] For example, firms such as Time-Warner, Sony, Disney, IBM, Western Union, AT&T, and Hughes Aircraft, which have generally been associated with information technologies, are incorporating cable television, videocassette recorders, videotext, and satellite transmissions into their packages of available services. These services interface with the entertainment sector and it becomes increasingly difficult to make clear distinctions between sectors within the international telecommunications community.

At the heart of the debate on international television flow lies the issue of the impact and effect on the viewers around the world. It is in this area that values and priorities are most often considered in research efforts. In the most general sense, participants in this debate are aligned in three camps. One camp argues that television's impact is immense and totally pervasive, requiring immediate formulation of national media policies to cope effectively with advancing influences. A second group maintains that the lack of empirical data precludes verification of the degree and nature of television's impact, thereby necessitating an intensified research effort allowing policy makers to base their decisions on accurate information. The third group asserts that national communication policies result in restrictions detrimental to the free flow of television programming and, although there is at present an imbalance, with time and fewer restrictions the process will right itself.

A primary cultural issue is the American model of commercial television programming possibly leading to consumerism and cultural homogeneity. Many countries where television was launched as a medium for education have subsequently moved towards commercialization of their television systems. Additionally, the link between cultural identity, language, and political conflicts is considered in the discussion devoted to linguistic effects.

Although researchers such as Colin Cherry document an increase in the number of languages used by international broadcasters, recorded declines in programs broadcast in minority languages in the United States and other countries elicit concern over possible homogenization of languages.[26]

The research on the psychological effects of television has produced variable results. While Charles Osgood's development of the semantic differential isolates meanings that are universally understood, Charles Holmes and Leonard W. Doob reported that visual symbols are not always transferable from one culture to the next. An indication that television serves as a vehicle for escapist fantasy may be found in research by Bradley Greenberg and Marta Colomina de Rivera, yet in a classroom setting, Milton J. McMenamin found that a teacher's effectiveness is reduced when translated into the television image.[27] Different conditions and intervening variables appear to produce different results. This confusion of results highlights the need for more complete research in this field.

Documenting the manner in which television programs serve to sustain outmoded stereotypes are the contribution of Luis Beltrán, who analyzed the effects of American programs in Latin America; Margaret Gallagher, who addressed global images of women in the mass media; among others. Because children are seen as having special media needs and as being easily molded by television messages, a number of scholars have taken issue with the impact of television on children and its possible policy implications. Resulting again in contending assessments of children's television are the works of Doris A. Graber, John Mayo, Luis Ramiro Beltrán, George Gerbner, and Joseph Straubhaar.[28]

Among the most critical debates are the questions of the impact of television violence on various segments of the viewing population, and of realities and television fantasies. Here, George Gerbner's work on television and with cultural indicators is most relevant.[29] Gerbner's studies are unique and important because they take the research and data far beyond familiar "children-and-violence" arguments, exploring wider and deeper ramifications. His conclusion, based on American television programming, is that heavy viewers of the prime-time programs are receiving a grossly distorted picture of the real world that they tend to accept more readily than reality itself – that there is evidence that television violence induces heavy viewers to perceive their world a more violent and more dangerous place than it really is.

Some of Gerbner's findings follow:

- Male prime-time characters on American television outnumber females by three to one, and women are portrayed as weak, passive, and submissive to powerful men.
- The elderly (people over 65) are grossly underrepresented in television programming.
- Television treatment of blacks is more one of image than of visibility.

- Heavy viewers greatly overestimate the proportion of Americans employed as physicians, lawyers, athletes, and entertainers.
- There is about ten times more crime on television than in real life.

Inherent in Gerbner's findings is the element of cause and effect, or the "chicken-or-the-egg" proposition. Is it television that makes heavy viewers view the world the way they do, or do the viewers come from that segment of the population who, by virtue of their environment and socialization, regard the world that way to begin with? Gerbner approaches the cause and effect questions through cross-sectional correlational analysis and sampling of heavy television viewers stratified across all ages, income and education levels, and ethnic groups. To change the trend, Gerbner suggests active, participatory roles for the viewers in the overall television production and distribution process.[30]

On a different note, the summary of a portion of a Nordic project about women in television suggests that there are two mutually dependent causalities determining the concepts of reality, and thus the concepts of women, rendered by television. They are: "a) the position of the media in society and the related managerial conditions, and b) the national and international news structure (which is generally derived from the economic structure of the society in question, but which is administered through a set of professional journalistic criteria and methods of preference)." This research states "that in many respects the women disagree with the existing principles of producing and editing – disagreements which would be of great impact even to the contents of the broadcasts if they were taken into account."[31]

Methodological questions regarding both flow and impact have also been at the center of television research literature during the last 15 years. For example, one of the first things that becomes obvious when reviewing the literature on global television flow is the lack of consensus on the appropriate means by which one should study and measure that flow.[32]

In the political arena, inquiry is directed toward the issues of sovereignty of the state, prior consent for foreign television broadcasts, and the role and extent of state control. Here, the nexus between the capacity to communicate and economic viability is evident. Once again, the importance of conducting additional investigations constructed to provide national leaders with reliable information on which to base their policy decisions is stressed. Paradoxically, there is evidence that those groups with the resources to sponsor such research are not committed to these efforts, and those who feel a dire need for additional information often lack the financial resources to gain it.

There are several factors that impede or facilitate the flow of television programs from one country to another. Mayo refers to an insufficient infrastructure in Latin American countries as inhibiting reception and adaptation of programs such as *Sesame Street*. On a more concrete level, this translates into a shortage of capital necessary to insure the backup materials and services that keep a broadcasting system in operation, as well as a lack of trained technicians, scriptwriters, actors, translators, producers and other essential staff, appropriate facilities, and interpersonal contacts. This combination of factors alone explains why so many developing countries find it easier to fill their broadcast days with canned American programs at a significantly lower cost than to attempt building their own viable production and distribution system.

By the same token, when communication and development goals are not clearly defined, many national leaders have joined the bandwagon praising Western technology to justify communications projects without carefully considering the purposes for which the technology is to be applied. A related factor is the rate at which innovations are diffused. The consequences of misjudgment are best illustrated by the Iranian revolution, where the modern communication system implemented by the Shah conflicted with the traditional communication networks of Iranian culture and value systems.[33]

As has been discussed, governments play an important role in the flow of television programming.[34] Some countries have implemented policies to gain greater local control over the production and distribution processes.[35] For example, Canada has stipulated that a minimum of 60 percent of the programs in a broadcast day must be Canadian in content and character.

Other relevant factors affecting the flow of television programming are competition, commercial motivation, ethnocentrism, language barriers, and the degree of cultural similarity between the producing and receiving countries.[36] Proximity of nations, especially in the case of Europe, tends to increase television flows, be it as a consequence of broadcast spillovers or formal exchange systems. Different standards for television line systems present technical barriers as well.

The question at hand is whether imported communication technologies ensure the transfer of the skills prerequisite for local production. It is not unusual to find countries in which the hardware for distribution of programs has been set in place while the means for production of software and programming have not been transferred. In those countries where local production systems are just getting off the ground, domestic television producers find themselves competing with slick foreign imports and Western-established standards of "professionalism." If national communication policies are to be devised, the conflict of interest between conventional notions of media professionalism and the desire to gain control over the production end of television flows must be resolved.

As communication models vary, so do their supporting assumptions. It is instructive to look at some of the common assumptions found in the literature on television flows. It should be remembered that differing worldviews lead researchers to ask different questions and to reach divergent conclusions in their work. Assumptions frequently made include:

1. Television is the most powerful medium and exposure assures impact.
2. The impact of television flow is especially powerful on women, children, and populations of the least industrialized nations.[37]

3. Uneven flow is bad and should be corrected through the formulation of national communication policies.[38]
4. Uneven flow is temporary and will balance itself out over time.[39]
5. Given the nature of the "product life cycle" of television transfers, a free flow of programs is more desirable than the imposition of national communication regulations and policies.
6. The present global system of television flows is perpetrated by the dominant Western producers of television programs (especially by the United States) to maintain the status quo.[40]
7. The transfer of technology may be considered effective if the format and original objectives of a given program are maintained, but the process can be overtaken by local media personnel.[41]
8. Neither the dominant Western model nor the socialist model of television infrastructures is sufficient to meet the communication needs of developing countries.[42]

**International Radio Broadcasting**

Since its inauguration in the 1920s, radio broadcasting has been a rapidly expanding part of the flow of information, and international broadcasting in particular has become a significant area of focus. Voice of America, for example, claims that 86 million adults listen to its broadcasts at least once a week and the British Broadcasting Corporation estimates its audience at 114 million regular adult listeners.[43]

In spite of the obvious significance of this medium in the international flow of information, little is known on a worldwide scale about the attention paid by external broadcasters to audience research. In much of the world, domestic broadcasters are no better informed about their audiences. The truth is that, as one writer suggests, "in some political contexts nobody really wants to know the facts that would be uncovered by audience research."[44] In a system in which positive feedback is highly valued as contributing to self-preservation, negative feedback indicating that the broadcasts are off-target may be ignored or suppressed.

The research in radio broadcasting is imbalanced in other areas as well. Little attention has been given to the use of international broadcasting in the transportation industry – aviation, terrestrial, and maritime – and to the commercial functions and stations. Additionally, there is very little known about radio broadcasting in most Third World regions, both of intraregional broadcasting and of South-to-North flows. Clearly, there is a need to step up research efforts in the neglected areas of radio broadcasting as it relates to the international flow of information.

International broadcasting can be defined as the purposeful attempt on the part of stations in one country to reach listeners in other countries. It is communication crossing national boundaries through technological and telecommunication channels, the latter enhanced by the introduction of satellite, making possible super-high-frequency (SHF) transmissions that are more rapid, higher quality, and more difficult to jam than other frequencies.

The flow has traditionally been from stations headquartered where policies and programming are created directly to the audience through relay stations located in foreign countries. There are, however, other types of cross-border flow. One is from international transmitters to domestic broadcasters who use portions of the external service to supplement domestic programming. This type of flow appears to be decreasing.

Another type of flow in international broadcasting is in the form of monitoring services, which function to collect and disseminate information that is particularly relevant to political decision-making and foreign policy objectives. It is estimated that this type of flow reaches larger audiences than can be reached by direct broadcasting.

The directions of international radio broadcast flow can be viewed in two distinct patterns. The first is a vertical flow, in which stations transmit to foreign audiences within and between East and West and from North to South. Although there is some intraregional broadcasting within the South – or the Third World – there is no effective South–North flow.

The second distinct pattern is circular broadcasting, in which beamed signals are intercepted and routed to alternate destinations. This is primarily used by monitoring broadcast services that provide information to policy and decision makers.

Of prime importance in the patterns of flow is the geographical distribution of broadcast transmissions and receiving sets. In 1986, the United States, Europe, Latin America, and the Middle East were the geographical regions with the greatest number of radio sets. In terms of hours broadcast per week, the list was essentially the same except for China replacing Latin America in the third position. The major broadcasting regions also produce the greatest number of multilingual services, with the Transworld broadcasting station providing programming in 70 different languages and dialects.[45]

There are three primary actors in the international flow of information through radio broadcasting: governmental actors and agencies, international institutions, and private organizations. The first, governmental actors and agencies, perform two roles, sometimes functioning as regulators and gatekeepers of the flow as well as actually participating in international broadcasting to serve their "national interests." International institutions play the same roles as governments on different levels and in differing degrees. In addition to operating broadcast facilities to transmit news and educational and cultural programming, organizations such as the United Nations have passed resolutions pertaining to global broadcast flow. While not exhibiting the enforcement capability of governmental regulations, such resolutions do have an influence, however major or minor, on UN member nations and broadcasters.

The third category, the private organization, would include religious, unofficial political, commercial, and educational organizations. This is the most diverse category of actors, and the types and purposes of their broadcasts are highly varied, ranging from missionary programs to language instruction and from ideological propaganda to entertainment sponsored by advertisers.

The purpose of the broadcast is a factor that influences both content and flow of international broadcasts. A major purpose of broadcasting is to inform and influence the receiver, whether politically, socially, culturally, or academically. Radio broadcasting is also used both as an instrument of "public diplomacy" and as an agent of psychological warfare.[46] For example, a 1981 study showed that Cuban international broadcasting covered diverse topics emphasizing news about Latin America and Africa in its North American broadcasts while the United States' Voice of America Spanish broadcast dealt primarily with US domestic and foreign affairs.[47] Within cultural and educational broadcasting, language instruction is the most prominent type of programming, although cultural programming featuring classical music is also popular.

Another factor influencing international broadcasting is technical capacity, which includes not only the actual technical facilities for production and distribution but also the ability to jam unwanted incoming signals. Additionally, multilingual capability is a factor which, when combined with technical capacity, increases the size and diversity of the audience.

The financial capability of both broadcasters and receivers is a factor that determines the amount and nature of the flow that is produced and disseminated, as well as influencing where it is sent. For example, the BBC had to drop its services in three languages because of budgetary constraints. The high cost of maintaining correspondents abroad and of hiring personnel, frequently required to be citizens of the receiving nation, restricts and limits broadcast flow. Additionally, the purchasing power of a specific audience is a factor in determining the type, amount, and feasibility of programming.

Geographic factors and technical and financial factors are often interrelated. For example, distance and natural barriers, such as mountains or atmospheric interference, not only directly influence technical equipment in terms of restricting its utility, but also increase the cost of maintaining or securing equipment that can overcome geographical barriers. Similar examples can be cited where the geographical barrier is not a natural phenomenon but rather a human one, such as a widely dispersed audience.

Governmental relations and regulation comprise another of the factors influencing broadcast flow. On the technical level, global flow is regulated to some extent by international and intergovernmental institutions and organizations such as the ITU, and by regional broadcasting organizations. Additionally, national regulations and diplomatic relationships have a direct influence on cross-border flows both in the content and the process aspects of flow.

Additional factors influencing broadcast flow include world events and crises as well as time. For example, there is a worldwide tendency for broadcasters to respond to crisis by establishing services or securing positions in the crisis area. This in itself directly affects content, volume, and direction of flow. However, the time involved in setting up such facilities and the time span of crisis activities have an equivalent influence.

Finally, human and ideological factors must be examined for their direct and indirect effects on broadcast flow. The ideological orientation of the producers is a definite factor in determining content, but a more subtle influence is ideological affinity or opposition within the sphere of operation. An even more subtle influence is the human aspect of production and distribution represented by technicians, service staff, and translators. Even though the ideology may be dictated by ownership, the human channels of flow production and distribution will influence not only the message content but sometimes even administrative policy, through the continual minor decisions made by staff and technicians every day in the context of personal mindsets.[48]

The impact of international radio broadcasting on receivers is an area of research that has largely been neglected, as was indicated previously by broadcasters' relative disinterest in audience research. Some work has been done, however, on what could be labeled "indicators" or impact. Jamming efforts usually indicate that the flow is having some kind of an effect not considered desirable from the point of view of regulatory institutions – be they political or social. Additionally, mail received by broadcasters is often regarded as an indicator of impact, although Bernard Bumpus of the BBC warns against drawing conclusions about audience size or reaction to programming based on listener letters.[49] Mail is, however, the primary source of feedback in some instances, especially where there is no audience survey.

In the area of regional broadcasting, infrastructure and technical facilities have been the focus of research. Audience studies have been carried out mostly in Europe, North America, the Soviet Union, and, to some extent, in the Middle East. Although the structure and technique of broadcasting is a line of inquiry in this area, few data are available on minor interregional transmission, broadcasting among Third World countries, and South-to-North broadcasting. There is significant imbalance in the research in this area and much of the data on regional and international radio broadcasting are prepared and distributed by the major stations, which have the financial resources to conduct research to serve their own purposes.

Study of religious broadcasting is another research area having received attention recently. Although religious stations are seldom included in listings of major broadcasters, Donald R. Browne states that at least four of them – Radio Vatican, FEBC, HCJB, and Transworld – figure among the top 20 international broadcasters in terms of hours broadcast per week.[50] They are also leaders in multilingual broadcasting, Transworld broadcasting in 70 languages and Radio Vatican in 30. In several Third World countries, specifically in Asia, religious broadcasting has continued to expand. Christian groups have received permission to operate broadcasting stations and are the major religious broadcasters in Indonesia, Australia, South Korea, Taiwan, and the Philippines. There are also major differences in methods and approaches within the groups of religious broadcasters. For example, whereas Christian broadcast stations are operated by religious organizations, Islamic broadcast stations generally operate as part of the national broadcasting authority within the Islamic societies.

A further area of research in international radio broadcasting is audience analysis. Until recently, most of the audience research on international broadcasting was conducted on listeners in Eastern Europe and the Soviet Union and little research was done on the US audience. A study conducted on feedback in international broadcasting by Fred Collins, David Gibson, and myself showed that the most common methodologies usually employed by international broadcast stations around the world are audience surveys, listener letter analysis, and listener diaries. Listener letter analysis was shown more likely to be employed outside of Europe and North America and the resultant research findings used more frequently to guide radio programming. Similarly, domestic broadcasters were more interested in estimates of audience size whereas external broadcasters were concerned with audience perception of the station and its credibility.[51]

A final category of radio flow research is programming and its flow internationally, which occurs either by direct broadcast or by program exchange among stations. The latter is controlled and coordinated by international organizations and, additionally, somewhat controlled by the receiving station, which links international broadcasting to domestic services. Programming has been extensively researched with a focus on content, sender, and receiver's socioeconomic status.

## Direct Broadcasting by Satellite

The major issues in certain facets of international communications have been transmuted in the last few decades. One of the primary elements underlying this change has been phenomenal technological innovations that have transversed various cultural, social, political, economic, and legal norms. Most recently, the issue of new communication technology, specifically in the form of direct broadcast satellites, has become increasingly prominent in discussions pertaining to international communication.

The technique has been used in several countries around the world and is being employed in the United States by television networks and cable companies. However, it is the possible use of direct broadcasting internationally and across national boundaries, especially without the prior consent of the receivers, that has stimulated the most controversy and debate in the international community and organizations. In 1982, the United Nations General Assembly endorsed a resolution emphasizing the importance of negotiating an international agreement on the subject, and outlined a set of principles for such an accord.

At issue is a new technique that relays satellite telecasts directly to residences without going through ground receiving stations. The main impetus behind the debate is the conviction in the world community that unregulated DBS poses serious threats to national sovereignty. Specifically, these perceived threats fall in the categories of propaganda, commercial domination, and cultural intrusion.

On the other hand, there are undeniable benefits to be derived from this technology. Broadcast satellites offer a cheaper and more flexible means of communicating messages over long distances. This technology also has the potential to open up contact with previously inaccessible areas. Because of the dangers and benefits inherent in this technology, DBS has sparked a heated international debate. The issue is complicated by the fact that direct broadcasting involves the use of outer space – an area that has never been adequately regulated. For this reason, these debates are perceived by many nations to be important in establishing precedents in international law. Crucial issues at stake here are the future of the administration of outer space, and the competing principles of national sovereignty and the free flow of information.

Direct broadcast satellites are not an essentially new form of communication; rather, they are the result of the development of the communications satellite. The direct broadcast satellite is a more powerful and versatile communications satellite that transmits a signal "directly" to an inexpensive receiver. There are two types of direct broadcast satellite systems: (1) reception of the transmissions into community receivers for rebroadcasting; and (2) direct reception by private sets via small antenna without the aid of a community or ground transmitter. It is this latter type that has caused much of the controversy because the nature of the former makes it more conducive to control and regulation.

The ITU radio regulations revised by the World Administrative Radio Conference for Space Telecommunications (WARC–ST) define a broadcasting satellite service as "a radiocommunication service in which signals transmitted or retransmitted by space stations are intended for direct reception by the general public."[52] The ITU radio regulations specify that the term "direct reception" shall encompass both individual and community reception. Individual reception, on the one hand, is defined as "the reception of emissions from a space station in the broadcasting-satellite service by simple domestic installations and in particular those possessing small antennae." Community reception, on the other hand, is defined as "the reception of emissions from a space station in the broadcasting-satellite service by receiving equipment, which in some cases may be complex and have antennae larger than those used for individual reception, and intended for use by a group of the general public at one location or through a distribution system covering a limited area."[53] A distinction must be made also within community reception as to whether the reception is direct or indirect. A direct community reception is one in which there is a transmission of programs from point A through the satellite to point B and point B is the site of a rebroadcasting facility that can immediately transmit the signal as a broadcast to individual television sets. If, at point B, the program signal is relayed further through terrestrial facilities to other cities from which the program is broadcast for general reception, the distribution is termed indirect community reception.

There are several problems related to the use of this type of satellite reception system. One of the major problems in the past has been economic in nature. In the beginning of satellite communication, terrestrial receiving stations required such large expenditures, from hundreds of thousands to millions of dollars, that the idea of having direct home reception was realistically inhibited. On economic grounds, direct broadcasting by satellite was not considered a viable alternative to the already existing terrestrial transmission networks, especially in the developed countries. It was not until the last two decades, through technological innovations in satellite design, satellite receivers, and reception antennae, that the cost of such a system has been reduced.

Furthermore, it had been thought that reception by large terrestrial stations with subsequent distribution by cable would be a more economical arrangement than direct reception by a large number of viewers using small terrestrial receiving antennae. In fact, it has been estimated that this latter arrangement offers the lowest per-viewer cost. For example, given a country with 16 million homes, each with individual satellite reception, the distribution cost would be approximately 50p per home per annum. This is considerably less expensive than a terrestrial network system. Additionally, the cost of an antenna, modulator, and receiver, assuming a production of one million units, would be between $250 and $500.[54]

A study in Italy has shown that to serve 98 percent of the population would require the construction of 45 UHF main terrestrial transmitters with 770 UHF relay stations. For a second program network with a coverage of 96 percent, the required construction would be 48 UHF main transmitters and 396 UHF relay stations. Assuming that the network would have a life span of twenty years, the overall distribution cost would be approximately $12.75 million per annum. A comparable satellite system, however, would only cost between $6 and $8 million.[55]

In the future, the cost of satellite broadcasting will diminish even more than it has in the past three decades. With the space shuttle system available, it is possible to use heavier satellites carrying more and more transponders. Formerly, in the event of a breakdown, it was generally impossible to intervene, and the satellite, although it may still have contained many elements in perfect operational condition, had to be abandoned. Flights for maintenance or repair, whether manned or automatic, were too costly in relation to the cost of the satellite itself. With the development of the space shuttle it is now possible to do maintenance and repairs in space and consequently, it is feasible to use components in the satellite with less expensive reliabilities.[56] The economic impact is enormous because the capital outlay will be amortized over a lifetime much longer than that of the existing satellites.

Additionally, it is realistic to assume that in the near future there may be enormous space stations assembled in low orbit using separately transported units, which, once the station is assembled, can be transferred into a geosynchronous orbit.[57] This could revolutionize broadcast satellite systems, since it would decrease the cost of space systems, open the possibility of more powerful satellites, and further lower the costs of receiving antennae by reducing their diameter size requirements.

Aside from the promises for the future, a second major problem that needs to be considered is the problem of orbital or spectrum spacing. Although there is physically ample space in the synchronous orbit for a very large number of satellites, there is a limitation on the proximity of their orbits. As a result of the increased number of communication satellites, a problem related to orbital spacing is "band capacity." The capacity of a band of frequencies is the maximum quantity of information which that band can convey.

A third major technical problem is that of "spillover." This problem arises when the transmission signal overextends or crosses the boundaries of one country into another. This causes numerous legal, social, and political problems that will be discussed later. It is doubtful that future technology can totally eliminate this problem. However, continuous technological improvements have gradually reduced the degree of spillover in some areas. Through the use of "spot" or "directional" beams, the area that a satellite signal covers has been drastically reduced.

Satellites offer several advantages over more conventional methods of communication. Because the satellites are located high above the earth, they cover a much larger distance than do traditional broadcast systems. In addition, there is no corresponding increase in cost for greater distances. A second advantage is that satellites are much more flexible than terrestrial systems, which rely on an infrastructure of cables and wires. In the first place, they do not require the costly physical networking of a region to establish communication ties. In the second place, satellite beams can be easily redirected to other areas whereas physical infrastructure is rigid. A third advantage of satellite communication systems is their greater capacity for carrying messages. Satellites can be used to transmit large numbers of any kind of electronic signal.[58]

In the industrialized countries, ever-increasing needs for regional and local television programs will take over terrestrial UHF or VHF bands and national programs will have to find either another new medium or higher-frequency bands. Thus, satellite broadcasting is also of interest in these countries and provides a means of replacing or transmitting additional national programs by making it possible for terrestrial networks to be used for new services.

The fear of many nations is that this technology will result in the unwanted reception of foreign programming. This outside programming can occur in two forms, which can be distinguished as unintentional and intentional spillover.

The first, as its name implies, refers to the accidental transmission of television signals between countries at border areas. This is often unavoidable because broadcast patterns cannot be made to conform with the configuration of international boundaries. This type of spillover occurs with any form of broadcasting. Progress is being made in attempting to avoid spillover problems by altering the shape of the broadcast pattern.

Underlying the question of intentional spillover is a widespread sense that the form and content of the television system in a country is an aspect of national sovereignty. The traditional notions of sovereignty, which have been expressed in geographic or spatial terms, are being redefined in terms of concerns about informational sovereignty as integrity. This concept reflects a recognition that all countries have, by national political decision, worked out their own arrangements for domestic television to fit their own special needs and situations. In most countries, including Europe, broadcasting has always been under government control. Either the national system has been directly operated by the state or by a state-owned corporation, or it has been strictly regulated by the state. For these countries, a system of international control represents no great conceptual extension.

One concern for the broadcasting of television programming across national boundaries has been the indication that the majority of this flow has been one-way – from developed to Third World countries. The introduction of direct broadcasting satellites to already existing international radio services and current television exports would seem to indicate an increasing volume of this one-way flow, rather than any equitable cross-national exchange of information. A related concern is the balance of the flow. The principle of free flow of information would be more palatable if it were not unidirectional, or nearly so. For these less developed countries, which are media-poor and information-poor in the Western sense, each external piece of information takes on great significance.

The fear expressed by many countries of being subject to unwanted political messages through DBS is not without precedent. The point at which the free-flow-of-information principle seriously violates national sovereignty and becomes offensive propaganda is, of course, subject to widely divergent interpretations. Most countries with the technical capacity have been engaging in international radio broadcasting for years. This is particularly true where the sending and receiving nations are politically antagonistic. To date, the only alternative nations have had to accepting these unwanted messages has been to jam the incoming signals. This measure is expensive and not entirely effective. Furthermore, jamming wastes the limited number of broadcasting frequencies.

There have been claims that nations would not be defenseless against unwanted direct television broadcasts. In addition to jamming, some writers have cited options such as forbidding illegal viewing, adapting sets to prevent DBS reception, or even shooting down offending satellites.[59] For obvious reasons, none of these alternatives is realistically workable. The only real option would be jamming, and it is even more difficult and expensive to interfere with television signals than radio signals.

The chief advantage offered by DBS over more conventional methods of television broadcasting is that the former method does not require elaborate ground infrastructure to be developed before an area can receive television transmission. For this reason, DBS may have more promise for those areas where extensive terrestrial broadcasting facilities do not exist. Additionally, for the countries having remote, sparsely populated areas where it is difficult and expensive to set up terrestrial broadcasting, the technology of DBS can be beneficial. It is projected that the use of direct broadcasting by satellite would greatly reduce the cost and time required to establish television networks. Formerly isolated areas could be connected simply by setting up community receivers. By establishing visual contact with formerly inaccessible regions, a country's leaders are provided with opportunities to promote national integration and development. Among current users of this type of broadcasting are Alaska, Northern Canada, Siberia, and the Japanese islands.

The problem of national integration is particularly acute in countries with regions and populations that are made remote by geographical, cultural, and linguistic barriers. By surmounting these barriers through the application of satellite communications systems, many national governments hope to unify culturally diverse and regionally scattered people under a single set of national symbols and values. In addition to promoting national integration, it is hypothesized that an all pervasive national communication system would afford national planners the opportunity to promote education and national planning.[60]

The first true direct broadcast satellite was the Applications Technology Satellite (ATS–6), which was launched by NASA in May 1974, and positioned in geosynchronous orbit over the west coast of South America. This experimental satellite was intended to demonstrate major advances in communication and spacecraft technology. It initially pioneered delivery via space of advanced educational and health services to many Americans in small towns in remote areas of the Rocky Mountains, Appalachia, and Alaska, where reception by ground facilities had been difficult and costly.

At the conclusion of the year of availability for the Home Educational Television experiment, ATS–6 was moved to 35° east longitude for the Satellite Instructional Television Experiment (SITE) for India from 1975 through 1976. This experiment took place under an agreement concluded in 1969 between the Indian Department of Atomic Energy and NASA. The primary objective of the SITE experiment was that television should be utilized in the developmental process as an instrument of social change and national cohesion, which should cater to both in-school and out-of-school learning, with priority on primary education. Additionally, it should be used to disseminate information about specific aspects of science, technology, agriculture, health, and family planning.

The educational programs achieved very high ratings in the Indian villages, while entertainment programs, drama, folk music, and folk dancing were less popular. The education was simplified and suited to the very limited experience and knowledge of the village people.[61] The experiment, more than anything else, was a hardware success story.[62]

A second experimental direct broadcast system was conducted in Canada and known as the Communication Technology Satellite (CTS). The CTS experiment demonstrated how a satellite system of this magnitude and scope could be used in conjunction with a well-developed terrestrial communication system, such as that existing in southeastern Canada. It provided valuable information on the utility of a high-powered communication satellite. Not only have the northern communities of Canada benefited from CTS, but so also has the nation's remote, underdeveloped areas – and the United States as well. The CTS experiment further demonstrated reception capabilities by compact, simple, and potentially low-priced receivers representative of the home-entertainment type of equipment that would be used for receiving television signals at home directly from a satellite.[63]

In the United States the Satellite Television Corporation (STC), a subsidiary of the Communications Satellite Corporation (Comsat), was granted a satellite construction permit for the nation's first direct satellite-to-home broadcasting service.[64]

The United States and Canada are not the only countries which have experimented with and established direct broadcast systems. European nations have already developed large-scale, fixed plans for direct-to-home television and radio broadcast services. European broadcast administrators are turning to satellite distribution out of desperation rather than choice, in an attempt to solve major and increasing problems they already face in their efforts to finance, produce, and distribute domestic broadcast programming.

The evolution of the issue of direct broadcast satellites illustrates changes in the nature of the debate on questions of international communication since 1970. These changes are in essence just reflections of larger alterations in the international geopolitical structure. More specifically, this is evidenced by the changes within the United Nations system, in the international economic order, and in the way traditional identities of national interests decompose and new ones emerge. From the beginning of the debate on direct broadcast satellites, many countries have been reluctant to accept this new communication technology without some form of control over its application. The political values these countries attach to such concepts as cultural integrity and national identity have taken precedence over what the United States and several other countries would consider more pragmatic values. It is clear that some of the more salient technical, legal, institutional, and political problems of this new technology are just beginning to emerge.

# Notes

1. International Commission for the Study of Communication Problems, *Many Voices, One World* (London: Kogan Page, 1980), p. 61.

2. Kaarle Nordenstreng and Tapio Varis, *Television Traffic – A One-Way Street?*, Reports and Papers on Mass Communication No. 70 (Paris: UNESCO, 1974).

3. Ibid., p. 30.

4. Elihu Katz and George Wedell, *Broadcasting in the Third World* (Cambridge, MA: Harvard University Press, 1977).

5. Russell W. Neuman, "Patterns of Recall Among Television News Viewers," *Public Opinion Quarterly*, 40 (Spring 1976), pp. 115–123.

6. John Robinson et al., "Comprehension of Television News: How Alert is the Audience?" paper presented at the Association for Education in Journalism annual convention, August 1980.

7. William C. Adams, "Covering the World in Ten Minutes: Network News and International Affairs," in William C. Adams, ed., *Television Coverage of International Affairs* (Norwood, NJ: Ablex Publishing Corporation, 1982), pp. 3–14. See also chapters by Haluk Sahin, Dennis K. Davis and John P. Robinson, and others.

8. William C. Adams, ed., *Television Coverage of the Middle East* (Norwood, NJ: Ablex Publishing Corporation, 1981).

9. Adams, ed., *Television Coverage of International Affairs*.

10. Ibid., pp. 3–14.

11. Ibid., pp. 15–44.

12. Ibid., pp. 45–65.

13. Ibid., p. 62.

14. Everett M. Rogers and Livia Antola, "Television Flows in Latin America," paper read at the Conference on Flow of Messages, Flow of Media in the Americas, Stanford University, Stanford, CA., December 9–10, 1982.

15. Ibid., pp. 7, 7a, and 8.

16. Chin-Chuan Lee, *Media Imperialism Reconsidered: The Homogenizing of Television Culture* (Beverly Hills, CA, and London: Sage Publications, 1980); Tapio Varis, *International Flow of Television Programmes* (Reports and Papers on Mass Communication, No. 100), Paris: Unesco Press, 1985; Preben Sepstrup and Anura Goonasekera, *TV Transnationalization: Europe and Asia* (Reports and Papers on Mass Communication, No. 109), Paris: Unesco Press, 1994; and US Department of Commerce, *The NTIA Infrastructural Report: Telecommunications in the Age of Information*, National Telecommunications and Information Administration, Department of Commerce, United Government, Washington, DC, 1991.

17. Graham P. Chapman, "International Television Flow in West Europe," paper read at the International Institute of Communication Annual Conference, Strasbourg, Austria, September 7–10, 1981.

18. Jeffery Johnson, *Structure of Swedish Television Broadcasting*, ITFP Discussion Paper No. 12, Cambridge University, 1980. Also *Mapping an Atlas of International Television Flow*, ITFP Discussion Paper No. 9, Cambridge University, 1979.

19. George Gerbner, "Television Violence: The Art of Asking the Wrong Question," *Currents in Modern Thought*, July 1994, p. 387.

20. Ibid., p. 389.

21. Ibid., p. 393.

22. Peter Gould and Anne Lyew-Ayee, *The Structure of Jamaican Television: A Pilot Study*. ITFP Discussion Paper No. 13, University Park: Pennsylvania State University, 1981.

23. Rogers and Antola, "Television Flows in Latin America."

24. Tomo Martelanc, *External Broadcasting and International Understanding* (Paris: UNESCO, 1977); Eduardo Contreras, James Larson, John K. Mayo and Peter Spain, *Cross-Cultural Broadcasting* (Paris: UNESCO, 1976).

25. Charles Fombrun and W. Graham Astley, "Telecommunications Community: An Institutional Overview," *Journal of Communication*, 32: 4 (Autumn 1982), pp. 56–68.

26. Contreras et al., *Cross-Cultural Broadcasting*, pp. 26–33.

27. Ibid., pp. 31 and 33.

28. See Doris A. Graber, *Mass Media and American Politics* (Washington, DC: Congressional Quarterly Press, 1980), pp. 97, 144, 146, 150, 274; and George Gerbner, *Violence and Terror in the Mass Media* (Reports and Papers on Mass Communication, No. 102), Paris: Unesco Press, 1988.

29. George Gerbner, Larry Gross, Michael F. Eleely, Marilyn Jackson, Suzanne Jeffries and Nancy Signorielti, "TV Violence Profile No. 8: The Highlights," *Journal of Communication*, 27: 2 (Spring 1977), pp. 171–180. See also G. Melisoek et al., eds, *Cultural Indicators: An International Symposium* (Vienna: Akademie der Wisenschaften, 1983).

30. Harry F. Waters, "Life According to TV," *Newsweek*, December 6, 1982, p. 140.

31. Else Jensen, "Television Newscasts in a Woman's Perspective," paper read at the International Association for Mass Communication Research Conference, Paris, September 1982.

32. Peter Gould, *How Shall We Classify Television Programs?* ITFP Discussion Paper No. 5, University Park: Pennsylvania State University, 1978. See also Peter Gould and Jefferey Johnson, "National Television Policy: Monitoring Structural Complexity," *Futures*, 12: 3 (June 1980), pp. 178–190.

33. Hamid Mowlana, "Technology versus Tradition: Communication in the Iranian Revolution," *Journal of Communication*, 29: 3 (Summer 1979), pp. 107–112.

34. Joseph D. Straubhaar, "Television and Violence in Brazil," paper read at the Northeast Conference on Latin American Studies, Dartmouth, NH, October 1980.

35. Haluk Sahin, "Ideology of Television: Theoretical Framework and a Case Study," in *Media, Culture and Society*, 1: 1 (1979), pp. 161–169.

36. Hamid Mowlana, "The Limits of the Global Village," *Intellect*, November 1974, pp. 122–124. See also John Mayo et al., "The Transfer of *Sesame Street* to Latin America," paper read at the Conference on Flow of Messages, Flow of Media in the Americas, Stanford University, Stanford, CA, December 9–10, 1982.

37. Luis Ramiro Beltrán, "TV Etchings in the Minds of Latin Americans: Conservatism, Materialism, and Conformism" *Gazette*, 24: 1 (1978), pp. 61–65.

38. International Commission for the Study of Communication Problems, *Many Voices, One World*.

39. Ithiel de Sola Pool, "The Changing Flow of Television," *Journal of Communication*, 27: 2 (Spring 1977), pp. 139–249.

40. Herbert J. Schiller, *Communication and Cultural Domination* (White Plains, NY: International Arts and Sciences Press, 1976).

41. Mayo et al., "The Transfer of *Sesame Street* to Latin America."

42. Hamid Mowlana, "Mass Media and Culture: Toward an Integrated Theory," in William B. Gudykunst, ed., *Intercultural Communication Theory: Current Perspectives* (Beverly Hills, CA: Sage Publications, 1983), pp. 149–170.

43. Statistics obtained from the VOA office of research and the BBC Branch Office in Washington, October 1996.

44. Sydney Head, *Broadcasting in Africa* (Philadelphia, PA: Temple University Press, 1974).

45. UNESCO Statistical Yearbook 1995. (Paris: UNESCO Press, 1995).

46. See Rutger Lindahl, *Broadcasting Across Borders: A Study on the Role of Propaganda in External Broadcasts* (Göteborg: C.W.K. Gleerup, 1978). For further reading in this area, especially from a geopolitical point of view, see: David M. Abshire, *International Broadcasting: A New Dimension in Western Diplomacy*, The Washington Papers, 4: 35 (Beverly Hills, CA: Sage Publications, 1976); Georgi Arbatov, *The War of Ideas in Contemporary International Relations* (Moscow: Progress Publishers, 1973); A.F. Panfilov, *U.S. Radio in Psychological Warfare* (Moscow: International Relations Publishers, 1967); Julian A. Hale, *Radio Power: Propaganda and International Broadcasting* (Philadelphia, PA: Temple University Press, 1975);

Donald R. Browne, *International Radio Broadcasting: The Limits of the Limitless Medium* (New York: Praeger, 1982); and James O.H. Nason, "International Broadcasting as an Instrument of Foreign Policy," *Millennium* 6: 2 (London, 1977). For a more recent example, see Glenn Hauser, "Monitoring the Falklands Crisis," *Popular Electronics*, 20: 94 (September 1982), pp. 94–96.

47. Howard Frederick, "Ideology in International Broadcasting: Radio Warfare Between Voice of America and Radio Havana Cuba," paper read at the 30th annual conference of the International Communication Association, Acapulco, Mexico, May 20, 1980.

48. For factors influencing the flow of radio broadcasting see: Burton Paulu, *Television and Radio in the United Kingdom* (Minneapolis, MN: University of Minnesota Press, 1981); Browne, *International Radio Broadcasting*; and Douglas A. Boyd, *Broadcasting in the Arab World: A Survey of Radio and Television in the Middle East* (Philadelphia, PA: Temple University Press, 1982).

49. Collins et al., "Feedback in International Broadcasting," p. 18.

50. Browne, *International Radio Broadcasting*, pp. 300–305.

51. Collins et al., "Feedback in International Broadcasting," p. 18.

52. H. Kaltenecker, "Direct Broadcasting by Satellite: An Overview of the Work of the United Nations," *EBU Review*, May 1977, p. 91.

53. Ibid., p. 92.

54. Ibid., p. 23.

55. Ibid., p. 45.

56. Rosetti, "Prospects Opened up to the Broadcasters by the Use of Satellites," *EBU Review*, May 1977, p. 29.

57. James Redmond, "Direct Broadcasting to the Home via Satellite: Possible Application in the United Kingdom," *EBU Review*, January 1977, p. 9.

58. Benno Signitzer, *Regulation of Direct Broadcasting from Satellite* (New York: Praeger, 1976), pp. 3–4.

59. O.W. Riegal, "Satellite Communication and Political Power," in George Gerbner, ed., *Mass Media Policies in Changing Cultures* (New York: John Wiley, 1977), p. 69.

60. Hamid Mowlana, "Political and Social Implications of Communication Satellite Applications in Developed and Developing Countries," in Joseph P. Pelton and Marcellus S. Snow, eds, *Economic and Policy Problems in Satellite Communication* (New York: Praeger, 1977), p. 135.

61. Ibid., p. 139. See also Snehlata Shukla, "The Impact of SITE on Primary School Children," *Journal of Communication*, 29: 4 (Autumn 1979), pp. 99–105.

62. For an excellent discussion of the significance of rural realities and values in intended effective communication exercises see K.E. Eapen,"The Cultural Component of the SITE," *Journal of Communication*, 29: 4 (Autumn 1979), pp. 106–111. Also see his "Social Impacts of Television on Indian Villages: Two Case Studies," in Godwin C. Chu, Syed A. Rahim and D. Lawrence Kincaid, eds, *Institutional Exploration in Communication Technology* (Honolulu: East–West Communication Institute, 1978), pp. 89–108.

63. Michael Schrage, "2 Firms Race to Space for Lead in DBS TV," Washington Business Section, *The Washington Post*, March 12, 1983, p. 1; and Michael Schrage, "2 Private Satellites Planned," Business and Finance Section, *The Washington Post*, BI, March 12, 1983, p. 1.

64. Eduard Haas, "Possible Applications of Direct Broadcast Satellite," *EBU Review*, May 1977, p. 39.

# 5

# Cultural Industry: From
# Books to Computers

The great acceleration in the flow of information across national boundaries during the last half century has been due, in part, to radical changes in the organization of international life resulting from tremendous activities in the spheres of cultural industries and marketing and commercial promotion, and also in the growth of scientific and technical messages. As we approach the twenty-first century there promises to be an ever-increasing international flow in the areas of advertising, film and sound recordings, video, book publishing, scientific and technical journals, and associated media. Unfortunately, communication research on these channels is sparse and far from systematic.

The disparity of study observed in these somewhat overlapping areas is due to at least three factors. First is the long tradition of communication research occupying itself with those channels that are conventionally in the province of classical mass media such as newspapers, news agencies, radio, and television. Second is the particular interests of economists, technology experts, and education specialists, who have examined these areas solely from the perspective of their respective disciplines, giving little attention to social and cultural impacts of such transactions. Finally, the short history of many of the new technologies – such as video, DBS (direct broadcast satellite), and the personal computer – has not provided sufficient time for investigation of the different dimensions or international ramifications of these media. For these reasons, research and writing on the international flow of information in the above listed commercial and cultural industries, as well as scientific and technical areas, is comparatively new.

## Books, Journals, and Educational Texts

The current transborder flow of books, scientific journals, and educational texts is immense. Both the production and trade of these materials have grown at unprecedented rates during the last three decades. However, the exact amount of the flow of books, journals, and related items has yet to be calculated. It is only through general observations and through estimates provided by the industry itself and by governments involved in exporting and importing such materials that the tremendous growth in the industry is discerned.

More is known about book production than about other printed material since statistics on world outputs have been calculated by various organizations including UNESCO. In the 16 years between 1955 and 1971, the total world production of books almost doubled, from 284,000 titles to 548,000 titles. The latter figure included 43,000 translations: 43 percent from English, 13 percent from French, and 10 percent from German and Russian. Most of the translated titles are from the regions of high production – North America, Europe, Oceania, and the former Soviet Union.[1] According to one estimate, 591,000 titles were published in 1979. Annual world production of book copies in 1983 was estimated to be about 10 billion.[2]

Between 1983 and 1994 the publication of books, worldwide, increased 40 percent. The largest producers of books in numbers of titles include the former Soviet Union, the United States, Germany, the United Kingdom, the People's Republic of China, India, France, Spain, Holland, and Italy. The number of titles produced in each of these countries has been increasing almost yearly since the 1960s. The countries of Scandinavia also produce a considerable number of books in terms of their population to book production ratios. Other big producers are Poland, Hungary, Belgium, Portugal, Switzerland, Austria, Canada, Australia, Brazil, Mexico, Argentina, South Korea, Egypt, and most recently, Iran.

Although these regions dominate the international markets for books, exports are not necessarily a large sector of their publishing industries. The United Kingdom, where 50 percent of the income of the publishing industry comes from exports, is the exception. Foreign revenues are important, especially in the field of technical, scientific, and professional publishing, but do not constitute a major portion of earnings. For example, in the United States, only 6 percent of the total annual output is exported.

In examining the basic available figures, it is immediately apparent that most of the world's books are published by only a few nations. Approximately 80 percent of all books are currently being published in the industrialized world. The countries of Europe alone account for nearly 50 percent of the world total. Although the industrialized countries make up only 35.6 percent of the world's population, they account for 83.1 percent of all book titles. The less industrialized nations, with 64.4 percent of the world's population account for only 16.9 percent of all book titles.[3]

Furthermore, although figures on the total number of copies produced are rarely available, there is obvious disparity in production-count totals, since the number of copies run per title in most Third World countries is lower than in the major book-producing countries of the West. Early in the 1970s, Africa, which produced a mere 1.7 percent of the world's book titles, accounted for only .15 percent of the copies printed during that year. During the same period, Asia produced 16 percent of the world's titles and only 2.5 percent of world copies. Although total production had increased by the end of the 1970s, the ratios had changed little by the beginning of the 1980s.

In 1976, Africa, with 13 percent of the world's population, Asia with 45.2 percent, and Latin American with 10.5 percent, accounted for only 1.9 percent, 16.9 percent, and 5.2 percent respectively, of all books produced in that year. While in the last two decades total book production, in terms of both title and copy outputs, has increased steadily, and in some cases dramatically, in the Third World, this vast region's percentage share of total world production has remained disproportionately low and has, in fact, declined. This decline is due to the immense expansion of book production in the industrialized world.

The statistics on book production show that approximately 65 percent of the people in the world experience a severe book shortage. Today in many parts of the world there is a great demand for scientific, technical, and educational books. Less industrialized nations continually import increasing quantities of books from industrially advanced countries, while the flow of books from the developing to the developed world remains slight. The nature of the book trade between these two regions is essentially an immense one-way flow.

Two other discernible patterns of flow are those between the nations of the developed world and those among the countries in the Third World. Large numbers of books are traded within Western Europe, as well as between the countries of Eastern Europe and the former Soviet Union, and between Europe, North America, Australia, and Japan. Of the latter, the greatest volume of trade is among the Europeans and across the North Atlantic. The largest transborder flow of books in the world is from the United States to Canada.

The majority of trade in books between Third World countries takes place in Latin America, the Middle East, and parts of Asia. The recent increase in trade among Third World countries is a positive development, since they spread the creative works, thought, and knowledge originating in the Third World, and usually at less cost than imports from the developed world.

During the 1950s and 1960s, while new technologies were lowering the cost of book production, the popularization and improvement of the paperback were increasing book sales and production. Additionally, the organization of publishing houses was changing through mergers. Although small, specialized firms could still enter the market, control of the publishing industry came to be concentrated in a few multinational corporations. The larger publishing houses had an advantage in inventory control, advertising budget, and distribution channels, and by producing greater numbers of books, they lowered the unit price and expanded sales. The 1970s saw even more mergers, this time across the media. IBM, ITT, RCA, Xerox, and GE are examples of corporations that initiated mergers of publishing houses and electronic corporations. There were also mergers involving the motion picture industry.[4]

Large publishing houses in capitalist countries have been able to make use of elaborate administrative and marketing arrangements to stimulate growth in industry sales. Advertising and other marketing devices have resulted in the expansion of foreign trade for European and American companies. Some mergers of firms across continents have taken place and many American firms have established subsidiaries in Europe. European firms are now beginning to establish themselves in the United States as well. Consequently, there is increased publishing of books in foreign languages for foreign markets, as well as co-publishing arrangements, especially between German, Italian, Swiss, American, and Japanese firms.

The state and conditions of book production and distribution have been altered considerably in Russia and the former republics of the Soviet Union after the collapse of communism. The former Soviet Union reported a total output of 1.7 billion copies of 83,000 titles in 1975, making it the largest producer of book titles and among the largest printers of book copies in the world. Book production and distribution were considered to be vital instruments for national development and therefore the government put much energy into the coordination of book production, publication, and distribution. The majority of books produced in the Soviet Union were in scientific, political, and social fields and usually printed in 20 different languages. Most were published in Russian, but a large number were translated from one Soviet language to another. The export of books was regarded as highly important, and between 1970 and 1975 alone the output of books in non-Soviet languages doubled in numbers of titles and tripled in numbers of copies, nearly all destined for export. Post communism and changing economic conditions combined with internal strifes have considerably altered the publishing industries in the former Soviet Union, especially in the Central Asian Republics.

The United States has consistently been among the top three publishers of book titles in the world, the former Soviet Union and the United Kingdom being the two other largest producers. The US is also the largest book importer in the world. Over 57,000 titles were released in the United States in 1977 and domestic sales reached $4.1 billion. Imports were valued at $300 million in 1981, and book exports totaled over $600 million, 410 million copies being shipped abroad. The US publishing industry benefits directly from the increasingly worldwide use of English as a second language, from the vast amount of scientific and technological research being done in the United States, and from rising school enrolment in Third World countries, especially where American publishers are actively promoting and marketing their products.

The United Kingdom, which published 48,158 titles in 1980, is the world's second largest producer of English books, as well as one of the top three world producers overall. Britain's 2,000 plus publishing companies include some of the largest in the world. For over two centuries this nation has been a top center of world publishing.

Another important book producing country is Germany. Frankfurt, although only the third largest book publishing center in Germany, is the site of the world's largest and most prestigious book fair. Holland's liberal trade policies, its excellent location, and its modern intercontinental communication facilities make this country a center for the importing and re-exporting of books from other European countries and from North America. Spain, which has been in the business of book exporting ever since the sixteenth century, is the world's fifth largest book exporter and a major supplier of books to Latin America. Another major center of world publishing is Japan, which in 1978 released 635 million copies of 43,973 Japanese books, making it the largest producer of books in Asia. Interestingly, some 63 percent of Japan's imported books come from the United States, and many American firms have established subsidiary houses in Japan to produce books locally in the Japanese language.

Among the less developed nations of the world, India, China, Brazil, Mexico, Nigeria, and Egypt are all important actors in book production and distribution. India is the world's seventh largest producer of book titles (18,000 in 1979), as well as the third largest publisher of English language books.

Books, scientific journals, and educational texts are acquired either through the exchange of publications or through direct purchase. International exchanges are usually conducted through either centralized or decentralized organizations to increase coordination and cooperation among those participating in exchanges. A centralized distributing center, generally the least costly method of exchange, considers the special needs of the libraries it represents, deciding the most fitting partners for exchange purposes, the quality and volume of consignment, and the subject matter of exchanges. A decentralized system of distribution, on the other hand, allows more relevant choices of partners, more rational selection of foreign or international subject matter, and possibly more rapid supplementation of items missing in library collections.

Direct purchases of dispatch are usually less costly than exchange, but are subject to barriers that limit their possibilities, such as currency limitations and import restrictions. It has been suggested that the ever-increasing cost of educational textbooks and scientific journals, especially in Europe and North America, greatly affect the acquisition budgets of individuals and libraries, and will continue to have a dramatic impact on the international flow of such material.

Although the number of scientific and educational texts has increased, especially in industrialized countries, no available research shows the extent or pattern of their flow internationally. The best estimates usually come from production/distribution institutions within individual countries, as well as from raw data on import and export of scientific and educational materials.

For example, a conservative estimate indicates that in the late 1970s, approximately 2,700 scholarly journals were published in the United States: that number has apparently been increasing at an average rate of 2 percent or 3 percent per year. Approximately half of the journals published in the United States deal with the humanities and social sciences, the remainder with the natural and technological sciences.[5]

In the 1970s and the beginning of the 1980s, the number of communication and media research journals began to increase. According to a published survey, the number of communication and media periodicals increased threefold between 1969 and 1980 to 534, nearly half being published monthly and quarterly.[6] The major centers for publication of communication and media research journals are the United States (70), Germany (32), Australia (31), Canada (27), India (25), Brazil (25), Japan (19), Belgium (14), Poland (13), and Russia (13). The recent phenomenon of "on-line journals" as well as the "electronic publishing" generally have been contributing to the proliferation of research publications, challenging the traditional resources of information.

There are both internal and external factors that impede the global flow of scientific journals and educational texts. Economic factors include surcharges on books sold abroad; shortages of foreign exchange; postage and customs; transport and other taxes; different levels of development between participating countries in publishing specifically and in overall development generally; and the monopolistic influences of national, international, and transnational book publishers and distributors.

Political factors affecting flow range from existing or proposed governmental policies to political ideology and the political climate. Cultural factors primarily concern the export of intrinsic cultural values within the content of publications, and the resultant perceived threat to the ethnic and national identity in importing countries. Examples include assumed literacy levels, the languages and alphabets employed in publication, translation barriers, the influence of the media employed, and the lack of a standardized classification system.

Among the technical factors impeding the flow are the gap in technological advancement, the lack of accurate statistical data, and the lack of coordination between centralized and decentralized exchange structures. Institutional factors include both censorship and national and international copyright laws.

Translation plays an important role in the international flow of printed material, the amount and type of translated material revealing much information about the circulation of books, journals, and educational texts both internationally and within nations. The success of translated material often depends upon acceptance in certain literary markets, overcoming language barriers, and overcoming ideological and governmental barriers.

Because the flow of books and scientific and educational material is an important part of the international exchange of information, some recommendations can be made to facilitate a flow beneficial to all participants. First and foremost, it is imperative that a universal classification system be established, both to expedite the flow of such material and to collect and compile data necessary to monitor and improve the flow. Second, the circulation of systematic scholarly content reviews would improve the accuracy and effectiveness of selection and exchange processes. Third, specific governmental and private policies should be encouraged to create more favorable conditions for indigenous publishing and increased cross-national exchange and sale. Such policies may include reduced transportation and postage fees, as well as customs regulations conducive to the exchange and sale of printed technical material. Finally, it is important to encourage increased international cooperation between and within the public and private sectors to facilitate and coordinate this most beneficial type of international exchange.

### Film and Sound Recordings

The international production and distribution of films and sound recordings is a major area of global information flow which has received relatively little attention from researchers. Although statistics on world film production are sketchy and imprecise, available data show the Asian countries in the top positions, India and Japan each producing approximately 400 films a year. A second group of producers includes Italy, the United States, and the former Soviet Union, which are each credited with 250 to 300 films a year. Countries producing up to 200 films a year include France, the Republic of Korea, Greece, Hong Kong, and Spain: and those nearing 100 films per year are Mexico, Germany, the United Kingdom and Pakistan.[7]

It is estimated that global production of long films varies between 3,400 and 3,500 per year, but this figure does not indicate the number of films distributed internationally. Most film producing countries, in fact, have little international distribution for their products and can rarely sell them outside of their own national market. Further, American films have had a dominant share of the international film market, and have joint ventures with a number of countries in Europe such as United Kingdom, France, Italy and Germany in production and distribution.

It is possible to compare the motion picture market with that of sound records, although the two forms of mass communication have very different characteristics. In the latter case, however, it is best to approach the market from the point of view of consumption rather than production because ample information on the consumption of records and CDs is more readily available. The dollar volumes of the two markets are similar, the world motion picture market being approximately $5 billion while the volume of world record market is approximately $6 billion.

In 1982, Thomas Guback and Tapio Varis collected data and analyzed the transnational film and sound recording industry, concluding that the "principal American motion picture firms constitute the only integrated, world wide network for theatrical film distribution."[8] This network facilitates global dissemination of television material as well, and results in negligible commercial distribution of foreign films in the United States. In addition, American films abroad have "cultivated patterns of public taste for decades, and this undoubtedly has facilitated the distribution of American television material."[9] These conclusions reinforce the necessity of examining a medium in terms of the broader global patterns and frameworks, especially since the communications industry is an integrated, interacting whole.

## International Advertising

In 1950, the United States was responsible for some 75 percent of all advertising generated in Western industrialized countries. However, as other industrialized countries, particularly Japan, Germany, the United Kingdom, and France, recovered from World War II and began to develop their own consumer goods for distribution in the world market, their share of global advertising increased. Nevertheless, the United States remains the leader in the global promotion and advertising of consumer goods and manufactured products, and sets the pace for the world:

> The rest of the world is rapidly emulating many of our advertising practices and by the year 2000 these will be the norm in a number of other countries around the world. In this sense, the U.S. may be considered to be a leading indicator of the developments that lie ahead in other parts of the world.[10]

Viewed in this light, the implications involving the flow of international advertising are indeed staggering. Not only does international advertising attempt to influence consumer patterns; it actually helps to create markets by encouraging development of mass advertising media. Thus, a review of the more dramatic changes in the world's major advertising agencies in recent years and the pattern of their involvement in the world economy will not only help identify what will probably occur in the years ahead in other countries but will also provide insights into future changes in the activities of transnational advertising agencies.

It has been said that transnational corporations can change the "cultural ecology" in a country through increased media ownership and penetration of foreign advertising. This creates a communication structure that transmits and reinforces the attitudinal conditions of the transnationals financing the system. Transnational corporations usually employ the services of either: (1) a domestic agency; (2) a company-owned agency in each country; (3) a large international agency with branches; or (4) a coordinating agency dealing with independents in the respective countries. Equally interesting, in most commercially significant countries of the world, five patterns of corporate expansion have emerged: (1) setting up a wholly owned national operation; (2) purchasing an existing overseas agency; (3) buying an interest in an overseas agency; (4) joining forces with overseas agencies to form third parties; and (5) setting up corresponding agency relationships.

Until recently, there was a paucity of the more specialized advertising media in many countries: but in the last two decades, especially in Western Europe and to some extent in Eastern Europe, the former Soviet Union, and the People's Republic of China, specialized media have developed to provide the industrial market with means of communicating with potential customers. In addition to advertising normally placed in the print media, many industrial markets are now reached through catalogs, direct mail, and trade fairs, all important promotional media in international industrial marketing. For example, motion picture cinema advertising is now becoming a popular tool for the international advertiser. In countries where quality newspapers and magazines are difficult to produce, cinema advertising is mildly successful. Many theaters sell commercial film time, and even serve as places for merchandising. Additionally, there are two related worldwide organizations: the International Advertising Service, which consists of 21 major advertising concerns booking commercials into more than 100 world markets, and the International Screen Publicity Association.

Economic factors are highly correlated with the basic institutional advertising structure of the transnational, which in turn influences the requirements for international advertising agency service. There are basically three ways in which the international advertising function integrates into the structures of transnational organizations. These differing structures in turn have a strong impact on the flow. The first is headquarters-created advertising, where headquarters maintains full responsibility and authority for all plans, creativity, production, media selection, placement, and budget throughout the world. Local market managers may make recommendations, but the ultimate decision-making authority rests with corporate headquarters.

The second structure involves advertising created locally under broad guidelines subject to periodic review. Advertising guidelines are set by corporate headquarters, but no prior clearance is needed for release. In this structure, there is an inherent controversy over the amount of control each party possesses since local experience is often deemed necessary, but multinationals are hesitant to delegate to distant advertisers the responsibility for the interpretation and presentation of the company, its ideas, its policies, and its products.

The third structure centers on locally created advertising, where copy, illustration, and layout are all subject to varying degrees of corporate conformity and control.

In some countries, no commercial television and radio advertising has been permitted. This is changing because of the enormous expense involved with local production when direct public subsidies are not available (advertising revenues can offset expenses), and a corresponding tendency toward construction of commercial radio and television stations. For example, Italy, which had no private local radio or television until 1976, currently has some 300 plus privately owned stations. In countries where advertising has not previously been permitted on government-owned stations there has been a softening of restrictions, for example in Belgium, where advertising is now allowed on state-controlled radio and television, even though television advertising is concentrated at the beginning and end of evening programs.

Of increasing importance in advertising is satellite broadcasting. It is estimated that the ability to reach all of Europe with a single message will stimulate new forms of activity by international advertisers, including the possibility of standardized messages covering several countries.

On the other hand, in several countries political factors, such as strict regulation through taxation and other governmental policies, have reduced the direct influence of international advertising agencies on the local scene. In Iran, for example, since the establishment of the Islamic Republic in 1979, the activities of international advertisers have been eliminated totally and the commercial aspects of national radio and television have been removed through constitutional provisions.

It is, however, evident that international advertising, by virtue of its volume, its expenditure, and its activities, plays an important role in the international market. Yet, research pertaining to the complex flow of international advertising remains scant, and there is a definite need for additional analysis in this area. As one reviews the existing literature and available data at the beginning of the 1990s, three general conclusions are apparent: (1) the United States is the model within the field of advertising; (2) the obvious sources of the majority of international consumer and industrial advertising are transnational companies and international advertising agencies; and (3) the flow of international advertising is mostly vertical, from developed and industrialized nations to the Third World.

The world's top 50 advertising agencies in terms of gross income and billings include, first, the United States agencies, followed by the Japanese, British, German, French, and Italian agencies. Based on total equity interest in foreign shops, the first 15 world agencies in the order of income and advertising expenditure were: (1) Dentsu, (2) Young & Rubicam, (3) J. Walter Thompson Co., (4) Ogilvy & Mather, (5) McCann-Erickson Worldwide, (6) Ted Bates, (7) BBDO International, (8) Leo Burnett Co., (9) SSC&B, (10 Foote, Cone & Belding, (11) Doyle Dane Bernbach, (12) D'Arcy-MacManus & Masius, (13) Hakuhodo, (14) Grey Advertising, and (15) Benton & Bowles.[11]

The total worldwide advertising trends in terms of advertising expenditures project that the United States will remain the leader in the world market by the beginning of the twenty-first century, followed by Japan, Germany, the United Kingdom, France, and Italy. In 1980 the total world wide expenditure on advertising was $110,000 million.[12] In 1994 this figure had increased to approximately $200,000 million. In 1985 the United States, the European Union and Japan spent $60,000 million, $20,000 million and $10,000 million respectively on advertising. These figures changed to $47,500 million for the United States, $60,000 million for the European Union and $22,500 million for Japan in 1994. The increase in expenditure in 1994 within the European Union (6.7 percent) remained, however, under that recorded for the United States (7.8 percent) and Japan (8.6 percent). In 1994 there was a clear upturn in advertising expenditure across the whole of the European Union. Advertising is tending to become the prime source of financing for television in Western Europe. At the same time television in Western Europe has become the main advertising medium within the European Union. Advertising expenditure in central and eastern Europe also rose sharply, a clear sign of growth markets, with Slovakia increasing expenditure by 79 percent, Poland increasing by 70 percent, the Czech Republic by 59 percent and Hungary by 34 percent over last year.[13]

The economic as well as cultural information powers of world capitalism, especially that of the United States, can be best examined by the worldwide network of major advertising agencies and by growing expenditures to advertise and promote their products on national, regional, and global scales. The strength of international advertisers lies in the fact that not only do they have a powerful influence over the international network of transnational mass media and the entertainment industry but their techniques and methods, developed over the past several years, are essential for the development and expansion of manufactured goods and commodities. Furthermore, their perceived "neutrality" in international politics and inter-state conflict, coupled with the desire of people almost everywhere for certain universality, cosmopolitanism, and consumption, provide the ingredients necessary for persuasive and informative strategies.

### Video, Computer, and Related Technologies

During the last three decades, developments in cable, cassette, video, computer, and satellite technologies have produced a scramble for profit on a worldwide scale through information, business, and entertainment programming, while also making possible an expanded use of these technologies to provide information services to the home. Additionally, the use of these technologies in social and political mobilization has also been tested. Such developments have brought about complexity in information handling, both in the vertical and the horizontal dimensions of systems. The consumption of new technologies generally, and of computer, video, and cassettes specifically, is increasing so rapidly, particularly in industrialized nations, that information regarding their use is nearly always outdated and meaningless.

Worldwide consumers spent more on video than any other new media technology between 1985 to 1995. The global figure for total video units increased from 168.96 million in 1987 to an estimated 300 million in 1994.[14] In 1987 the countries that had a higher than 50 percent penetration figure of video in television households included Australia, Bahrain, Hong Kong, Iceland, Ireland, Kuwait, Lebanon, Malaysia, Netherlands, New Zealand, Nigeria, Panama, Qatar, Singapore, United Arab Emirates, United Kingdom and the United States.[15] These figures representing both the industrialized and less industrialized countries reflect the fact that middle-class homes are increasingly likely to have a video as well as a television set, a trend continuing in the 1990s. The influence of video on cinema attendance continues to be a debatable subject. However, as a number of studies show, in many countries of the world video does not so much replace cinema as operates as an adjunct to it.[16]

Because of confusion surrounding regulations in the video industry as well as import and foreign exchange restrictions, piracy is rampant, especially in Asia, Africa, and Latin America. In the industrialized countries of Europe, however, and in such producing countries as Japan and the United States, the public use of new technology continues to grow at an accelerated pace. For example, a survey conducted by the Electronic Industries Association for the Consumer Electronics Manufacturers Association in 1995 indicated that 88 percent of American households owned videocassette recorders.[17] The same survey showed the following household ownership of consumer electronic products: television, 98 percent; home radios, 98 percent; telephones (corded), 96 percent; answering machines, 60 percent; telephone (cordless), 59 percent; home CD players, 48 percent; personal computers, 40 percent; cellular telephones, 21 percent; and home fax machines, 8 percent. Another survey in 1995 showed that the rate of growth of personal computers in the industrialized world is growing as rapidly as did the videocassette recorders a decade earlier. There were a total of 150 million personal computers worldwide in 1995.[18]

The onrushing wave of video, cassette, and tape technology threatens to bring down many established social and political bulwarks throughout the world. With pornographic films a fact of life on the video circuit, and with political messages taped through cassette and related technologies, censorship threatens to become certainly different and somewhat irrelevant. Similarly, in many parts of the world, defense by government and industry of the monopoly of film and television broadcasting may appear increasingly meaningless as alternative programs become available. The social utility of these new innovations, however, will depend largely on the accompanying structural changes within communication systems and national and local policies; otherwise, their implementation on a world scale will most likely perpetuate existing media commercialization.

Aside from the economic and commercial considerations, educational and political implications of this type of information flow can be quite profound, having lasting impact and consequences. In the 1970s, prior to the Iranian revolution, the exiled Ayatollah Khomeini sent his messages through telephone and tapes to Iran, where they were copied by the thousands on cassette tapes and distributed to the masses through the informal and traditional communication network. This method of information flow provided both the credibility and excitement of oral messages, and the permanence and accessibility of written messages.[19] In 1984 a videograph in Asia reported that

a videotape cassette labeled "Playboy Lovers," smuggled through customs, is later seen in many Philippine living rooms for its political, not sexual, content. Most of the pornographic material has been erased and replaced by a taped copy of a Japanese documentary on the assassination of opposition leader Benigno

Aquino, Jr. Other illegal tapes of Japanese and U.S. newscasts are passed around, recopied over and over on home recorders as Philippinos supplement the bland news given by their own mass media.[20]

Another major technological advance that gave impetus to the search for appropriate nomenclature was videotex, the generic name for home retrieval systems. In videotex, the merger of information reception, communication transmission, and the computer was thought to be complete. This new electronic data retrieval business was expected to boom. As one leading US business journal pointed out, "A giant home information industry is taking shape in the plans of hundreds of companies, many of them among the largest U.S. corporation. By 1990, they are confident that videotex will be big business."[21]

There are two types of videotex. The first is the simple broadcast version, teletext, which continuously transmits a finite amount of information on the unused portions of TV transmissions. Users receive the desired information whenever they want by entering a code into their modified television sets. The second type of videotex is the interactive view data service, which links a home terminal or computer either by cable or telephone lines to a giant information bank. However, the videotex technology did not expand as was expected due to the rapid advances in other computer and electronic technologies, such as the Internet.

The distribution of a limited number of advertising dollars has caused concern among publishers. While video services duplicate traditional services such as newspapers, they can be updated more easily and at lower cost. Businesses that have traditionally provided such services will soon experience shrinking revenues that may force their closure.

The convergence of countless industries on the informatics sector is certain to have a profound impact on the economic market as we know it today. In the United States, with such diverse actors as Citibank, AT&T, Time Inc., CBS, Fox Cable Communications, Dow Jones, Sears Roebuck, and American Airlines all competing in the informatics arena, limitations placed on community news ownership by the Federal Communications Commission, for instance, are totally irrelevant.

Thus, any new communication policy will have to deal with all industries that can be potentially linked to the digital system. It must also be recognized that the US system is one of the few that will be operated for the benefit of commercial interests. In Canada and the European countries, the system will generally fall under the jurisdiction of the post, telegraph, and telephone Ministries, which would then operate it for the benefit of the government itself. It is in this context that a call is made for an information policy to regulate this highly diverse and burgeoning field.

## The Internet Elite

A few years ago, the Internet was just an experimental collaboration of the US Defense Department and US academia. But it grew exponentially as users all over the world discovered the advantages of linking their computers together to share software, exchange electronic mail, and discuss complicated scientific problems.

The Internet seems like magic. Pioneer users established huge electronic databases, and then threw open access to anyone in the world who had a computer, a modem, and the will to access the information. Largely free from government control, and run on a completely decentralized basis (it was designed that way to help it survive a nuclear war), the Internet seemed like the perfect free lunch. No one was in charge of running it, but somehow it ran. Anyone could use it without paying for the privilege. Universal access was a reality, and the most distant user could access the system as easily as a New York tycoon or a Harvard researcher.

As talk of the Internet's benefits trickled out to the world, something unanticipated happened: it began to interest casual users. During the 1980s, the worldwide population of people with access to personal computers mushroomed from a handful to literally hundreds of millions. Popular magazines and newspapers breathlessly promoted the benefits, and its use doubled monthly. By the 1992 US presidential campaign, the Internet was considered important enough to merit speeches by vice presidential candidate Al Gore. Among the most over-hyped inventions of the twentieth century, the Internet today is envisioned by many as the precursor to the information superhighway.

And the hype only increases. Many enthusiasts consider the Internet as not just a way to link electronic databases, but as an entirely new way for people to interact. It is hailed as a return to the equality of the eighteenth-century pamphlet. The most obscure user is free to post views on the system's bulletin boards or to establish a forum, bypassing the monolithic press and media barons. Interaction between people will be forever changed, these enthusiasts claim, because anyone anywhere can communicate with anyone else, at any time.

Lately, however, a note of discontent has sounded. Even though the Internet has moved from the back pages of computer magazines to the covers of mainstream magazines, not everyone has been seduced by its allure. Critics have focused on three shortcomings: potential controls over content; the potentially disenfranchising effect of communication that is available only to the upper and middle classes; and the profound social impact of communication that takes place through an electronic intermediary. Each of these concerns is taken all-too-cavalierly by technological gurus and policy-makers, who seem intent on boosting the Internet no matter what its cost to society.

*Control Over Content*

Theoretically, anyone can post information, but the reality is that the main content of the Internet – the huge databases containing electronic information so important to people's daily lives – is controlled by governments, corporations, and academic institutions. Their control was less significant when the system's major purpose was to link together academic and government researchers. Now that the Internet is becoming an important source of world knowledge, the ease with which it is possible to alter information – or merely to shade the truth by selectively culling out unfavorable information – is a real concern. This concern is deepened by the recent trend of large corporations to establish their own Internet sites, especially on the fast-growing World Wide Web. There are proposals to privatize the Internet. Some see the privatization and commercialization of the network as a threat to its continuing availability for educational purposes. Who will be the custodians of the world's information?

*Disenfranchisement*

Although the Internet supposedly is available to anyone with a modem and the will to use it, the profile of users is skewed by race, gender, income, and age. Studies show that more than 80 percent of all users are computer-literate, middle-class males under the age of 40. Access may be unlimited in theory, but it is restricted by the cost of technology and the steep learning curve for computer neophytes. Although in 1995 for the first time Americans spent more money on home computers than they did on television sets, such purchases were confined to middle- and upper-class families. If electronic communication is the future, what will become of the vast majority of people who can only stand by and watch the worldwide exchange of electrons?

*Social Implications*

Finally – and most profoundly – there are the disturbing social implications of a future in which human communication increasingly takes place through electronic media. Since the invention of the telegraph and telephone in the nineteenth century, more and more discourse has taken place through impersonal electronic intermediaries rather than through natural face-to-face communication. Despite these changes, however, personal communication still remained paramount. Whether at work or on daily errands, people still needed to interact.

But the Internet could change that. Researchers are working on electronic substitutes for the daily interactions we take for granted. Work will be done at home and transmitted by modem; shopping will be done over the World Wide Web and paid for by debits to our electronic bank accounts. Even entertainment will take place through the computer screen.

Chat lines linking together devotees of certain hobbies long have been a fixture of the Internet. With the growth of consumer interest in the on-line world, electronic dating services, sexual chat forums, and even casino gambling are all available today at 28,800 bauds per second. Soon, there will be very little that cannot be accomplished from the comfort of our own homes.

But is a world split between an elite minority of information-empowered people interacting electronically and a majority mired in information poverty in anyone's best interests? Do we really want to choose between a "successful" but soulless electronic existence and disenfranchisement?

The Internet is not an unmixed blessing. It gives the computer-savvy individual access to information; at the same time it raises an insurmountable barrier to those who cannot avail themselves of the new opportunity. It allows people to bypass the chokehold that the global media giants have on political discourse – and disseminate underground materials advocating actions like the Oklahoma City terrorist bombing. In short, the Internet may fulfill the dreams of its boosters and reorder human interaction, but that reordering may not be a good thing. All dreams should be closely examined before being fulfilled.

**Conclusion**

Some aspects of the cultural industries discussed in this chapter direct our attention to the influence of the information universe, the symbolic environment that shapes the perceptions and behavior of actors at all levels of the international theater. There is greater significance to such a symbolic environment, which is nourished by various international, cultural, and knowledge production industries, including book publishers, movie distributors, advertisers, public relations practitioners, and purveyors of electronic technologies and data. An analysis of the commercialization and economization of culture and knowledge provides a basis for explaining information imbalance in terms of the economic milieu.

Alongside the universe of material trade, production, distribution, and value adding, there is a parallel or perhaps coterminous universe of cultural and knowledge trade and cultural production and distribution, adding value to culture and culture exporting. Not only do these universes impinge on each other, but they offer "currencies" that are acceptable tender in each other's realms, and sustain mutually supportive growth. One cannot hope to market a new product without disseminating knowledge of it, creating a demand, and shaping the cultural environment to accept it. The ability to control the means of production and international distribution of cultural products, then, is the key to larger markets and greater productivity and prosperity in an international system that has eschewed "gunboat" coercion, to some extent, in favor of the utilization of cultural industries as persuaders.

**Notes**

1. *UNESCO Statistical Yearbook, 1974* (Paris: UNESCO, 1975), pp. 663–668.
2. *UNESCO Statistical Yearbook, 1982* (Paris: UNESCO, 1983), p. 790.
3. Ibid., see Table II.

4. For a full historical account of changes in the industry as they occurred in the United States, see Lewis A. Coser, *Books: The Culture and Commerce of Publishing* (New York: Basic Books, 1982).

5. The Report of the National Inquiry, *Scholarly Communication* (Baltimore: Johns Hopkins University Press, 1979), p. 38.

6. These figures were computed from Sylwester Dziki, *World Director of Mass Communication Periodicals* (Cracow: Press Research Center and Bibliographical Section of IAMCR, 1980).

7. *UNESCO Statistical Yearbook, 1982*.

8. Thomas Guback and Tapio Varis (in collaboration with José G. Hanton, Heiberto Nuraro, Gloria Rojas, and Boonrah Booyahetmala), *Transnational Communication and Cultural Industries*, Reports and Papers on Mass Communication No. 92 (Paris: UNESCO, 1982), p. 31.

9. Ibid., p. 31.

10. Robert J. Coen, "Vast U.S. and World Wide Ad Expenditures Expected," *Advertising Age*, April 19, 1982.

11. Ibid., pp. 9–12.

12. This has been computed from the projected statistics published in *Advertising Age*, April 19, 1982.

13. *European Audiovisual Observatory Statistical Yearbook 96* (Strasbourg: European Audiovisual Observatory, Council of Europe, 1995), pp. 275–287.

14. Manuel Alvardo, ed., *Video World-Wide: An International Study* (Paris: Unesco Press, 1988), p. 323; and *Screen Digest*, August, 1994, p. 15.

15. Alvardo, ed., *Video World-Wide: An International Study*, p. 323.

16. Krister Malm and Roger Wallis, *Media Policy and Music Activity* (London: Routledge, 1992), pp. 43–44, 167–168.

17. "Who Has What?", *New York Times*, June 22, 1996. Section E, p. 2.

18. John Greenwald, "Battle for Remote Control." *Time* (special issue), 145: 12 (Spring 1995), p. 70.

19. Hamid Mowlana, "Technology versus Tradition: Communication in the Iranian Revolution," *Journal of Communication*, 29: 3 (Summer 1979), pp. 107–112.

20. John A. Lent, "Videography in Asia: Revolution, Resistance and Reform," paper read at the Howard University Communication Conference, Washington, DC, February 17, 1984, p. 1.

21. "The Home Information Revolution," *Business Week*, June 29, 1981, p. 83.

# 6

# Political Economy of Information:
# Transnational Data Flows

An important trend in international economic activities during the past two decades has been the increasing role of data communication. Information-intensive industries such as banking, insurance, airlines, multinational business, and news agencies are heavily dependent on the instantaneous availability and dissemination of data around the world. In order to transmit vital management information, manufacturing and trading firms operating in more than one country must facilitate reliable lines of data communication between the parent organization and its subsidiaries. Governments, as well, rely on data links via satellite and cable for military, diplomatic, and technical communication and decision-making.

These types of international communication, commonly known as transborder data flow, were made possible by the development of computer communication systems, linking sophisticated computers in one country to affiliated computers in other countries, and through them to remote terminals. Providing for cost-effective and speedy data processing, storage, and retrieval at virtually any location, the merger of computer and telecommunications technologies is, in fact, the precondition for the emergence of transborder data flow.[1]

In recent years, many nations have become concerned with the growing international network of computers facilitating the storage, transmission, manipulation, and retrieval of enormous amounts of information. This information ranges from personal data on private citizens to financial information and data on scientific and technical processes. The number of industries involved in such activities is rapidly growing.

In short, the computerized supply of financial and commercial information has become a major and growing source of profit. There are no accurate statistics on the total amount of such transactions worldwide, but it is estimated that the lucrative transborder data flow industry is a multibillion-dollar enterprise.

The United States leads the way in the field of communication and computer technology, and American producers of equipment and software dominate the world market. Currently, the United States is responsible for the majority of worldwide transmission and processing of data.[2]

Of course, at this point, there are many nations without the technical development to build their own computer systems. An important question for these countries is whether it would be in their interest to subscribe to an international data network where they will clearly play a client role.

Opinion is divided on this issue. On the one hand, it is argued that information networks offer less developed countries cheaper and more effective access to the latest scientific and technical know-how from the developed countries.[3] Others claim that Third World countries find themselves in dependency relationships, suggesting that the information that is transferred to the Third World is often "ill-suited to the resources, needs and climates of the developed world."[4] For example, francophone Africa has much of its information on credit and insurance stored in French computers. As a result, "a computer-poor country depends on a dominating, computer-rich neighbour even for vital information about itself."[5] This is paralleled by an earlier observation that in the process of technology transfer and know-how, "ninety-eight per cent of the scientific and technological research at present is being undertaken in the advanced industrial states – drawn on their own experience. Only one per cent of the research is directed at the special problems of developing countries."[6]

Specifically, transborder data flows are defined as the transfer of digitally encoded units of information for processing, storage, or retrieval across national boundaries. To qualify as transborder data flow, the technical process must involve (1) transmission, (2) storage, and (3) processing. Traditional telephone and telegraph by themselves provide transmission, but provide neither storage nor processing. Storage of data opens convenient access to large databases, and processing allows manipulation of data in various forms and orders. This definition excludes transborder data flows resulting from media products, such as news broadcasts, television programming, and conventional telecommunication services.[7]

These technical distinctions are important, as they relate to the roots of problems peculiar to transfer data flows. For example, laws affecting personally identifiable data did not appear until the development of technologies involving data processing and storage. In addition, transborder data flows are normally of a proprietary nature and are based on contractual relationships between parties. Thus, electronic media products that involve mass diffusion are not considered as part of transborder data flow.

It is important to understand the nature of transborder data flow in the context of its participants, content, patterns, and direction. To assure that this innovation is used to benefit humanity in its global environment, we must examine the various issues surrounding transborder data flow, including the implications on communication policies, and determine the direction of future research.

## From Transborder to Transnational

The major actors in the flow of data across national boundaries are states, intergovernmental organizations, and nongovernmental organizations such as private communication carriers, data processing service bureaus, multinational corporations, and transnational associations.[8] Depending on their particular interests in transborder data flow, these participants may promote or restrict the flow of information, with widely varying strategies and methods for maximizing interests. It is precisely this complex of conflicting interests that makes it so difficult to achieve widespread policy agreement on transborder data flow.[9]

States and multinational corporations are the most significant actors in transborder data flow. They are heavy users of international computer communication systems and own, operate, and manage domestic communication networks that send and receive international data traffic. In the United States, computer communication systems are operated largely either in-house by private organizations, or by data processing service bureaus for private customers. In other nations where communication services are state-operated, data communications are provided through facilities of the post, telegraph, and telephone (PTT) authorities.

Intergovernmental organizations are a second set of significant actors in transborder data flows. Although their actual use of computer communication is quite limited, these organizations provide an arena both for regulating data communication technologies and for debating and resolving conflicts about the transnational flow of data. The International Telecommunications Union (ITU), a specialized agency of the United Nations, performs planning, standard setting, and coordinating functions for international communication facilities ranging from telephone and telegraph to broadcasting and data communication. Although the ITU operates no communication facility, administrative conferences held under its sponsorship have considerable authority over such practices as the allocation of radio spectrum frequencies.

The International Telecommunications Satellite Organization (INTELSAT) operates its own system of communications satellites. INTELSAT membership currently stands at 136 states, each owning an investment share in the system proportional to its use of the satellites.

Other international organizations taking an active role in transborder data flow include the Organization for Economic Cooperation and Development (OECD), the Council of Europe, and the Intergovernmental Bureau of Informatics (IBI). These organizations are specifically involved in the issues and controversy surrounding this burgeoning new field.

In addition to governmental actors who sometimes own and operate communication facilities, there are a number of private communication carriers and international data network organizations. International record carriers such as RCA Global Communications, ITT World Communications, and Western Union International jointly own and operate transnational communication links with American Telephone and Telegraph (AT&T) and state-owned PTTs. International data networks such as SWIFT (interbank transfer system) and SITA (airline networks in Europe) provide customized communication services to specific groups of subscribers.

Another type of nongovernmental actor in transborder data flow is the data processing service bureau. As a consolidation of specialized communication carriers providing data transmission and processing, these organizations offer international computing services directly to a wide variety of users in any state that has transmission capabilities and permission to access the network.

Multinational corporations purchase and use large amounts of data services, as well as using internal international data transmission for management purposes. Information-intensive organizations such as banks, credit firms, and commercial airlines are the heaviest users of external services, while manufacturing firms must internally transmit and consolidate vast amounts of data for corporate decision-making. Additionally, some corporations use high-speed data communication for international currency speculation.

A final set of nongovernmental actors includes national and transnational associations such as the National Endowment of Science and the Smithsonian Institution. These organizations produce and disseminate scientific or bibliographic data through international computer communication networks.

## Diversity of Data Flow

The use of transnational computer communication systems is largely determined by a variety of needs for a given actor. The content, patterns, and directions of transborder data flow reflect the specific tasks assigned to each data communication according to the diversity of the actors' needs.

Eric Novotny has identified four types of data flow content:[10]

- *Operational data* consist of transborder data flows supporting organizational decisions or sustaining certain administrative functions. Multinational corporations, for example, use such information to coordinate geographically dispersed business functions.
- *Financial transaction data* represent the information resulting in credits, debits, and transfers of money that are distinct from operational data containing financial information. While the unrestricted flow of financial data permits convenient financial arrangement, it also makes it difficult for governments to control currency speculation.
- *Personally identifiable data* contain information relating to credit and medical histories, criminal records, employment and travel reservations, or simply names and identification numbers. Personally identifiable data may also appear in operational or financial transaction data.
- *Scientific and technical data* include experimental results, surveys, environmental or meteorological measurements, and economic statistics. Bibliographic databases and software to process raw data are also made available to the international scientific community through computer-communication systems.

As shown in Figure 6.1, patterns of transborder data flow movements also fall into four generic types.[11]

- *Consolidation flow* describes a simple subsidiary relationship in which a subsidiary entity in country A transfers information one-way to a headquarters user in country B. The headquarters consolidates such data from a number of subsidiaries.
- *Distribution flow* occurs when a centralized entity distributes data to several subsidiary entities. Applications of this type of flow include updates to local databases, orders and financial reports, and similar instructions or information transmitted to subsidiaries.
- *Transnational network flow* commonly involves transborder processing such as a service bureau arrangement in which subsidiaries in one country use host computer facilities in another. Two-way traffic occurs since the main purpose of accessing the host is to use its databases.
- *Multinational network flow* is a more complicated pattern in which data flows are characterized by multiple-user, multiple-host interactions. Information and processing can be centralized, distributed, or both. Large data service bureaus or time sharing networks typically operate in this manner.

In this process, a more important consideration is whether a particular type of data flow arrangement poses legal compliance problems. Generally, regulatory conditions are influenced greatly by the directions of transmission, the geographic location of processing and storage functions, and, most important, the location of the user.

Although there have been few attempts to measure the aggregate volume and direction of transborder data flows, heavy concentration of satellite and submarine cable communications in the North Atlantic area and between the United States and Japan indicates the predominance of transborder data flow within the industrialized West. Yet even within this area there are disparities. Canada, France, and Sweden particularly feel that they are too dependent on the United States to supply data processing products and services, and that much valuable information is being deposited in the United States without an equal flow in the reverse direction.[12]

This directional pattern is further reinforced by the uneven distribution of computer communication technologies among nations. The limited data processing capacity available in "computer-poor" countries, many of which are located in the Third World, makes it necessary for them to export raw data for processing and to re-import the processed data. As data flow out to be processed, with them flow revenues and, consequently, business and jobs in the information industry.

As Figure 6.2 indicates, this cycle in international data flow is analogous to cycles in other trade areas where industrially less developed countries export raw materials to industrialized countries for processing and then purchase back the more costly finished products. Noticeably lacking is the

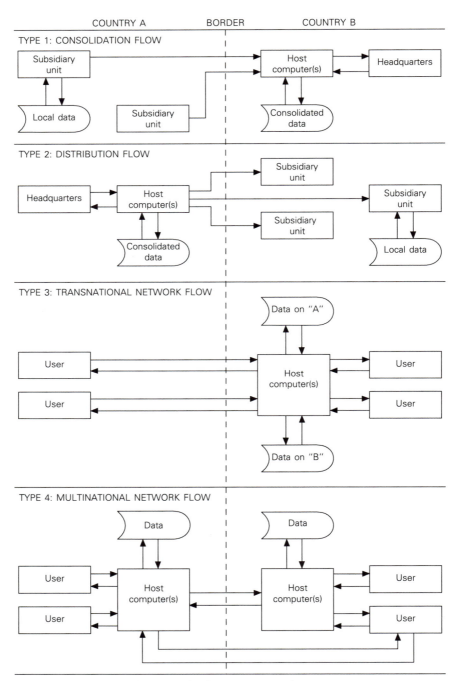

Figure 6.1   *Patterns of transborder flow movements (Eric J. Novotny,
"Transborder Data Flow Regulations: Technical Issues of Legal Concern,"*
Computer/Law Journal, *3:2 (Winter 1981), p. 111)*

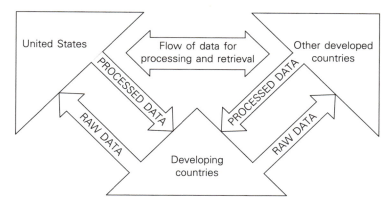

Figure 6.2   *Directions of transborder data flows (Rein Turn, ed.,*
Transborder Data Flows: Concerns in Privacy Protection and Free Flow
of Information, *Vol. 1, Report of the AFIPS Panel on Transborder Data
Flows (Washington, DC: American Federation of Information Processing
Societies, 1979), p. 5)*

exchange of data among developing countries. In the absence of effective
communication to integrate and represent the interests of the Third
World, their dependency relationships with the industrialized world are
exacerbated.

## From Privacy to Sovereignty

The issues and controversies in transborder data flow, although wide-
ranging and seemingly unrelated, reflect the general context of conflicting
interests among actors and participants in international computer communication. In one of the early studies on transborder data flow, Allen
Gotlieb, Charles Dalfen, and Kenneth Katz in 1974 suggested that the
issues of computer communication should be viewed in light of the "tension
between the conflicting state interests in protecting, conserving, and
controlling information on the one hand, and of importing, exporting, and
exchanging ideas on the other – both in pursuit of state goals and in
support of national policies."[13]

This perspective was shared by Novotny in 1981:

> Competition between the exclusive interests of information control and the
> inclusive interests of unrestricted transfer of information across national
> boundaries is the taproot of the controversy. Inclusive interests include principles,
> practices, and policies grouped under the general term "free flow of information."
> These policies promote increased sharing, use, enjoyment and exchange of
> transborder data flows. Principles, practices, and policies that represent exclusive
> interests are grouped under the term "sovereignty over information" and promote
> controlled use, restricted access, conservation, denial and decreased transfers of
> information.[14]

In the process of balancing the competing benefits of promoting and restricting the flow of information, transborder data flow encounters a diversity of problems. The first issue to emerge from transborder data flow activities regarded the protection of personal privacy – the rights of individuals regarding the collection, storage, dissemination, and use of information about them. When the development of computer communication technologies in the early 1970s made it possible to store a large amount of personal information in foreign databases bound only by the statutes of the host nation, a number of countries began to realize the need for laws and policies to preserve the privacy of their citizens.

While regulations vary from nation to nation, most countries follow the principles of privacy protection contained in the Code of Fair Information Practices:[15]

1. *Openness*. There must be no secret personal data record keeping systems.
2. *Individual access*. There must be a way for individuals to find out what personal data are on record about them and how the data are used.
3. *Individual participation*. There must be a way for individuals to correct or amend personal data about themselves.
4. *Collection*. There must be limits on the kind of personal data organizations may collect and the method employed.
5. *Use*. There must be a way for individuals to prevent the use of their personal data for purposes other than those for which they were collected.
6. *Disclosure*. There must be limits on the external disclosure of personal data that record keeping organizations may make.
7. *Information management*. All record keeping organizations that create, maintain, or use records of personal data must implement data management policies.
8. *Accountability*. Record keeping organizations must be accountable for their operations regarding personal data.

Privacy protection and fair information laws, however, are not implemented by all nations. Virtually all of the concern about computer-processed personal information has been in the democracies of the North Atlantic area. Most other states do not have political traditions or economies that require the legal arrangements for computer-processed personal data.

Additionally, the privacy rights of an individual in one country may be incompatible with those in another nation to which personal data are exported. The potential legal problems and conflicts arising from the different levels of privacy protection worldwide have prompted several international bodies to establish a standard. In 1980, the OECD "Guidelines Governing the Protection of Privacy and Transborder Data Flows of Personal Data" were adopted by 18 of the 24 member governments.[16] In the same year, the Council of Europe adopted the "Convention for the Protection of Individuals with Regard to Automatic Processing of Personal

Data."[17] While the OECD guidelines are voluntary and intended to provide an interim standard without creating unjustified obstacles to transborder data flow, the Council of Europe Convention seeks to enforce common principles of fair information practices among its members. The United States, judging that transborder data flow problems and resulting policy positions are in an early stage of development not warranting binding agreements that are potentially disruptive of economic interactions, has been critical of the Council of Europe Convention.[18]

Another issue in transborder data flow is the question of national sovereignty, which arises when vital information affecting national decision-making is processed and stored in foreign databases. National sovereignty – a country's ability to influence the direction of its political, economic, and sociocultural changes – may be severely impaired if knowledge about the full range of alternatives open to a given country in a given situation is restricted because of limited access to relevant information or an underdeveloped capacity to apply the necessary technology.[19] Sudden interruption of critical data inflow by computer breakdown, natural disaster, political pressure, or the outflow of sensitive data for processing in "data havens" (countries with lax or no data protection laws) could expose a country to foreign manipulation.

Prompted by fears of vulnerability, many states are leaning toward more pronounced restriction of transborder data flows. A study by the Canadian government concluded that "the government should act immediately to regulate transborder data flows to ensure that we do not lose control of information vital to the maintenance of national sovereignty."[20]

Perhaps the most significant impact of computer communication technology on national sovereignty is the transformation of the concept of sovereignty as expressed in geographical terms to information sovereignty.[21] As the role of information in management expands, it is increasingly recognized as a resource over which a state must exercise control. Transborder data flow, however, has been an elusive problem for states. It has been suggested that nations measure political sovereignty by control over resources, including information. Unregulated transborder data flow diminishes this sovereignty.

Yet when it comes to the regulation of internal information flows, states do assert power. In the name of national security, governmental authorities reserve broad powers to engage in interception of telecommunications and monitoring of automated data.

A nation's sovereignty is threatened not only by other nations, but by multinational corporations, probably the most powerful non-state actors in transborder data flow. A primary threat is in the context of international currency speculation. Empowered with a computerized global banking system, multinational corporations are capable of bypassing national monetary policy. A study by the French government reported that nations no longer control the international cash flow and credit distributed through specialized networks. They concluded that it was impossible to implement "a coherent financial policy" because worldwide electronic currency transfer makes exchange systems "volatile."[22] The continuous development of new technologies is likely to intensify the threats to national sovereignty and the corresponding reactions of states.

Another major issue in the recent debate over the economics of transborder data flow is the growing belief that information is a commodity that should be taxed and regulated as it crosses national boundaries. In order to protect the domestic information industries and markets from foreign penetration, a number of countries have erected economic barriers including tariffs, discriminatory pricing, inconsistent technical standards, monitoring of information, excessive government regulation, and restriction of entry into markets. France, in order to impose a duty on information flows, had proposed a system for their classification according to retail value.[23] However, the proposal never materialized due to the new round of trade negotiations under the World Trade Organization (WTO). Tymshare, an American computer firm, estimated that the cost of subscribing to a Japanese public communication service is about ten times more than using the fixed-cost, dedicated telephone line.[24]

Governments also deter the flow of information by non-tariff barriers, such as regulations requiring registration of databases (Sweden), processing of data within the host country (Germany), purchase of domestic computer and communications equipment (Brazil), and limiting the use of private lines (Japan).[25] Many business leaders are concerned about the economic impact of privacy data protection statutes that risk disclosure of proprietary information to an unwarranted third party, as well as the possible protectionist motives that underlie the passage of such laws.[26]

US government and businesses perceive these barriers to transborder data flow as serious threats that affect not only the operation of individual enterprises but the efficiency and growth of entire industries such as banking. Canadian banking regulations, for example, require banks to process and maintain copies in Canada of all data pertaining to Canadian customers, thus compelling foreign firms to establish unnecessary data processing facilities within that country.[27] As competition intensifies among the information industries, these kinds of problems in transborder data flow are likely to be debated in terms of international trade.

The impact of transborder data flow is not limited to the small circle of Western industrialized states. To the extent that information is a basis of power, access to information and ability to utilize it can give some nations political, economic, and social advantages over others. Third World nations fear that underdeveloped computer technology and lack of access to the international data market will block their participation in the growing information-bases world economy, and perpetuate their dependence on the developed world.

As a report by the UN Centre on Transnational Corporations (UNCTC) points out, transborder data flow presents an enormous potential for both assisting and hindering the Third World development process.[28] Providing instant access to a diverse pool of up-to-date knowledge, transborder data flow may give developing countries more information on alternatives and contribute to a more efficient international allocation of resources which, in turn, will accelerate productivity and economic growth. On the other hand, the current imbalance in the international data market and the corresponding levels of computer technologies indicate that transborder data flow has reinforced the international division of labor – Third World nations supply raw materials (data) to the developed nations and receive processed goods (data) in return.

Sophisticated capital-intensive technologies such as computers and telecommunications tend to integrate the multinational corporate system, and deepen the dependence of the Third World on hardware, software, training, and administration supplied by that system.

It is in this context that several international forums began to reflect Third World concerns for a more equitable distribution of data and technologies. In 1978 IBI cosponsored with UNESCO an Intergovernmental Conference on Strategies and Policies in Information (SPIN), where developing nations discussed methods of decreasing their dependence on the United States and Europe for data processing, communication services, and products.[29] In 1980, IBI hosted a Conference on Transborder Data Flow Policies which initiated International Working Parties to conduct research on topics such as data protection, national sovereignty, and the economic impacts of transborder data flows.

Increasingly at issue in these forums is the assumption that the free flow of data across national boundaries is beneficial to all. Herbert I. Schiller has noted that the free flow of information has been and is a "myth." There are "selectors and controllers," who "shift and shape the messages that circulate in society."[30] The fear and frustration of Third World nations are exacerbated by multinational corporations that now select and control large segments of world data flows.

At a 1982 Conference on New Technologies and the New International Information Order, Cuban delegates called for an alternative order in the international flow of information. They advocated rejection of free flow on behalf of establishing "autonomous, coordinated national communication policies, articulated to educational and cultural sectors . . ."[31] With the current economic and political situations surrounding transborder data flow, however, Third World nations are likely to follow a different path, where they will strike a balance between total acceptance and total rejection of the free flow doctrine.

The increasing realization of the critical role of computer communication technologies in economic and social development has prompted several industrialized and developing nations to prepare comprehensive strategies for the utilization of information resources and industries. Since transborder flow involves a variety of economic and political issues, national communication policies are likely to reflect each country's view of the international flow of information.

While transborder data flow issues have grown, from initial concern over privacy protection to concern for national sovereignty and trade, the literature on data flow has also grown substantially in volume and scope. The relatively large number of policy-oriented studies suggests that inquiry into the nature of transborder data flow originated in states searching for appropriate measure to incorporate this new communication activity in national planning for economic and social development.

The current controversies concerning transborder data flow can be attributed largely to the inability of the current international legal regime to accommodate changes resulting from the rapid development of computer communication technology. The concept of national sovereignty can no longer be considered in geographic terms alone. Information is increasingly viewed as a commodity that can be bought, sold, and taxed. Conventional means of privacy protection are challenged by the capability of computers to process and store large amounts of data at any location. The concept of copyright is going through a fundamental change because of the ability of computers to write, revise, edit, and modify programs and texts without generating paper copies.

In light of these developments, there are several possible areas of future research. First, there is a pressing need for the formulation of an international legal infrastructure. Although the proponents of "free flow" fear that international agencies will result in more, rather than less, restriction on transborder data flow, they admit the necessity for multilateral agreements to facilitate international information trade.

While developing and implementing international agreements, it is important to establish the current status and future direction of information technologies. Most American researchers argue that premature decisions creating binding agreements would hinder future technological development and economic activities. They believe that the world would be best served by "fluid conflict rules" and "a broad framework for resolving difficulties that arise from the diversity of national rules and regulations."[32]

On the other hand, European and Third World nations believe that computer communication technologies have reached the stage where they should be controlled by states to protect their interests. In order to regulate the economic aspect of transborder data flow, it has been suggested that the World Trade Organization (WTO), formerly known as the General Agreement on Tariffs and Trade, (GATT) be applied. Some believe the WTO could serve as a "flexible multinational forum that can broaden its mandate to accommodate new trade issues, including international data flows."[33]

While a report by the UN considers this relatively undefined legal environment as the "favorable preconditions for a cooperative approach,"[34] others express skepticism. Any formulation of international legal infrastructure is likely to occur as an attempt to balance the conflicting needs and demands of states.

A second research concern mandates the empirical examination of the content of transborder data flow and resultant impacts. Due to the proprietary nature of data flowing across national boundaries, it is difficult to identify precisely what data are flowing and with what effect. The vast majority of data flow is private and beyond public scrutiny. Yet, a study conducted by the Japanese government in 1982 indicates that empirical analysis of transborder data flow is not impossible. The report, prepared by Japan's Ministry of Post and Telecommunications, measured the quantity of data flow in and out of Japan, classifying flows by industry (i.e., trading firms, banking, and air transport).[35] This type of research is increasingly important to verify the generally observed characteristics of transborder data flow.

There is additional research interest in the impact of transborder data flow on the Third World. UNCTC has been particularly active in monitoring transborder data flow issues from this perspective. In a report to the Secretariat, UNCTC identified an effort to determine how transborder data flow "could be used by host countries to assist them in negotiating advantageous contracts and agreements on the whole range of their interactions with developed countries in general and transnational corporations in particular."

Subsequently, UNCTC launched a country case-study project, for which Brazil and Japan submitted reports.[36] Although the United States prefers to pursue the debate over transborder data flows in forums more representative of developed countries such as the OECD, it agreed to participate in the UNCTC project.

In the larger context of the international flow of information, transborder data flow represents a wide range of issues yet to be explored. As the rapid development of new technologies continues to change traditional economic and political perceptions, fundamental changes in the structure of global communication are expected. Scholars of transborder data flow will play an important and challenging role in instituting these changes.

## Trade and Information Services

As the new horizon of communication technology expands, all sides speak about the potential benefits of new innovations for humanity if used according to particular prescriptions. The most enthusiastic supporters see technological advances as the harbingers of a new age of increasing and equitable development. Others see them as the new means by which the rich will become richer at the expense of the poor if their application is not carefully directed at a change in the status quo.

Remote sensing, as defined by the United Nations Committee on the Peaceful Uses of Outer Space (UNCOPUOS), is "a system of methods for identifying the nature and/or determining the conditions of objects on the Earth's surface, and of phenomena on, below, or above it, by means of observations from airborne or spaceborne platforms" (UN Document A/AC.105/98, 20.1.72). Thus the term "remote sensing" refers not only to sophisticated satellite sensing activities such as Landsat, but also to conventional aerial photography operations. Although this definition includes other satellite systems (i.e., meteorological satellites and Seasats), the most controversial system remains the US Landsat system. The ability of these satellites to sense and "photograph" nations from a sunsynchronous orbit of 705 km without the knowledge or permission of the nations being sensed, combined with the enormous amount of information produced concerning natural resources, has sparked the ongoing debate over issues such as national security and national sovereignty.

The technology of remote sensing by artificial earth satellites has potential value in a number of areas. In fact, to many, the benefits of remote sensing are overwhelming. By repetitively providing synoptic imagery of the earth's surface, remote sensing can be helpful in such areas as resource management, land use analysis, water quality study, disaster relief, crop predictions, and protection of the environment. As in the area of direct broadcasting satellite technology, the United States with its Landsat program is in the dominant position in this area, although the former Soviet Union has, in recent years, made significant advances.

As early as the 1970s, remote sensing became an issue of debate within the United Nations' Outer Space Committee. An earlier proposal by France and the Soviet Union had mentioned the sovereignty of the state over, not only its resources, but the information regarding these resources. The proposal emphasized the principle that a sensing state should have the "prior consent" of the sensed state before transmitting remote sensing data to a third state, based on the assumption that remote sensing was not the exploration of outer space, but the exploration of the earth from outer space.[37]

Advocates of strict regulations over remote sensing support their position with Article III of the Outer Space Treaty, which establishes the obligation of states to perform activities in the exploration and use of outer space in accordance with international law, including the United Nations Charter. In 1974, Brazil cosponsored with Argentina an even stricter proposal for remote sensing regulation than that supported by the Soviet Union and France. Not only did the proposed treaty claim that information about natural resources should be included under a state's sovereign rights, but it also "would prohibit any remote sensing activity relating to natural resources under national jurisdiction without prior consent."[38]

The United States was strongly opposed to both the France/Soviet Union and Brazil/Argentina draft treaties, indicating that "free and open dissemination of data derived from remote sensing has no legal basis."[39] The United States was not opposed, however, to the institution of a mild set of guidelines. In a working paper submitted by the Canadians in 1976, an effort was made to find a middle ground between those who supported "free and open dissemination" of all data, and those who called for strict regulations to be applied to dissemination for economic and political reasons. The question of how to establish some sort of international body to coordinate and oversee work in remote sensing also received attention at several meetings of UNCOPUOS. While the debate on this matter continues, a certain degree of consensus has been reached on a number of principles. It was agreed that remote sensing should be carried out:

1. for the benefit and in the interest of all countries;
2. in accordance with international law;
3. to promote international cooperation and maximize the availability of benefits;
4. to prevent phenomena detrimental to the natural environment of the earth;
5. by states which provide technical assistance to other interested states;
6. with the United Nations playing a useful role in coordination of remote sensing activities;
7. with information indicating an impending natural disaster being made available to affected states as soon as possible;
8. without the use of data intentionally to the detriment of other states.

It is safe to say that as the technology grows, efforts to establish legal principles and to facilitate cooperation in this area will continue. It is also probable that the interest of commercial enterprises in the West (especially in Germany, Japan, and the United States) in operating their own remote sensing satellites will continue to cause increased concern in the Third World.

With the launching of Landsat D on July 16, 1982, the capability of the US to transmit high resolution images to its ground receiving stations increased significantly due to the addition of a new thematic mapper (TM) to the multispectral scanner (MSS) already in use in Landsats 1, 2, and 3. The new system is designed to accept 300 earth scenes a day with each scene covering 13,255 square miles of land area. Scenes from the MSS sensor contain 32 million picture elements, or pixels. Those from the TM contain 300 million pixels. Under ideal conditions, the MSS sends 200 scenes a day and the TM sends 100 scenes a day through the ground system. Every portion of the earth, with the exception of the polar areas, undergoes this scrutiny every 16 days through the scanning of successive swaths on each orbit, each measuring 115 miles wide.

The space shuttle also comprises part of the US remote sensing equipment. Its second test flight in November 1981 clearly demonstrated the shuttle's ability to collect remote sensing data on a worldwide basis for earth-related research.[40]

The importance of Landsat imagery lies in its varied applications. These applications include: agricultural production; rangeland management; forest management; water resources management; geologic survey and mineral and petroleum exploration; cartography; land use (urban and regional) planning; demography; environmental protection; marine, resources, oceanography, and coastal engineering; disaster warning and assessment; and desertification. These diverse applications are made possible by Landsat's ability to detect sediment patterns in coastal waters, heat stress in crops indicating disease, rock structures that indicate mineral or oil deposits, as well as detailed surface imagery. The SIR–A flight in November 1981 was successful in identifying an ancient river system under the Sahara Desert, using radar images that exposed features as deep as 16 feet below the arid sand.[41]

There are numerous ground stations currently operating outside the United States that receive Landsat data directly from the relay satellite. Most of these stations are owned by Argentina, Australia, Brazil, Canada, India, Indonesia, Italy, Japan, South Africa, Sweden, and Thailand. In addition to these countries, many other nations have made use of the information, available on the open market through the EROS Space Center in Sioux Falls, South Dakota. These nations generally buy the imagery either outright, or in conjunction with development aid through the World Bank or USAID.

For example, the government of Upper Volta, working with the World Bank, is using Landsat to identify areas that can support nomadic tribesmen migrating southward because of drought conditions. A Regional Remote Sensing Center has been set up in Ouagadougou under the authority of a management committee composed of the 11 member countries: Benin, Cameroon, Ivory Coast, Ghana, Guinea, Upper Volta, Mali, Mauritania, Niger, Senegal, and Sierra Leone. In 1981, the center had already trained 90 participants in remote sensing data interpretation.

Additionally, other nations have had access to and made use of remote sensing information. The EROS Data Center has sole imagery to 127 countries. Thailand has proposed regional usage of the data generated by its ground station in addition to current domestic uses. Sixteen countries of distinct geographical territories are wholly covered and six more are partially covered. In conjunction with the ASEAN countries, Thailand could serve the entire area.[42] This proposal is in keeping with NASA's original intention in expanding earth station coverage. Nations with ground stations are encouraged to develop their own markets for the imagery to defray some of the operational costs.

Foreign use of Landsat imagery constituted only 33 percent of all data sold in 1981, and 25 percent of all data in 1982. One of the largest domestic users continues to be the US government. However, since the commercialization of this technology in the 1980s both in Europe and the United States, private satellite firms have been active in the exchange of data and images on an international level.

The Department of Defense has relied heavily on Landsat imagery in the last decade to compensate for the failure of its own sophisticated weather satellite system. Of two military weather satellites in polar orbit, "one is spinning uselessly out of control." The primary instrument on the second satellite has failed. "A third Air Force weather satellite was destroyed when its launching rocket failed."[43] During the Falklands War, Landsat provided the only high-quality satellite data available. Since US spy satellites primarily focused on the Soviet Union, they did not range to the south, or were too high in space when passing over southern areas.

In private application, the US Commerce department's National Oceanic and Atmospheric Administration (NOAA) satellite data on sea temperatures, ice, and wind conditions can be transmitted via radio facsimile to Alaskan king crab fishermen aboard their boats.[44]

There exists no comprehensive listing of the actual users of remote sensing data. Apparently, Landsat data is stored haphazardly on various computer tapes interspersed with tapes of aircraft photography and other information. According to officials, a request for a list of users filed a couple of years ago was turned down by the Department of Interior, which decided that it violated the Privacy Act.

There is no readily available information on the former Soviet remote sensing efforts. The countries in Europe do have their own system of satellites: Intercosmos. For the first time, in 1976, it was indicated that some of the Intercosmos satellites were capable of remote sensing. This ability had already been attributed to Soviet Soyuz and Salyut spacecraft.[45]

The Japanese have developed their own MOS–1 (Marine Observation Satellite–1), the first of a planned series of land and marine observation satellites. Japan launched MOS–1 in 1986, and the readout and processing of sensor data is done at the earth observation center where Landsat readout and processing currently occurs. Additionally, the Japanese Earth Resources Satellite–1 (JERS–1) was developed by Japan primarily for purposes of geological mapping and resource evaluation.[46]

## Planetary Resource Information Flow

The issues involved in remote sensing are numerous. In the economic sphere, the transition of remote sensing from an experimental project by NASA to an exploitable market commodity under the auspices of the US Commerce Department illustrates the rapidly changing context in which this resource is viewed.

The transfer of the operational system to the Commerce department's NOAA, and Comsat's takeover of the system complete with the weather satellites, have resulted in a state of flux that make it difficult to pinpoint exactly who is responsible for what services and information.

Although the general consensus is that there does not at present exist a market that would make commercialization of the Landsat system economically feasible, the Metrics, Inc. study indicates that the field could be extremely lucrative. Frederick Henderson of Geosat, a cooperative venture of large private corporations that use Landsat data, states that "the technology is way ahead of its applications."[47] As Henderson speculated in the 1980s, the market has now, in the 1990s, split into two separate fields: the operation of the satellites themselves, and the "value-added" interpretation of the data for customers like oil companies and agricultural firms.

It has been suggested that industry generally tries to obscure its sales through third parties such as consulting firms or cooperatives like Geosat. Mineral and petroleum companies will further try to cover up their interests by "overbuying" (buying imagery in three or four different states to distract any observers from their true interest in a small five-mile-square area). State and local government purchases are also obscured by buying from academic institutions. The institutions, in turn, further muddle the picture by replicating what they have bought and swapping with other institutions.

Another economic consideration is the cost to other countries of constructing and maintaining ground stations. It takes between $4 million and $7 million to build the station, and $1 million and $2 million annually to operate it. Additionally, there is a $600,000 US government charge for data access. Thus, although the US position on remote sensing advocates free dissemination of the information, the cost often determines a nation's ability to participate in data use.

An additional cost is interpretation fees. Landsat offers would-be users (foreign governments or private companies) interpretation assistance for a fee ranging from $1,000 to $3,000 per frame. The users of this service are primarily the US government, but 30 percent are private industry, largely oil and mineral exploration firms. In spite of the stiff fees, Landsat imagery remains one of the most cost-effective means of obtaining the information sought. Satellite image analysis costs only about 16¢ per square mile, as opposed to aircraft film interpretation, which is about $1.30 per square mile.[48] These figures may have changed somewhat because of recent price revisions, but the comparison with aircraft film is still appropriate.

The institutional and political factors in remote sensing revolve primarily around the US government. The shift of operations from NASA to NOAA in the Department of Commerce has introduced a new philosophy about the nature of the program: that it should at least break even, or perhaps show a profit. Admittedly, the Landsat program was initially designed as an experimental program, and it was difficult for NASA to keep up with the proliferation of ground stations and demand for imagery. The emphasis in NASA was on innovation and further refinement of the existing system rather than data production on a regular basis. The latest discussion of privatization of the system reflects acknowledgement of this weakness, but merely proposes government subsidization of a private corporation, rather than a government agency. Commerce Secretary Malcolm Baldrige's April 14, 1983 testimony before the House Committee on Science and Technology seemed to reflect a determination of the US government to turn the system over to the private sector, despite considerable evidence discouraging this move.

The legal issues involved in remote sensing are numerous and complex. In examining some of the literature produced in this area over the last three decades, it is evident that many of the suggested approaches for dealing with these issues through an international body have lost their pertinence because technical advances have made them obsolete. Similarly, the lack of consensus on the issue has forced inaction in establishing a regulatory system, resulting in the adoption by default of the US position of free dissemination. Nevertheless, a brief overview of some of the most significant statements can demonstrate the complexity of the area.

In 1968, the United Nations established the Committee on the Peaceful Uses of Outer Space partly to assist in the normalization of ongoing sensing practices. The Scientific and Technical Subcommittee of UNCOPUOS called attention to the use of remote sensing techniques for the planning of global resources in 1969.

An ongoing controversy in this forum has been the issue of national sovereignty. Two types of suggestions have been offered to deal with the reservations expressed by nations opposed to "free dissemination." The first involves a technical solution that envisages the development of a space–ground system confining the satellite's observations to a specific nation's frontiers, and a "'dump' coded telemetry" to each country individually and exclusively. A procedural solution would establish a nation's priority access to data about itself, prior to general release after a preestablished lapse of time.[49]

The US, on the other hand, has traditionally advocated a policy of "open skies," and asserts that infringement of sovereignty and related issues are all moot points. To impose limitations on dissemination would be detrimental to two predominant benefits of satellite sensing: the broad-era, synoptic view of natural characteristics and of environmental and resource factors that may be multinational in scope; and the timely availability of dynamic data important to the international community as a whole in matters requiring concerted action (as in the case of monitoring crops).

The policy of the US is that the space systems of any nation are national property and have the right of passage through space without interference. Indeed, the US regards the purposeful interference with the space systems of any nation as an infringement upon the sovereign rights of that nation.

William Lazaras describes the dilemma of developing nations in this regard when entering negotiations with transnational corporations, even when both have access to Landsat data:

> Even with the best information provided by the most honest, competent foreign consultant, expatriate expert or national resource analysis department (a highly idealized hypothetical situation), an LDC is likely to be at a disadvantage in its ability to use the information effectively in a negotiation. Local ground experience, even if it is incorporated in the negotiating process, is often more than outweighed by the multinational's access to print, graphic and computer data bases which may include, in addition to the best available analyses of Landsat data, highly sophisticated geological projections, contracts and negotiations in other countries and high level decision-software for handling all the data.[50]

Thus, the crucial distinction between "primary data" and "analyzed information" can make a considerable difference in the ability to take advantage of remote sensing imagery, even if it is freely disseminated, as proposed by the US government. Free dissemination does not guarantee equal access to information, even as "free flow of information" does not mean "balanced flow." However, with the widespread participation in use of Landsat imagery in the last 20 years, and no regulation over reproduction of scenes already purchased, the sovereignty and security issues disputed by many developed countries are, indeed, moot.

The technical factors involved in remote sensing are fairly obvious from the previous section of this chapter. The primary impact of the technical aspects has been in the policy-making area, where technological advancements have preceded any coherent consensus on collection and distribution of the data in question. Since these data are also freely disseminated to those who can pay, any proposals for restrictions through the United Nations will have again been too late to be effective.

The impact of the flow of this information is evident in its many applications. Undoubtedly, the number of nations that have been enriched through use of remote sensing imagery are many. The examples mentioned in this work only scratch the surface of the applications of data in the last 20 years. In all fairness, the availability of the data has, in all probability, resulted in some exploitation of developing nations by multinational corporations with the personnel and experience to extract the most analyzed information out of the primary data. The international political ramifications of remote sensing data are considerable as well.

Although the effect of the flow on private industry is impossible to measure because of the obscured buying practices mentioned earlier, the fact that the largest percentage of buyers is industry indicates that the data are valuable in a variety of areas. Herbert Schiller sees an insidious link between the private sector and government funding in the area of remote sensing. Citing the Geosat Committee, Inc., as an example, he criticizes the US position as catering to private interests and use of the "open skies" policy as a shield for commercial exploitation of the information. Geosat is an organization sponsored by tons of US and non-US international oil, gas, mineral, and engineering–geological companies, and "coaches" NASA on the technical interests of its members. As mentioned earlier, it acts as a screen for corporate purchases of imagery through third-party buys. Perhaps Schiller's most revealing quotation is from the testimony of Dr. Irwin Pikus:

One [problem] concerns the question of sovereignty over information pertaining to natural resources. We find that many developing countries guard their natural resources quite jealously and are considerably concerned that advanced countries might be able to exploit them to their disadvantage. That has motivated a number of countries to assert sovereign control and sovereign claims over information and data concerning their natural resources that, of course, we can't agree with and it is a claim put forth strongly by a number of developing countries . . . we do not consider the question of sovereignty over information in the hands of others.[51]

Pikus presents the US position as refusing to consider the issue of national sovereignty (except US sovereignty) entirely.

The purpose and intention of this vertical information flow is purely technical. It is only when the impact of the data is considered that value assumptions come into question. The literature in this area reflects this split. The literature divides into approximately three different areas: (1) technical works on issues or problems of a specific scientific or engineering interest, (2) reports of field projects and efforts in technology transfer, and (3) cost–benefit forecasts or works on the potential or prospects for the technology in developing nations.

The first of these categories encompasses the majority of the literature available today on remote sensing. These works range from do-it-yourself manuals on remote sensing film interpretation to extremely technical treatises on the workings of the multispectral scanner and the thematic mapper. Most of the information from NASA falls into this category.

The second category, also easily identified, is composed of government statements on remote sensing and governmental proposals for applications. It seems that even as governments are criticizing the omniscience that remote sensing data bestows upon the user, they are jostling in line to be next.

The third category is equally represented in US government and in foreign material. Noticeably missing, however (with the exception of Herbert Schiller's work), is any criticism of the technology on a specific level. The issues being raised currently by the proposed transfer of operations to the private sector need further study and analysis.

Thus, remote sensing is anything but a clear-cut issue. Because of the numerous factors involved and the fluid state of current developments, it is impossible to predict its future even a year from now. Suffice it to say that remote sensing is here to stay, and the heated debate over its use may ultimately be decided by similar contemporary issues in international communication.

The benefit of these new technologies are now available on a widespread basis, but policies to deal with them do not exist. It is here that policies must be developed before the benefits are negated. An all-pervasive problem on national, international, and global levels has been the continual lag of social institutions behind technological progress. It is now generally agreed that application of a set of principles, born out of narrow national circumstances, to the operation of technologies with overwhelmingly global implications is at least a pretentious and self-serving approach. This, at least, is illustrative of the view of those who take a cooperative rather than a competitive approach to international utilization of satellite technology.

The economic and political implications of the knowledge acquired by remote sensing are obvious. The ability to predict agricultural failures and food dependencies, for instance, can influence political judgements and international market bids.[52] The conditions under which private corporations have agreed to the takeover of the remote sensing operation illustrates the economic and institutional aspects of this technology. These conditions include: (1) giving away the existing facilities free of charge, (2) governmental obligation to undertake future research and development, (3) governmental assurance not to enter into any competition as well as to guarantee a fixed market for remote sensing data, and (4) government management of the international negotiations that global remote sensing activities necessitate. For the moment remote sensing activities in the United States are the domain of NOAA, but the government's intention to turn the activity over to the private sector is also being entertained. In fact, this commercialization of space by the United States private firms is well under way.[53]

## Notes

1. United Nations Centre on Transnational Corporations (UNCTC), "Transnational Corporations and Transborder Data Flow: An Overview," paper presented at the Seventh Session of UN Economic and Social Council Commission on Transnational Corporations, Geneva, August 31–September 14, 1981, advance copy, June 1981.

2. W. Michael Blumenthal, "Transborder Data Flow and the New Protectionism," paper delivered before the National Computer Conference, Chicago, IL, May 6, 1981, p. 6.

3. For example, see Jonathan B. Tourtellot, "A World Information War?" *European Community*, January/February 1978, p. 15.

4. See John H. Clippinger, Review of Ithiel de Sola Pool et al., *Datanets and the Third World*, in *Telecommunication Policy*, June 1, 1977, p. 264.

5. Tourtellot, "A World Information War?" p. 140.

6. Hamid Mowlana, "The Multinational Corporation and the Diffusion of Technology," in Abdul A. Said and Luiz R. Simmons, eds, *The New Sovereigns: Multinational Corporations as World Powers* (Englewood Cliffs, NJ: Prentice Hall, 1975), p. 83.

7. Eric J. Novotny, "Transborder Data Flow Regulation: Technical Issues of Legal Concern," *Computer/Law Journal*, 3: 2 (Winter 1981), p. 107. See also Mark B. Feldman and David R. Garcia, "National Regulations of Transborder Data Flows," *North Carolina Journal of International Law and Commercial Regulations*, 7: 1 (Winter 1982), p. 1.

8. See Eric J. Novotny, "Transborder Data Flows and International Law: A Framework for Policy-Oriented Inquiry," *Stanford Journal of International Law*, 16 (Summer 1980), pp. 150–156.

9. Rein Turn, ed., *Transborder Data Flows: Concerns in Privacy Protection and Free Flow of Information*. Report of the AFIPS Panel on Transborder Data Flows, 1, Washington, DC, Federation of Information Processing Society, Inc., 1979, p. 39.

10. Novotny, "Transborder Data Flows and International Law," p. 156.

11. Novotny, "Transborder Data Flow Regulations," pp. 111–112.

12. Novotny, "Transborder Data Flows and International Law," p. 152.

13. Allen Gotlieb, Charles Dalfen, and Kenneth Katz, "The Transborder Transfer of Information by Communications and Computer Systems: Issues and Approaches to Guiding Principles," *American Journal of International Law*, 68 (1974), p. 227.

14. Novotny, "Transborder Data Flows and International Law," p. 145.

15. Rein Turn, "Privacy Protection and Security in Transnational Data Processing Systems," *Stanford Journal of International Law*, 16 (Summer 1980), pp. 71–73.

16. Organization for Economic Cooperation and Development, "Guidelines Governing the Protection of Privacy and Transborder Flows of Personal Data" (Paris, 1980).

17. Council of Europe, "Convention for the Protection of Individuals with Regard to Automatic Processing of Personal Data" (Strasbourg, 1980).

18. United States Congress, House of Representatives, 96th Session, Committee on Government Operations, "International Information Flows: Forging A New Framework," December 11, 1980 (Washington, DC: Government Printing Office, 1980), p. 28.

19. United Nations Center on Transnational Corporations, "Transnational Corporations and Transborder Data Flow," p. 28.

20. Ibid., p. 29.

21. Hamid Mowlana, "Political and Social Implications of Communications Satellite Applications in Developed and Developing Countries," in Joseph N. Pelton and Marcellus S. Snow, eds, *Economic and Policy Problems in Satellite Communications* (New York: Praeger, 1977), pp. 124–142.

22. "Madec Expects TDF Dividends for France," *Transnational Data Report*, 5: 6 (September 1982), p. 291.

23. United States Congress, "International Information Flow," pp. 13–19.

24. Feldman and Garcia, "National Regulation of Transborder Data Flows," p. 14.

25. United States Congress, "International Information Flow,' p. 24.

26. Feldman and Garcia, "National Regulation of Transborder Data Flows," p. 14.

27. Joan Edelman Spero, "Information: The Policy Void," *Foreign Policy*, Fall 1982, p. 143.

28. United Nations Centre on Transnational Corporations, "Transnational Corporations and Transborder Data Flow," pp. 24–27.

29. Turn, ed., *Transborder Data Flows*, p. 29.

30. Herbert I. Schiller, *Who Knows: Information in the Age of Fortune 500* (Norwood, NJ: Ablex Publishing Corporation, 1981), p. 20.

31. "Technology, TDF and the New International Information Order," *Transnational Data Report*, 5: 4 (June 1982), p. 206.

32. Ithiel de Sola Pool and Richard Jay Solomon, "Intellectual Property and Transborder Data Flows," *Stanford Journal of International Law*, 16 (Summer 1980), pp. 117–129.

33. Spero, "Information", p. 153.

34. United Nations Centre on Transnational Corporation, "Transnational Corporations and Transborder Data Flow," p. 36.

35. "Japan Investigates TDF," *Transnational Data Report*, 5: 8 (December 1982), pp. 421–423.

36. "UNCTC Pursues Corporate TDF Impact," *Transnational Data Report*, 5: 7 (October/November 1982), p. 322.

37. Valerie Hood, Mary E. Kimball, and David A. Kay, *A Global Satellite Observation System for Earth Resources: Problems and Prospects*, The American Society of International Law Studies in Transnational Legal Policy No. 15 (Washington, DC: West Publishing Co., 1977), p. 48.

38. Hamilton DeSausur, "Remote Sensing by Satellite: What Future for an International Regime," *The American Journal of International Law*, 71: 4 (October 1977), p. 720.

39. "U.S. Presents Guidelines for Remote Sensing of the Natural Environment From Outer Space," *Department of State Bulletin*, 72, March 31, 1975, p. 421.

40. J.W. Beck, "Earth Sciences and Land Remote Sensing – Applications in Development," paper read at the First Intergovernmental Meeting of Space Technology Experts, New York, February 4–5, 1983, p. 8.

41. John Nobel Wilford, "Spacecraft Detects Sahara's Buried Past," *The New York Times*, September 27, 1982, p. 1A.

42. Sanga Sabhasri et al., "Remote Sensing Activities in Thailand," paper read at the Regional Meeting on Remote Sensing in Southeast Asia, Bangkok, Thailand, March 23–24, 1981, pp. 9–10.

43. Robert C. Toth, "Pentagon Can't Get Its Weather 'Spies' to Work," *Los Angeles Times*, September 27, 1982, p. 1A.

44. "Remote Sensing Aiding Alaskan Fisheries," *Satellite Week*, March 2, 1981, p. 4.

45. Gijsbertha C. Reijnen, *Utilization of Outer Space and International Law* (Amsterdam: Elsevier Scientific Publishing Co., 1981), p. 63.

46. Kioshi Tsuchiga, "Land Remote Sensing Technology of Current Status and Future Prospects of Japan," paper read at the First Intergovernmental Meeting of Space Technology Experts, New York, February 4–5, 1983, p. 4.

47. Michael Schrage, "Scanning the Globe for Private Profits," *The Washington Post*, April 3, 1983, p. 1H.

48. William M. Feldman, "Remote Sensing in the Development Process – UNCSTD Initiative," memo to Sander Levin, July 13, 1979, p. 2.

49. *Resource Sensing from Space: Prospects for Developing Countries.* Report of the Ad Hoc Committee on Remote Sensing for Development, National Academy of Sciences, Washington, DC, 1977, pp. 146–147.

50. William Lazaras, "Landsats, Minerals and Development: A Qualitative Notion of the Down-side Risk," Massachusetts Institutes of Technology, Cambridge, MA, 1980, pp. 21–22.

51. Schiller, *Who Knows*, p. 118.

52. Ibid, pp. 130–131.

53. See Michael Schrage, "Consortium Plans Private Satellite Venture," *The Washington Post*, September 8, 1983, D1, p. 1.

# 7

# International Interactions:
# Travel and Tourism

The worldwide explosion of communication and transportation technologies in the past three decades has led to a corresponding increase in contact between peoples of different nations and cultures. As changes in technology and communication have extended the boundaries of virtually every human enterprise, a number of people are becoming acquainted with the international dimensions of their activities by personal contacts and direct interactions rather than through the mass media. Links between cities and villages no longer require urbanization as a precondition to participation. Money and data can move through telecommunications and computers without any bankers ever leaving their offices or customers their homes. Goods can be purchased without buyers leaving their residences. In short, technology has made possible the global exchange of information without requiring the participants to venture from the center of their activities and life.

Many activities, however, now involve a second layer or type of information flow: human movement. Business people traveling around the world; professors and students attending conferences and academic institutions; immigrants in search of a new country; refugees seeking asylum; military and diplomatic personnel on assignment; and tourists in pursuit of novelty, pleasure, or rest are all potential channels of communication, particularly disseminating a great deal of cultural information.

In today's world, many people become involved in international activities as diverse as those in which they are involved domestically. Although international flow of information in technological–human channels has become multidimensional, international activities, which have originated from very specific geographical locations within nations, are very unevenly distributed.

## The Foreign Relations of the Public

Unfortunately, nearly all traditional international relations research has been carried out on the level of the national unit, emphasizing only (1) high- and middle-level policy makers, including formal institutions and bureaucracy, and (2) diplomatic, political, economic, and military aspects of international relations. Consequently, with the exception of a few studies,[1] the attitudes of the public toward foreign policy and the public's role in the entire realm of international communication have been neglected.

The mobility of people across national boundaries has historically been one of the most important factors in the international flow of information. In past centuries, especially in the last 500 years, human flow across national and cultural boundaries took the form of explorers, traders, merchants, colonists, missionaries, and armies, as well as prisoners of war. These flows are themselves quite revealing of the historical context within which such phenomena occurred among nations.

To illustrate the significance of the human flow across boundaries, one can cite the fact that in human communication, in addition to the message, the whole machinery and system of communication is being moved as well. When individuals move from one location to another, they transfer not only their physical bodies, but also a whole host of previous experiences, ideas, attitudes, beliefs, opinions, motivations, and goals. Despite the increasing importance of communication technologies in international relations and communication, and their profound impact on national, international, and cultural systems, it is a central thesis of this study that the development making current communication research different, and in some ways more valid than in the past, is and shall be the inclusion of human factors in international exchange.

It is, therefore, argued that the human being must be viewed as a central component in the entire process of message producing and distributing. The human being must be viewed as both a message and a channel of international communication. Individuals as media for international communication become most important in the light of the view that feedback is more instant, and communication is perhaps more complete and lasting, when it is executed on an interpersonal level. While this realization may appear elementary, it is a benchmark of what may heretofore be the most important efforts in research on the global flow of information.

The classification of the types of human flow across national boundaries is extensive and only a few will be reviewed at length in this study. In general, nine broad channels of human movement can be identified, each accounting for a variety of activities in international relations. They are: (1) migration and refugee movements; (2) movement of labor and professional personnel across borders; (3) tourism; (4) military, diplomatic, and intelligence ventures; (5) educational, scientific, and cultural exchanges and conferences; (6) business and financial travel and meetings; (7) mass media, popular culture, and performing arts; (8) sports; (9) voluntary organizations.

### International Tourism as a Mode of Communication

In the past, research on international tourism has focused on the economic aspects: market surveys, financial analysis, and logistical reports. It has now been recognized that tourism is a powerful medium affecting cultural change and international relationships. However, few hard studies have been conducted, and researchers are divided on the issue of effects being positive or negative. Many of the studies in the field of tourism do not directly link it to international communication and flow of information. Therefore, researchers must attempt to trace the history of tourism studies and document the evolution of the field as a growing component in the importance of international communication.

There are three key factors whose continued influence has shaped the tourist industry. First, developments in transportation provide rapid mobility at an affordable price. Second, communication technology brings images of the world close, evoking a desire for more. And third, the development of industrial production and a market economy provides the surplus money and time for individuals to explore the world beyond their front doors, and also furnishes the marketing apparatus to plan and sell travel as a desirable escape.

A fourth factor could be identified in the symbiotic relationship between tourism and all other forms of communication. As communication regarding travel increases, both formally through market and nonmarket information sources and informally through interpersonal contact, the volume of tourism increases. When that occurs, there is further dissemination of information and a spiralling effect is set in motion. All of these factors working together are primarily responsible for the boom in tourism since the 1960s.

Four major actors shape the roles in international tourism. The first, of course, is the tourist. The role of the tourist is especially important in that it is changeable and directly affects the type of cultural interaction and information flow that will occur. The tourist can be a part of the "mass," traveling and interacting only with the false fantasy world created for him or her. At the other end of the spectrum, the tourist can be somewhat of a drifter, traveling individually and observing or experiencing first hand the true culture of the host country.

Two important factors in determining the role of these actors are their reasons for traveling and their sources of information. Tourists travel for a variety of reasons, including enhancement of social status, transcending feelings of isolation, a search for reality and authenticity, escape, and pleasure. Further, information sources are not necessarily objective and unbiased. Obviously, travel magazines and literature are promotional rather than factual. Studies show that the advice of friends is considered more credible, but that, too, is certainly a non-objective information source.

The second actor is the host national or the "local." Again, we must make a distinction between those participating in the industry's fantasy world and those outside it. "Local color" is often the creation of marketing, and the host nationals who are employed by the tourism industry do not necessarily interact with tourists in a representative manner. Those

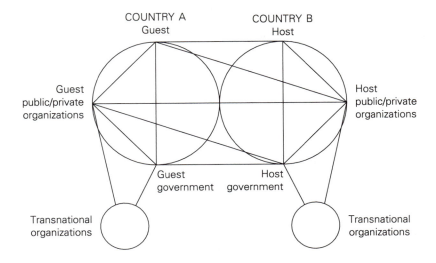

Figure 7.1   *International tourism relationships: patterns of information flow and influence*

nationals outside the industry may show a somewhat different face to tourists and some are even likely to be hostile. Nevertheless, an accurate reflection of people and culture in a foreign land is not apt to be obtained through interaction with nationals employed by the tourism sector.

Third are the corporations and individuals who make up the industry itself: travel and tour agencies, travel publications, airlines and transportation services, hotels, restaurants, shops, and all their personnel. These are the actors who design, package, and sell the complete experience that we have referred to as fantasy. These individuals and transnationals create the experience and image that sells, and then proceed to make that the reality for the tourist.

Finally, governments play an important role in tourism both as industry participants and as regulators. The latter engendered the former when in the process of regulation, governments became aware of the economic impact of tourism. They began to be active participants in the industry, forming travel ministries and information bureaus as well as developing policy conducive to attracting tourists (see Figure 7.1).

Regulation does at times, however, serve to protect the host and limit tourism, as can be seen in the strict government control of the tourist sector in certain countries. Some governments act to limit visas and specify travel modes, routes, and destinations. The tourism sector is limited not only geographically, but economically as well, and only authorized merchants may accept specially minted tourist money.

Although the public and private organizations of developed countries affect the people and governments of developing nations through investment and employment, resulting in a variety of dependency relationships as well as economic growth, the communication flows among participants in the tourism interaction are not necessarily one-way, nor does a message always end after passing between two parties. Interactions are possible at all stages, especially in cases of face-to-face communication. A major key to the outcome of a tourist interaction process is the nature of the relationship between the individuals involved. Several anthropologists have suggested that important factors influencing the quality of interaction are the types of tourists and the motivations that lead them to visit a particular country.[2]

One widely quoted theory of motivation for travel is Abraham Maslow's well-known "hierarchy of needs."[3] Here, after the basic human physiological and social requirements are met, people turn to satisfying self-realization needs. It has been argued that the wealth and leisure available in the Western industrialized nations have enabled individuals to turn their attention to the need for developing their own potential, seeking aesthetic stimulation, and building their character. More commonly cited reasons for travel and tourism are simply relaxation, pleasure, education, and culture. This explanation, as it applies to modern mass tourism, however, ignores the external information and promotion coming from the tourist industry around the world, as well as the consumer and consumption orientation of this phenomenon in modern life. Further, it overlooks the escapist nature of the process from the viewpoint of alienated individuals in today's industrialized world.

One of the few actual studies of tourist's motivations was a consumer marketing study of travelers to the Pacific.[4] Equally applicable to the Caribbean region, it found that "vacationers were most concerned with creature comforts such as accommodations and climate, with some interest in recreational facilities and less interest in cultural items." A vacation travel-attitude survey, based on personal interviews with 1,005 heads of households, indicated that the most important factors in determining American travel destinations (after elimination of visits to relatives and habitual repeat visits to one locale) were, in order of importance: beautiful scenery, a chance to get a good rest, good sports or recreational facilities, a chance to meet congenial people, and outstanding food.[5] The fact remains that in today's mass tourism, agents of the tourism industry are instrumental in the entire process of encounter, since they act as intermediaries between the tourists and the host country. As gatekeepers, they are the potential suppliers of information and indeed tourist-agenda setters. Research shows that the allocentric "drifters" are the first to discover a potential tourist locale.[6] They are followed by the "explorers," then, finally by the largest group, the "mass tourists."

Mass tourism is large-scale commercial and institutional tourism. It depends on the tourist establishment of hotel chains, travel agencies, travel industries and in some cases is government-sponsored. Mass tourists are processed as efficiently, smoothly, and quickly as possible throughout all phases of the trip. A mass tourist is allowed to take in the "foreigners that he seeks without experiencing any discomfort."[7] The mass tourist thus travels in a world of his or her own, failing to become integrated into the host society. Of the three groups just noted, mass tourists have the greatest potential for stereotyping and being stereotyped by the host country. Thus, in the 1950s and 1960s, when Americans more than any other nationality were economically able to travel around the world, they became more visible as a single group overseas. The cultural clash of this type of encounter was highly responsible for the term "ugly American," which was used for the American overseas. In the 1970s, Arabs traveling in England, and Japanese in the Far East and elsewhere, were targets of much local resentment.

The degree to which tourist interactions will affect a host society can be predicted using a functional framework consisting of such variables as temporal, spatial, communication, and cultural factors. For example, regarding the temporal factor, it has been hypothesized that the longer visitors remain in one area, the stronger the possibility that they will have greater penetration and encounters. The spatial factor will determine the degree of contact between the tourists and their hosts. Communication variables could include such factors as language, symbols, and nonverbal behavior. Cultural variables will account for ethnic characteristics, color, religion, and behavior. Such variables might allow policy makers and promoters to predict the degree of effect tourism will have on the host country as well as the visitors themselves. Further, sociocultural variables might give information as to the direction of impact.

**Tourism as an Integrated Industry**

In the past, tourism was considered – largely by those outside the field – as a provincial, peripheral area of domestic and regional studies dealing primarily with commercial and business analyses and applications. Today, however, the multibillion dollar international trade in tourism and travel-related services has created an important sector of economic and cultural activity. Furthermore, integration of communication technologies into the tourism industry is involving tourism in the areas of technology transfer and international trade in services, central areas of international political debate for the 1990s and twenty-first century.

International tourism evolved in a climate of expanding world trade and rising production, employment, and income in virtually all industrialized countries.[8] Tourism ranks as the largest industry in the world in terms of employment (101 million people, one of every 16 workers) and ranks in the top two or three industries in almost every country on nearly every measure. In virtually every country, the industry is as large as – and in many countries larger than – the entire agricultural sector or major manu-facturing industries (autos, electronics, steel, textiles) considered integral parts of economic policy. Complex interindustry interdependence of tourism products and services indicates that each million dollars in travel sales generate close to $2 million in aggregate output.

Between 1986 and 1999, international trips (counting all trips across international borders regardless of duration) are predicted to increase from 500 to 910 million, with real travel spending (excluding fares) rising from $109 to nearly $200 billion at constant 1985 relative prices and exchange rates.[9] Projected figures for the year 2000 are 532 million in world international tourism arrivals and $304.3 in receipts (excluding international passenger fare payments).[10] The accelerated numbers of international travelers and frequency of travel are accompanied by increasing wealth, cross-cultural exposure, and rising expectations of the frequent traveler in market-oriented economies.

Today, the international tourism infrastructure stands as a symbol of modern international relations in all its aspects by means of tourism's integration into the complex world of global political, economic, and trade relations (see Figure 7.2). The complexity of the tourism infrastructure, therefore, and the methods used in understanding the integrated nature of its growth are becoming central international relations policy concerns.

**Telecommunications and the Tourism Industry**

Telecommunications has now become a pivotal factor in international relations and a central issue in the changing global systems. One of the areas in which this telecommunications trend can be observed clearly is the international tourism infrastructure in which a number of economic and political issues converge (see Figure 7.3). This convergence is generating a new range of forces for cooperation and coalition formation as well as for increased interdependence and dependency in the division of labor in the tourism industry. The most recent major developments indicative of these changes include:

1. A rise in formal and informal national and international alliances and coalitions within the private sector and between public and private institutions involved in the globalization of travel and tourism.
2. A progression toward political and economic regionalism through increased levels of negotiations for new intergovernmental policies in such areas as international trade in tourism-related services and free trade and investment agreements.
3. The emergence of informal or quasi-international welfare systems in tourism in response to world economic crisis, resulting in corporate consolidation and the globalization of the communication and financial industries.

The increasing involvement and prominence of mixed-sector alliances and coalitions in the international system, particularly those in the tourism

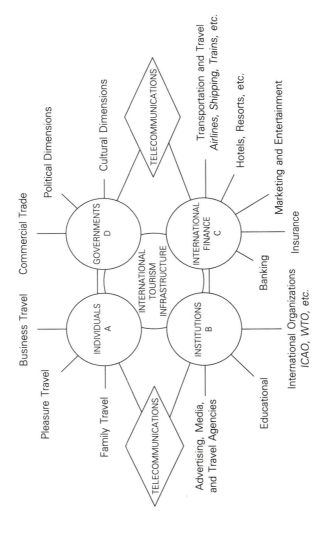

Figure 7.2 *Integrative model of tourism as international relations*

the policy level. Such arrangements have been promoted largely by transnational corporations in the interests of both maintenance and expansion of international trade and investments.

International financial institutions and telecommunications firms, within the structure of international tourism, consolidate into larger units through acquisitions and cross-ownership. The traditional labor-incentive sector of tourism, (i.e., booking and travel agencies) is being threatened with the loss of its traditional role. This is due to the fact that major transnational companies, through new integrative telecommunications techniques, are establishing the potential for direct market contact with tourism consumers, thereby bypassing the need for travel agents and other small intermediaries. Faced with industry-wide unemployment, large firms and transnational corporations are under pressure to make new arrangements to maintain the traditional sectors of international tourism through provision of technology access and indirect subsidies and benefits. At the same time, these large corporations are continuing to establish new relationships with the emerging market dominance of corporate business travel consumers.

On April 9, 1990, for example, under the auspices of the American Express Company, the World Travel and Tourism Council (WTTC) was formed, comprised of nearly 50 Chief Executive Officers (CEOs) from the world's leading travel and tourism companies. Being a CEO of a company was a membership prerequisite along with the payment of a $10,000 fee. The WTTC is financed by contributions from member companies and has an annual operating budget of $1.5 million. With dual headquarters in Brussels and London, the WTTC represents the first attempt by powerful global corporations – uniting diverse companies from within the industry – to cope with rising demands and issues in a changing international environment. Principal objectives of the WTTC include protecting the multi-billion dollar information capital tourism investment and promoting tourism's economic significance as the world's largest industry. In other words, the formation of the WTTC grew out of the rise in importance of the tourism infrastructure as a global instrument of economic power and of the ripeness of the international system for market expansion through telecommunications. The WTTC style is action-oriented as a public policy lobbyist coalition on the transnational level. The strength of the WTTC lies in the fact that there is direct participation by CEOs who shape the WTTC agenda, formulate policy, and speak out for the group at highest levels of international government and nongovernment interaction. "Therein lies our difference and our capacity to elevate industry issues onto national agendas." In short, the recent cross-sector alliance and coalition-building process has coordinated unprecedented collective thinking and mobilization toward political participation at the highest-ranking executive level of the tourism industry.

Thus, the convergence of telecommunications technologies with transnational banking and investment is contributing to the genesis of new supernational economies of scale in the tourism infrastructure and to the formation of oligopolies in the transnational trade of information capital.

## Tourism in a Global Context

Communication Technologies and transnational finance are central factors in the international interactions linking tourism to international relations; these relationships are heightened or altered strikingly by political, socio-economic, or cultural instability or conflict. War is an unfortunate occurrence but at the same time provides an opportunity to examine the relationship of certain phenomena to international relations through their response to changes in the international system. During the 1980s, for example, events such as regional and international conflicts ranging from the Lebanese civil war and that country's invasion by foreign troops, the Iran-Iraq War, upheavals in Eastern Europe and the Soviet Union, and worldwide terrorist attempts, all had profound effects on international tourism.

The psychological effect of terrorism in the context of the Persian Gulf War, more than in any other period in history, had direct impact on international tourism. Countries such as Egypt, Israel, Turkey, Jordan, Morocco – some as far as 4,000 miles east of Kuwait – were perceived to be "too close" (by Western standards) to potential danger and experienced large drops in their visitor counts. The precipitous decline in tourism affected national foreign policy strategies. Israel and Egypt even canceled, as fruitless, their national tourism promotion campaigns scheduled for winter 1990. Sharp declines in US visitors, fearful of terrorist activities on trans-Atlantic routes and in international airports, were devastating to London hotels, which experienced declines in occupancy rates between 25 and 50 percent in February 1991, forcing properties to lay off employees and close floors, a trend reflected by hotels in most major European cities.

As a result of the Persian Gulf crisis, the integrative role played by telecommunications technologies and transnational finance in the international relations policy field has become virtually an established theme. The collateral damage experienced by the international tourism industry during the Persian Gulf War was to a large degree attributable to these technological and financial links. As a device for monitoring the increasingly integrative effects of political instability on the international economy, international tourism provides a useful barometer.

In today's global economy, instruments such as communication, organizational and advertising skills, and manipulation of travel markets have become important sources of power. Thus, countries which foster transnational firms, such as the United States, Germany, and Japan, are becoming more powerful in the international scene, as are emerging regions such as the Asian-Pacific. Added to this, American and European long-time experience in marketing and advertising techniques are becoming crucial elements in intangible sources of power. The increasing level and geographic distribution of such international interactions are contributing to the erosion of the conditions upon which traditional conceptions of national sovereignty are based. It is not that the importance of nation-states as coherent units and dominant participants in world politics is disappearing. Rather, it is that the conditions underlying contemporary interactions are changing, shifting the political processes at times away from tradition, intergovernmental definitions in the direction of linkage strategies and agenda setting characterizing new transnational and transgovernmental relations.[13]

From the perspective of national sovereignty and economic power, the direction of this flow is of critical concern. It is producing a continuous erosion of the traditional notion of national sovereignty, especially in the areas of information flow and telecommunications. This, coupled with the growing trend toward consolidation in tourism, telecommunication, and banking industries, is changing the international regulatory environment of the international tourism infrastructure with profound effects on regional and domestic policies.

A significant pattern of flow in world tourism is North–South, from the more industrialized to the less industrialized countries. Many of the Third World nations are virtually tourist-free, while some Third World regions receive a disproportionate share of travelers. These latter areas constitute the "pleasure periphery": a tourist "playground" belt surrounding the industrialized zones of the world, normally two to four hours' flying time from the big urban centers and usually in the direction of the equator and sunny climes. The North American periphery includes the Caribbean countries, Mexican resorts, and the Pacific Islands. The Europeans head for Mediterranean destinations. There are also countries such as Kenya and India that draw thousands from the United States and Europe.

The present patterns of tourism support the theory that information flow between a mother country and a colony or former colony will be largely one-way.

A second issue that specifically concerns the center–periphery pattern of tourist flow is cultural imperialism. The exposition here is the same as in all the other types of information flow discussed: the dominant center overwhelms the underdeveloped peripheries, stimulating rapid and unorganized cultural and social change (Westernization), which is arguably detrimental. Further, the influence is all the more potent for its proximity: rather than seeing images of affluent Westerners on television, host nations are intimately involved in assuring maintenance of that high standard of living when Westerners travel abroad. Frustrated expectations take on a whole new meaning when the "haves" are in the resort hotels next to the dilapidated homes of the "have nots."

On the other hand, it is argued that such interaction stimulates positive development, that it is a catalyst for necessary cultural change. It is currently unclear whether the positive and negative impacts balance out. Two things, however, are clear. One is that tourism will continue to be a growing source of communication among nations. The other is the recognition of a desperate need for research on tourism that goes beyond the usual economic and financial concerns.

In the final analysis, of course, whether tourism is a negative or positive force in the country depends on one's value judgements, national aims, national communication policies and objectives, and finally on individual definitions of development. However, there is increasing evidence that the growing quantity of tourist encounters does not necessarily mean increased quality of relationships. The world of technology has expanded, and so has the perceived physical world with all its diversities and colors, but whether people's emotional capacities have also been expanded remains a big question: the potential for communication does not automatically bring people to a sense of personal involvement with one another.

Conclusions, at least for policy recommendations, are limited by the lack of empirical studies in the field of tourism from a sociocultural perspective. The fact remains that tourism will continue to be a growing source of information flow among and between nations and cultures. The potential for cultural impact increases with the number of tourists, and is particularly strong in the case of travelers from industrialized countries flowing to lesser developed regions: both of these points are forecasted trends.

**Impact and Effects**

The impact of tourism as a global flow of information can be seen on three levels: global, societal, and individual. As mentioned previously, tourism is now the single largest contributor to international trade, affecting not only global economic relations, but political and social relations between and among nations as well. Worldwide organizations and societies of professionals employed in the travel industry have been established. The movement of people around the globe cannot help but have far-reaching ramifications, many not yet fully understood.

On the societal level, the emphasis has increasingly shifted from a focus on economic impact to concern over cultural and social effects. Although the flow of information between societies is two-way – the tourist passes information about his or her own culture as well as receiving and relaying information about the host culture to friends at home – the social and cultural influence of tourists from developed nations on underdeveloped periphery nations is unsettling.

On the third level of impact, the individual, personal images are created or reinforced, on the part of both the traveler and the host. Individual interaction is deemed by the participants to be the most credible source of information on cultures and peoples. It is at this level that stereotypes are either broken or irrevocably reinforced.

It should be pointed out that communication interaction occurs not only within the levels of impact and effect, but between them. For example, individual tourists have interaction with governments internationally as they cross many national borders en route from one country to another. They interact on a societal level with the culture and history of a specific nation or with the bureaucracy in securing a visa. Finally, tourists have personal interaction with the individuals with whom they come in contact.

Keeping in mind the levels of interaction and impact, we turn now to two key issues that are currently the subject of heated debate. The first is image portrayal. It is argued that the travel industry purposely distorts the true image of a society and people to create a marketable image. This false marketable image, or "pseudo-image" as Daniel J. Boorstin calls it, is the conglomeration of everything the industry thinks the potential tourist desires.[14] The industry then goes to great lengths to provide the fantasy it sells, creating a tourist paradise and isolating it from the actual host society. Hence, false images and inaccurate information are perpetuated. The French become the greatest lovers, the Germans are typed as unfriendly, Polynesian islanders are thought to wear grass skirts and live in grass huts. Mexican fishermen are believed to be fishing with nets as their progenitors did, and Africans are stereotyped as uncivilized savages living happily in their primitive cultures. Such pejorative and sometimes patronizing images create substantial barriers to international interaction, and in the case of the Third World, become obstacles to real social, economic, and political development.

## Notes

1. Chadwick F. Alger's "Foreign Policies of the United States Publics," *International Studies Quarterly*, XXI: 2 (June 1977), pp. 277–317, is one of the few studies in this area.

2. Erik Cohen, "Nomads from Influence: Notes on the Phenomenon of Drifter Tourism," *International Journal of Comparative Sociology*, 14 (March–June 1973), pp. 89–103; Nancy H. Evans, "Tourism and Cross-Cultural Communication," *Annual of Tourism Research*, 3 (March–April 1976), pp. 189–198; and Valene Smith, "Tourism and Cultural Change," *Annal of Tourism Research*, 3 (January–February 1976)), pp. 122–126.

3. Donald E. Lundberg, *The Tourist Business* (Boston, MA: CBI Publishers, 1980), p. 1. See also Louis Turner, *Multinational Companies and the Third World* (New York: Hill and Wang, 1973), p. 24.

4. Louis Turner, *Multinational Companies and the Third World*, p. 102.

5. Ibid., p. 104.

6. Cohen, "Nomads from Influence," p. 90.

7. Lundberg, *The Tourist Business*, p. 256.

8. Willbald P. Pahr, "Report of the Secretary-General of the World Tourism Organization," presented to the First International Tourism Forum, October, Lausanne, (Madrid: World Tourism Organization, 1989), p. 3.

9. Anthony Edwards, "International Tourism Forecasts to 1999," *The Economist Intelligence Unit*, London: The Economist Group of London, 1988, in "World Travel Overview, 1988/1989," *Travel and Leisure* (New York: American Express Publishing, 1988), 16.

10. David L. Edgell, Sr, "Charting a Course for International Tourism in the Nineties: An Agenda for Managers and Executives," Washington, D.C.: US Department of Commerce (US Travel and Tourism and Economic Development Administrations), February 1990, 41.

11. Hamid Mowlana and Ginger Smith, "Trends in Telecommunications and the Tourism Industry: Coalitions, Regionalism, and International Welfare Systems," *World Travel and Tourist Review*, 2 (1992), p. 163.

12. Hamid Mowlana and Ginger Smith, "Tourism, Telecommunications, and Transnational Banking: A Framework for Policy Analysis," *Tourism Management*, 11: 4 (1991), pp. 85–106.

13. Robert O. Keohane and Joseph S. Nye, "Complex Interdependence, Transnational Relations, and Realism: Alternative Perspectives on World Politics," in Charles W. Kegleyji Jr and Eugene R.W. Wittkopf, eds, *Global Agenda: Issues and Perspectives* (New York: Random House, 1992), pp. 257–271.

14. Daniel J. Boorstin, *The Image* (New York: Harper Colophon, 1961), pp. 86–107.

# 8

# Human Flow Across National Boundaries: Intercultural Communication

Educational, artistic, scientific, and scholarly relations in general, and the particular interests of economic, political, and cultural groups and individuals, as well as of the nation-state, comprise a significant aspect of international and global flow of information. Since World War II, and especially in the last 30 years, we have witnessed a historically unparalleled expansion of significant activities in the area of international cultural and scientific contact and transfer.

That the flow of educational and cultural information is an important part of the current pattern of international relations cannot be denied. Such channels of information and communication offer to business, the diplomatic community, and foreign policy institutions an instrument the potential of which is enormous and only yet beginning to be felt. International education and cultural activities, however, are not simply instruments of foreign and economic policies; they are an essential part of what foreign policy, international economic and political relations in general, and international communication in particular are all about. In today's world, they are also inseparable from the stream of information provided by other national, regional, international, and global channels such as the mass media, telecommunications, and a score of political and economic institutions.

At the same time, the unprecedented expansion of worldwide communication capabilities resulting from advances in communication technologies has not yet created the "global village" these capabilities were expected to create. Therefore, it is of increased importance and concern to both researchers and participants in the international field that we construct a meaningful bridge to facilitate understanding and harmony among the peoples of the world. In short, because they concern themselves more with quality than quantity in communication, international education and cultural exchanges can reflect alternative paths to international political and economic communication. Furthermore, these types of information flow are directed toward specific individuals who are leaders and potential leaders in their communities, and eventually provide the necessary ingredients and contexts for other types of messages to be received. Finally, it has been hypothesized that such educational and cultural flow of information may contribute to the development of a common ground of shared interests between nations, on which cooperative effort can be built.

In the fields of international relations and international communication, much attention has traditionally been given to military, economic, diplomatic, telecommunications, and mass communication policy, while educational and cultural policy have received relatively little intellectual attention or systematic analysis. Yet the tradition of exchanging students, scholars, artists, and even athletes is an age-old international practice. It is important to note that both private and public exchange programs have increased to an unexpectedly high level since World War II, and especially since the 1960s, when a number of countries in the less industrialized world were added to the list of independent nations. The growth in the significance of such activities as an element of national policy has paralleled increases in the frequency of exchanges over the last three decades. Today, the educational and cultural aspect of international affairs is not only more apparent but considered to be more important than ever before.

In terms of information flow, the altered character and significance of international education and cultural interchange can be attributed to:

1. changes in the nature and sources of technological innovation;
2. changes in techniques of rapid distance communication and in the size of audiences exposed to messages;
3. changes in the nature and sources of the transfer of technology from materials, machines, and objects, to skill-oriented training and research;
4. changes in the perception of the epistemology, philosophy, and methodology of arts and sciences worldwide, particularly the "explosion of knowledge";
5. recognition of educational and cultural flow as an aspect of national development policy (especially in developing countries), and, in many cases, as part of political and ideological policies (especially in industrialized countries);
6. expansion of business and trade across national boundaries and the emergence of a diversity of transnational actors;
7. increases in the number of intergovernmental and nongovernmental organizations, as well as the number of the institutions and individuals engaged in educational, cultural, and artistic activities.

Information flow through human movements, such as educational and cultural activities, is more pronounced because it lends itself to both international and intercultural communication. Quite simply, international communication theoretically consists of communication across national boundaries and between countries, whereas intercultural communication occurs anywhere between people of different cultures. In practice, however, the two are often identical, since communication crossing national borders frequently involves different cultures. For example, the exchange of performing artists not only necessitates a crossing of national borders but requires contact with people of different cultures.

**International Conferences**

Conferences – both at the regional and international level – play a significant role in international communication and international relations. The conference mechanism provides a forum for the exchange of information, discussion, debate, and negotiation between governmental and nongovernmental actors. The review of literature in this area suggests a potential for research contribution, since few empirical studies have been conducted to assess the information flow in, and emerging from, conferences.

The importance of potential studies in this area can be illuminated by examining the recent growth of international conferences. Such growth is due largely to overall growth in the number of international organizations as well as to increases in air travel, rapid technological growth, and simultaneous translation capabilities. Consequently, the number of international conferences increased exponentially from three in 1853 and just over 100 by 1900, to more than 2,000 in 1953,[1] reaching well over 5,000 in the early 1990s.

In 1967, there were about 4,000 international meetings.[2] In the fields of science and technology alone, the last 40 years have seen a tremendous increase of meetings held throughout the world, from 5,800 in 1958[3] to over 12,000 in 1992. Although few attempts have been made to analyze the trends, ample data for such analysis do exist in the form of calendars and directories of international meetings and records of conference proceedings.[4]

Informal exchanges of scientific information at a conference, however, are unrecorded, and the "invisible college" nature of a scientific conference is difficult to document. Many of the papers that are presented are not published, many of the speeches are not recorded. Although some studies have been done on the exchange of scientific information in general, there has been little systematic research effort regarding international conferences. Information is available on the evaluation of international conferences or on organizing conferences, but this explains little about the flow of information occurring during and subsequent to such meetings. Yet, the international flow of scientific information is very important.

Additionally, international conferences are a valuable resource focusing public attention on issues of worldwide importance. They facilitate communication on vital issues and provide an area for negotiations that can lead to policy formation and international agreements. They also provide open forums for developing countries to voice their needs and demands. Still, not only is most scientific and technical information in the possession of the industrialized countries, because of educational and financial opportunities, but those nations also possess more scientists and technical experts than the rest of the world.

There are a variety of cultural, economic, political, legal, social, institutional, and technological factors that influence the flow of information at international scientific and technical conferences. These factors are inter-related and often overlapping. For example, the geographical location of the conference is an important factor in the amount and the direction of the flow of information at and from it. It is difficult to get precise data on the most frequently selected locations for conferences: the information exists for individual organizations but aggregate tallies are unavailable. A listing of the geographical locations of headquarters for international organiz-ations, however, showed that most are located in the United States, while France, Belgium, the United Kingdom, and Switzerland offer the next most popular sites.[5]

*The Yearbook of International Organizations* notes how many times a country is listed as a member of an international organization, including both nongovernmental and intergovernmental organizations. In general, countries listed more than one thousand times include Canada, the United States, Austria, Belgium, Denmark, Finland, France, Germany, Italy, the Netherlands, Norway, Spain, Sweden, Switzerland, the United Kingdom, Australia, and Japan.[6] The high cost of attending international conferences cannot be overlooked, nor can the allocation of funding by governments and organizations for particular individuals and groups to attend.

Cultural factors play a paramount role in the flow of information at international scientific and technical conferences. Obviously, language, interpretation, and semantics are very important. Surprisingly enough, little research has been done on simultaneous translation at international con-ferences and how this affects the flow of information. English is, increas-ingly and unquestionably, the language of science throughout the world, and consequently the main language of international scientific conferences as well. One writer even advocates the use of simultaneous English-to-English translation for non-native speakers, which suggests that, although some conferees may have a good understanding of written English through knowledge of scientific books and journals, they may not be comprehen-sible in discussions with English-speaking conferees.

Political factors affecting the flow of information at international scien-tific conferences are often potentially volatile, many resulting from current political events and the compatibility or incompatibility of contending ideologies. For example, largely as a result of the ill treatment of the dissident Sakharov, as well as the former Soviet actions in Afghanistan and Poland, the United States Academy of the Sciences, following the Reagan administration's political and economic sanctions against the Soviet Union in 1981, imposed a moratorium on joint symposia and other high-level contact with the Soviet Academy of Sciences.[7] In another decision, three weeks before the conference of the Society of Photo-optical Instrumenta-tion Engineers in San Diego in October 1982, the Defense Department announced that nearly 100 papers scheduled for presentation would have to be withdrawn because they contained sensitive technical information.[8] Soviet scientists had been invited to the conference and the government saw this as a threat to national security. Access to the information, it was felt, would enable the Soviets to skip costly research, perhaps developing early countermeasures to American military advances.

Similar restrictions have been imposed, on grounds of security reasons, not to grant visas to a number of scientists and scholars from countries with whom the United States has unfriendly relations, such as Iran and Cuba. In the words of the former Deputy Secretary of Defense Frank Carlucci, speaking in the early 1980s when the Cold War was still at its height, "By the very nature of our open and free society, we recognize that we will never be able to halt fully the flow of military technology to the Soviet Union. Nevertheless, we believe that it is possible to inhibit this flow without infringing upon legitimate scientific discourse."[9] Many examples could be cited to illustrate similar restrictions on the flow of scientific information imposed for political and security reasons by governments around the world.

Historical and cultural factors, as well as past colonial ties, indirectly influence the flow of scientific information, particularly in the case of British Commonwealth countries, where the influence of Western science and research is strong. According to one observer, Indian scientists participate in international conferences almost as much as they participate locally:

> The structural linkages of the Indian science and technology system indicate strong built-in flows of scientific ideas and technical information, as well as cultural and ideological orientations, from the West. These tendencies are constantly reinforced through higher education, scientific technical books and periodicals, and professional seminars and conferences which are so common place in free and democratic India . . . This linkage is . . . its greatest strength but it is also (part of) its greatest weakness . . . its alienation from the reality of India.[10]

Conference reports were previously mentioned as one of the key aspects of information flow connected to an international conference. Such reports are probably the most tangible evidence of the activity of international organizations, both nongovernmental and intergovernmental. This is due, in part, to the fact that the report of a conference may, for some time, be the only literature available on the subject until various papers and writings find their way into scholarly and professional journals and texts.

More recent studies of international conferences tend to focus on computer-assisted conferences, teleconferencing, and videoconferencing. It is quite likely that with technological advance, the forms of conferences will continuously change in the decades to come. A surprising number of international organizations have been involved with computer conferencing. However, there is little written evaluation of the nature and quality of information flow through such conferences. Telecommunications and computer-assisted technologies can partially substitute for both meetings and conventional laboratory-style team research. Such practices will conserve scarce resources, especially for the smaller and poorer countries. Although team research conducted through electronic media will be subject to the same cultural, linguistic, and political difficulties of other kinds of international scientific cooperation, observers believe it will receive governmental support if it shows proven benefits and cost reductions. Recent developments in communication and computer technologies can now provide an economically attractive alternative to face-to-face conferencing, but it seems unlikely that teleconferences will replace the scope and meaning of direct personal contact.

## International Educational Exchanges

Each year thousands of high school and college students, teachers, professors, researchers, vocational and technical trainees, conference delegates, and cultural performers travel to foreign countries to study, work, or perform. Although most exchanges are participant-sponsored, many international exchanges and human movements in the sphere of education and culture are funded by governments, foundations, transnational corporations, and educational institutions. In many cases, these organizations support international exchanges because they believe exchanges can create better international understanding and promote world peace. In spite of such beliefs and the resultant activity in the international exchange of persons, there is little systematically acquired or coherent knowledge of exchange interactions themselves, or of their functions and effects.

In the United States, research in the area of international exchanges has focused primarily on the practical concerns of exchange agencies. Therefore, the studies of exchange programs are "mostly specialized and non-cumulative, largely devoid of replication so that past studies might reinforce or modify presumed knowledge, predominantly 'episodic,' i.e., focusing on present data with little regard to comparison with related other data, and thin in the evolution of fruitful concepts and the building of theory."[11] These observations were made by Michael J. Flack of the University of Pittsburgh at the 1980 US–German conference on "Research in International Educational Exchange." Flack began his overview of research in the United States on international exchange with a review of his 1976 study, *The World's Students in the United States*. This study, a survey of almost 550 publications and studies on international educational exchange, concluded that the literature on exchanges is "quantitatively large, methodologically uneven, conceptually and theoretically unfocused, topically wide ranging but seldom interrelated . . . , in policy recommendations scattered, ad hoc and unconcerned about implementation, in research recommendation broad, seldom mutually related, encompassing a wide spectrum and within it emphasizing some recurrent themes while ignoring others."[12] Flack identified further characteristics of international exchange research in a review of literature published since 1974–5. These characteristics include an increase in the number of publications, a decrease in analytical studies, and an attempt to apply the ideology of international exchange to a "global perspective of the cultural transformation processes in mankind."[13]

Flack's critique of exchange research is bolstered by the similar observations of Spencer and Awe in 1970 in their study of 262 publications from 1960 to 1967 on international educational exchange. Like Flack, Spencer and Awe noted that exchange studies exhibited inadequate research design and a lack of research on "students' objectives in undertaking foreign study, [and] institutions' and nations' objectives in providing opportunities to study."[14] According to Spencer and Awe, "most studies do not refer to, or take into consideration, psychological or cross-cultural problems or research performed on general second-cultural variables, nor do they relate to the American abroad."[15] These studies reviewing exchange literature all emphasize the variety and abundance of available research, but, more important, note the need for more effective, comprehensive, and analytical research.

On a more general level, we can divide research and literature on the educational and cultural aspects of human flow and movements across national boundaries and cultures into four specific categories. The first involves comparison of demographic information collected on international exchanges. A clear example of this type of study is the annual publication of the Institute of International Exchange (IIE), *Open Doors*, which provides statistics on foreign university students and scholars studying in the United States, and US university students and scholars studying in other countries.

Studies in this first category of research are basically concerned with numeric and demographic trends in international exchange. These statistical reports provide a broad representation of the international exchange of persons, but do not answer questions regarding the quality and effects of exchanges. In short, it is difficult to abstract propositions from studies in this first category, since it is primarily descriptive, with data collected for the purpose of illustration rather than systematic analysis.

The second type of research involving the flow of people through educational and cultural channels is concerned with questions of image and attitude change as well as the effects of participating in international exchanges. This set of literature is oriented toward the generation of sociopsychological theory on attitude change and adjustment in a foreign culture. A discussion of these studies touches such topics as personal contact and interpersonal relations, the impact of academic failure and success, the sojourn experience and the "U curve" phenomenon, misunderstanding in communication, and cross-cultural norm conflict and adjustment.

For example, in his analysis of exchange research, Richard Merritt looks at the changes in attitudes and predispositions of foreign students toward their host country after living there for a time.[16] The impact of a foreign culture on travelers in general was reported by Ithiel de Sola Pool in "Effects of Cross-national Contact on National and International

Images."[17] Still other researchers have studied the influence of perceptions and differing experiences in assessing the professional utility of various exchange programs. Frederick Barghoorn and Ellen Mickiewicz conducted such a study in their survey of American scholars, scientists, businessmen, government officials, and others who had visited the Soviet Union under various exchange programs.[18] The different perceptions and experiences that individuals brought to the exchange were, in essence, reflections of their culture, which influenced their opinions on the value of the program.

Herbert Kelman's study "The Problem-Solving Workshop in Conflict Resolution" looks at the role of culture in terms of its influence on the perceptions and attitudes that individuals from conflicting countries bring to a research workshop designed to develop and test ways to resolve international conflicts.[19] It is important to note that the real utility of the workshop approach described by Kelman – and in a similar study carried out by Leonard Doob attempting to employ a modified form of sensitivity training in an international setting – is said to depend on the "ability to specify the points in foreign policy decision-making and international politics at which the attitudes and perceptions of certain individuals make a difference and to develop procedures specifically suited to the occasion for which they are introduced."[20] Once again, the attitudes and perceptions of individuals may be thought of as a reflection of their culture.

Research on cross-cultural encounters is growing, especially in the United States, Canada, and Japan, but the focus is on sociopsychological concepts rather than the process and content of information flow. For example, Richard W. Brislin's documentation of face-to-face contact experienced by students, scholars, immigrants, and diplomats shows how cross-cultural adjustments can be effected.[21] Earlier studies by John W. Bennett and Robert K. McKnight concentrated on the Japanese student in a new cultural environment in the United States, and his or her relationship with cultural and historical changes in Japanese society.[22] Later studies by Tamar Becker showed two distinct patterns of attitudinal and behavioral changes on the part of foreign students in the United States: (1) the U-curve pattern of students from highly industrialized countries, and (2) a reverse pattern for representatives of less industrialized countries for whom the involuntary return home would be perceived as a threat.[23]

The existing literature, however, provides little information or theoretical clues to the ways information is conveyed to foreign students and visitors in a host country. The author and Gerald McLaughlin's study is one of the few examining the information-seeking habits of foreign students in the United States. Foreign students indicated that they use the media, particularly newspapers and television, as a main source of information about American culture, but that interpersonal communication and contact with Americans remains the primary factor determining their attitudes towards the United States.[24]

A somewhat different focus is portrayed in research concerning the effects of foreign students as mediators of culture on their return home. Much emphasis has been placed on the effects of a foreign culture on the student, but little research has explored the student's impact on his or her own culture as well as on the country and culture he or she is visiting. For example, contact with the host country, through travel, lectures, conferences, meetings, and discourse through political demonstrations and public gatherings has been neglected in the study of the international flow of information.

A third category of study and research in the area of educational and cultural flow deals with the impact and effect of international exchanges on national and international development. Demographic studies show that a great number of students from developing nations are educated at universities in developed and industrialized countries such as the United States, France, Germany, and the United Kingdom. Leaders of developing countries hope that these students return home to assist in the development of their nation. Unfortunately, this is not always the case. A number of studies have documented the continuing and increasing problem of trained professionals, scientific specialists, and students from developing countries remaining abroad after studying or working in industrialized countries.[25] This phenomenon, labeled the "brain drain," has resulted in attempts by countries to institute precautions insuring that students and scholars return home upon completion of their study. There are those who argue for unrestricted mobility of the factors of production, asserting that absorbing educated people from the developing countries into the production and information stream in the developed world will result in raising world output and welfare. On the other hand, some view the educated elite, their professional skills, and vital information as critical to the growth process; their transfer is seen as detrimental to developing nations. This latter group perceives the brain drain as evil, and a threat to the stability and growth of the developing world.

This hidden subsidy of the rich by the poor has been occurring since the end of World War II. According to a multinational study by the World Health Organization, for example, India is the world's largest exporter of medical professionals.[26] In 1980, more than 15,000 Indian doctors representing some 13 percent of the total physicians of that country were working abroad, a government investment loss estimated at $144 million. Another study showed that in 1976, the United States saved $100,000 for every trained student imported from India.[27] Further research estimated that profits from foreign workers between 1961 and 1972 were $30 billion for the United States, $1 billion for Canada, and $3.5 billion for Britain.[28]

The fourth and final category of research and studies in the area of human flow views the process of international education and cultural exchanges as a fundamental aspect of scientific information and the worldwide explosion of knowledge. Many social science disciplines, such as psychology, anthropology, sociology, and political science, have included the study of educational and cultural contacts on personal levels as a laboratory for comparative and cross-cultural studies, as well as a testing ground for universal applicability of hypotheses and theories.

The direction of the flow of international educational exchanges – that is, the international flow of students and scholars – can be illustrated by a review of demographic studies provided by such organizations as UNESCO and the Institute of International Education. Several characteristics emerge from the data gathered on this type of human flow across national boundaries.

The first characteristic of the flow of educational exchange is the continual increase in the number of people involved. The number of university-level exchange students around the world rose from 489,000 in 1970 to 802,677 in 1979, nearly doubling in a nine-year period.[29] These statistics do not, however, include the thousands of secondary-level exchange students on programs such as Experiment in International Living (EIL), American Field Service (AFS) International/Intercultural Programs, and Youth For Understanding (YFU) in the United States. YFU has exchanged nearly 100,000 students in the past 32 years. AFS, founded in 1947, operates in 62 countries and exchanged thousands of students between 1954 and 1986. The Experiment in International Living pioneered youth exchange, initiating the home-stay in over 40 countries.

These are only a few of the many programs involved in youth exchange among and between the various geographical as well as ideological regions of the world. Exact figures of worldwide participation in these programs have not been compiled, but given their large number, they represent a substantial addition to the increased flow of educational exchange, and are growing yearly.

Second, the United States has gradually become the major center of foreign students subsequent to World War II as it has gained importance as a world power. Prior to that time, the United States received few foreign students, the major recipients for foreign students being the United Kingdom and France. In 1979, the United States hosted 286,340 students, more than twice the number studying in France, the number two host country; that figure included approximately 34 percent of the university-level exchange student population. By 1981, well over 300,000 foreigners were studying in American universities and colleges. According to the Institute of International Education, that figure was more than doubled by 1990, when foreign students accounted for at least 10 percent of US college enrollments.

A third characteristic (although somewhat overshadowed by US dominance in the field of educational exchange) is the tendency of students from less developed countries to study in those developed countries which have strong historical, linguistic, and cultural ties with their native country.[30] For example, the number of students from French-speaking Africa attending universities in France reflects the strong ties of these two regions. France clearly hosts the majority of students from Africa. Sizeable numbers of students from Algeria, the Congo, Morocco, Senegal, Tunisia, and the United Republic of Cameroon attend French universities. Although the United Kingdom has lost many of its foreign students to the United States, it still receives the majority of students from Zambia, Zimbabwe, Sudan, Brunei, Cyprus, Iraq, Malaysia, Singapore, Sri Lanka, and Malta. It is not surprising to find that the Soviet Union led in the number of students from Bulgaria, Czechoslovakia, the German Democratic Republic, Hungary, Poland, Cuba, North Korea, Laos, and Mongolia. Germany maintains the largest foreign student populations from such less developed countries as Botswana, Afghanistan, Indonesia, and Turkey. Clearly, in choosing a country in which to study, students from less developed countries use a number of criteria including the reputation of its universities, its world status, and its linguistic, cultural and historical ties to the student's native country.

Another important criterion for choosing a country in which to study is the availability of financial aid. The majority of students studying in the United States do not receive any financial aid. Generally speaking, home governments and foreign private sponsors provide only 16 percent of the students with funds. Another 15 percent received US funding. The United States also ranks behind its major European allies and Japan "in the percentage of its national budget allocated to public diplomacy efforts."[31] Indeed, US expenditures have decreased in recent years, while Germany, Japan, and Britain all increased their appropriations for these activities. Although the United States has spent hundreds of millions of dollars on educational aid overseas in the past, it now appears to be educating mostly the middle- and upper-class ranks of the developing world.

Another important characteristic of the flow of information through educational exchanges concerns the tendency of less developed countries to educate a large percentage of their students abroad, while only a fraction of the student population in developed countries studies abroad. The overwhelming majority of these students participated in programs lasting only a semester or a year. American students rarely complete their university education in other countries.

Another characteristic concerns the content of foreign study. A review of the major study fields of exchange students reveals that students from developing countries concentrate on the sciences, while students from developed countries go abroad to study the humanities and social sciences.

The last characteristic of the flow of educational exchange is the large number of students who emigrate to their host country. This brain drain exists not only for the developing countries, but for some developed countries as well. Countries as diverse as South Korea, the United Kingdom, and India suffer the loss of highly qualified individuals through emigration, a consequence partly of social, political, and economic conditions in the countries of emigration, and partly of immigration policies in receiving countries. At the same time, one must remember that outflow is a direct result of conscious decisions made by individuals.

**Effects of Intercultural Communication**

The characteristics reviewed above raise many questions regarding the effects of international educational exchange. Of the four types of educational exchange research and literature examined in this chapter, the second and third types of studies (image and attitude; effects of international exchanges on development) are primarily concerned with the effects of exchange.

The image/attitude studies examine the effects on the individual. Viewing educational and cultural exchanges as part of the global flow of information, a major question is whether or not educational exchange produces positive image/attitude changes toward the host country. A variety of answers have resulted from the ensuing research. Herbert C. Kelman discovered that "favorable change is facilitated by the joint occurrence of two conditions: genuinely *new information* about the country and people must be provided in the context of a *positive interaction* between nationals of the participating countries,"[32] Richard Merritt's work builds on Kelman's premise with a number of additional conditions necessary to increase the likelihood of a foreign student having a positive image of and attitude toward the host country. These conditions include a greater similarity between the countries, more favorable attitudes of the host country towards the student's native country, a greater amount of interaction between the student and nationals, and the close friendship of a host country national.[33]

The contrasting studies of Anita Mishler suggest that exchange students will develop a "more complex and differentiated image of the host country [as a result of their exchange experience]."[34] An exchange student in the USA may develop positive feelings toward Americans, but this will not necessarily imply an automatic positive view of American national policies and behavior. Indeed, given the diverse opinion of Americans regarding their country's national and foreign policies, there is no reason to believe that a foreign student's experience will determine his or her opinion of government policies.

Cross-cultural contact enables persons to understand the complexities of another society and empathize with persons of another culture. The ability to understand other cultures may represent the cornerstone of international understanding and world peace. Evidence of international understanding resulting from educational exchange was discovered in Barghoorn and Mickiewicz's study of Soviet–American exchanges. This study demonstrated that exchanges "gained confidence in the possibility of coexistence . . . [and] increased tolerance of the social and political system of the other.[35] This learning opportunity, however, is available to only a few persons from particular countries. The number of students from developed countries studying in less developed countries is slight. Thus, persons in industrialized countries have little chance to understand the cultures of the less developed world. Moreover, exchange students from developing countries studying in developed countries represent, for the most part, the elite of their nations. They provide their hosts with an undifferentiated and incomplete picture of their cultures. As a result, the diverse societies of developing countries are often misrepresented in the industrialized world. In sum, where the most misunderstanding occurs, a lack of substantial two-way exchange exacerbates misperceptions.

Foreign students, because they are an important link in understanding between their home country and host country, are valuable sources of information in international and intercultural communication. They represent their native culture and may be the only contact many host nationals have with that particular culture. Likewise, their fellow nationals may experience a foreign culture only vicariously through the related experiences of the students upon their return home. For these reasons, it is interesting to study the attitudes of foreign students toward their host and their home countries, general changes in these attitudes, and the reasons for the changes. It is also interesting to examine the crystallization of the diverse experiences that students carry back to their homelands and incorporate into personal value structures. Equally, as part of the two-way flow of information, it becomes important to study the impact of these students on the host country and the types of information, images, and attitudes generated by the host country's citizens as a result of such interactions.

To determine some of the probable effects discussed here, it is necessary to examine the kind of background foreign students bring with them. Important cultural factors include structure, values, and personality, from which come the complex of motivations and expectations that will determine the students' reactions to the host country. Because the self-image of an individual is so complex, it is helpful to isolate three components and determine how they are affected. These components are nationality, socioeconomic background, and the structure of culture.

It has also been argued that educational and cultural exchanges on a person-to-person level will assist nations and cultures in the foundation of "bridge leveling," that is, the development of a horizontal field of communication. In most cases, intercultural communication takes place between "communication partners" who share much in common. For example, scientists, artists, athletes, and technicians have a common profession, a similar level of education, and/or common interests and motivations with their counterparts in other cultures. Horizontal lines of communication develop in spite of vertical barriers that are erected between cultures because of the cognitive distance of different world views or frames of reference.

The importance of educational exchange as an overall aspect of foreign and national policies has been well documented in recent years by several reports in the United States, France, Germany, and Britain. For example, in its 1980 report, President Carter's Commission on Foreign Language and International Studies states that educational exchanges are consequential to national interest and essential to an aware and involved citizenry in the United States. The report specifically discusses four types of international educational exchanges: high school students and faculty exchanges, study abroad programs for college and university students, foreign students in the USA, and exchanges of college and university faculty. The commission addresses the strengths and weaknesses of the program in each of these four areas, and concludes by suggesting ways to increase participation in educational exchanges.

In the area of international exchanges for high school students and teachers, the commission reports that "exchanges at this level contribute enormously to foreign language acquisition and cross-cultural interaction." It suggests that exchanges of teachers should have greater priority and more support because of the multiplier effect, assuming that experience abroad affects what and how teachers teach, as well as their perceptions and attitudes toward other countries and cultures.[36] However, in 1978–9, the year in which most of the commission's findings were based, a marked decrease in the number of teachers and countries involved in the direct teacher exchange was noted. In that year, the program involved only "six foreign countries and one hundred thirty two US teachers, all of whom went to the U.K., Canada, West Germany, New Zealand and Switzerland,"[37] compared with the 45 countries receiving US teachers some 10 to 15 years previously. The Office of Education administered Fulbright programs contributing to school exchanges, but also tended to "neglect the non-western world, or enrolled far too few participants to produce a major impact."[38] The commission's report cited cutbacks in federal funding, decreasing foreign language proficiency in the United States, decline in foreign language teachers, and the restricted job market for teachers in the US and other industrialized countries as the major factors responsible for the reduced number of high school teachers participating in exchange programs. The commission concluded that more international exchange opportunities and available funds were needed, but that "American attitudes towards foreign language and international studies must also become more positive if this situation is to change."[39]

In its discussion of study abroad programs for college and university students, the commission acknowledged their importance in strengthening the interest and competence of US college students in foreign languages and international topics, explaining that experience abroad can have a "life-long impact on values and on concern for and understanding of other cultures." In fact, research on the impact of study abroad, a field in which more research is needed, suggests that it may be most important in terms of the personal experience of living in another culture and interacting with the people of another country. An Antioch College study showed that Antioch students who had studied abroad were "subsequently much more likely than their fellow students who stayed in the US to complete their degrees, to read the foreign press, to buy books published abroad and to enter careers which take them overseas."[40] The commission's findings, however, indicate that there seem to be several deterrents that prevent an increasing number of American college students from taking advantage of study

abroad programs. Higher costs for international travel and living abroad
(depending on the location), diminished funds for graduate study abroad,
and higher tuition fees for foreign students all conspire to make American
study abroad more difficult. The report also regretfully noted that, in
contrast to the increases in the number of US students going to the less
developed countries in the 1970s, fewer students do so now probably
because of increased travel costs and "the waning of 'Peace Corps' spirit
among students in recent years."

The commission recognized the thousands of foreign students studying
in American colleges and universities as a valuable resource for educating
Americans about other countries, and as a pool of talent increasingly
recruited by multinational corporations after they finish their degree
programs. Noting that foreign students provide an indispensable contact in
developing commercial and financial links between the United States and
the rest of the world, the commission sees their education in the United
States as an "investment important to American national interests." In
addition, involving foreign students in educational programs with
Americans can produce positive feelings toward people from other cultures,
facilitate learning about them, and counteract the cultural stereotyping
typical of anti-foreign attitudes.

Lastly, the commission addresses the area of international exchange
between college and university faculty. Access to and the advancement of
knowledge in a foreign language and international studies, in addition to
providing specialists with training and experience, are some of the needs
served by this type of exchange. The report notes, however, that recent
surveys indicate:

> fifty-seven percent of over half of American academics have never traveled out of
> the U.S. for professional reasons. Of those who do, sixty-six percent are in
> medicine, forty-five percent in the social sciences, and fifty-eight percent in the
> humanities. The percentage of college and university faculty traveling to non-
> western countries is miniscule compared with the nearly thirty-four percent
> travelling to English language countries, mainly the U.K. and Canada.[41]

The unavailability of funding – especially of the Fulbright program, the
major federally funded international exchange program related to international studies – reduced stipends, and reduced grant periods are factors
limiting the participation of many academics in exchange programs. In
addition, Fulbright awards in non-Western countries are predominantly for
teaching, with only a few for research. "Of those research grants awarded
in 1977–78, ninety-five out of one hundred and eighty-eight were for
Western European countries."[42]

The report of the commission concludes by recommending a program for
continuing financial assistance, appealing not only to the federal
government, but also to the state governments and the higher educational
institutions themselves. The commission's findings also suggest improving
the access of US researchers and scholars to developing countries and those
geographical areas currently underrepresented.

Another area of impact of educational and cultural flow through human movement across national boundaries and among cultures is the issue of "dependency" or "dominance" and its possible effect on national and international development. Again on the positive side, studies have shown that a foreign education can indeed assist national and international development, particularly if it is based on a sound educational and developmental policy. For example, Richard Myer's survey of the developing countries' alumni of four US universities revealed that these alumni were employed in organizations that "played a very important (54%) or moderately related (37%) role in national development. Also, the alumni indicated that their "U.S. education received almost full (21%), much (48%), and some (26%) professional use."[43]

On the other hand, the current theme of international debate has been the uneven flow of information in the world community. The pattern of the flow of information consists of two-way communication between developed countries and the one-way dissemination of information to the developing nations from the industrialized world. It is also argued that this flow pattern is replicated by the international exchange of persons. Thousands of students from the developing world study in the industrialized nations each year. These students learn about their host countries' theories, philosophies, technologies, and methodologies. Although students gain a more differentiated picture of their host country, they are also influenced by the culture in which they lived. Many returnees become separated mentally and spiritually from their native cultures, thus inhibiting their ability to assist in national development. Thus, educational exchanges that do not consider the national developmental goals have been linked to the reinforcement of this dependency syndrome.

This dependency and penetration have been best illustrated in the United States–Iranian cultural relations prior to the Islamic revolution.[44] The last period of the former Shah's rule in Iran, 1953–78, can be characterized as a period when the United States–Iranian cultural and educational relations became truly multidimensional from the American side. To a score of US governmental institutions active in Iran during this period were added many university and corporate programs in such fields as business, management, education, marketing, advertising and mass media, sports, and entertainment. The number of Iranian students studying in the United States increased rapidly and there was hardly a modern institution in the Iranian metropolis that was not under the influence of American higher education and corporate training. By now, the United States had replaced France and Britain as a major source of Western cultural, scientific, and educational values in Iran.

In 1977 there were approximately 300 American business and educational organizations involved in some aspect of educational and business training in Iran. Thus, the most active and aggressive period of United States–Iranian cultural relations took its course at the time that most of Iran's cultural, educational, religious, and traditional institutions were under extreme repressive measures of the former Shah. Iran was a fertile ground for the implantation of American educational structures and values. With a Western development model in mind and sufficient oil reserves in hand, the Shah's government oversaw the establishment of 74 direct links between American and Iranian universities and had adopted the American system of education as a template for its future. At the same time, large numbers of Iranians who were educated both in Iran and the United States or Europe took their permanent residency in Europe and the United States. For example, 160 out of 315 physicians who graduated from the University of Teheran Medical School in June 1966 were permanent residents in the United States a decade later, with more in Britain and Europe.

Several Iranian universities had moved in the direction of an American University model. The chancellor of the Pahlavi university, on one occasion, summarized the significance of this relationship: "We tried deliberately to adopt Western technology and to train the needed manpower for creating a new government system . . . of greatest importance was the formation of a homogeneous faculty trained in the American system of education." During this same period, Iranian students flocked to study in the United States. As late as 1971–2, there were only 6,365 (4 percent of total foreign student enrollment). By 1975–6, there were more Iranian students (19,000, or 11 percent) in US universities and colleges than from any other country. Just before the revolution in 1978, even that total had almost doubled to 36,220 (15.4 percent). In 1978, it was estimated that 66,000 Iranian students enrolled in various colleges and universities in the United States alone, while the total number of college students in Iran did not exceed 120,000. At one time, Iran taught its elite the French language and with that came the whole of French thought, French literature, and French methods. During the 1960s and the 1970s, American English prevailed. By the mid-1970s, important signs of the revolution were beginning to develop on college campuses in Iran and among Iranian students overseas. Thousands of Iranian students, scholars, and scientists abroad, as well as their American and foreign counterparts who were residing in Iran, had become a significant aspect of the United States-Iranian, and in fact worldwide, information flow.

Had the direction, content, and intensity of this type of information flow been taken into account in the analysis of the development in Iran and the region, the Western analysts and the students of politics who were surprised by the revolution in Iran and its outcome would have had a better picture and understanding as the events unfolded. In fact, the two dominant views of what was "really" happening in Iran prior to the downfall of the Shah – the first seeing Iranian culture and society under the complete domination of the West and the second proclaiming the path of development in Iran as an inevitable and irreversible trend toward secular modernization under the Shah – proved inaccurate. The analysts of both of these views based their evaluations on official information, media content, and economic data. Both dismissed Islam and the information generated and circulated through the traditional religious and national centers as well as the students and academic institutions as less significant. Similar misperceptions about the Iranian climate stemmed from a number of otherwise expert and credible sources in the academic field in both the United States and Europe. The study of the Iranian revolution underlined the importance of an appreciation of the flow of information through educational, cultural, and traditional channels and the total communication system in another culture.

## Traditional Communication

Traditional communication models focus on technologically oriented channels of mass media. Information such as news is seen as flowing through mass communication channels from a sender to many recipients. Traditional studies also emphasize the content of such information flows. In the interpersonal model, by contrast, the individual is at once the message, channel, sender, and recipient of communication when the individual moves from one culture to another, from one nation to the next. The crucial question in international flow studies of interpersonal communication should be what happens to such an individual in such a setting where feedback is much greater than in the passive, one-way flow of mass communication.

Several considerations for inquiry can be identified in analyzing interpersonal communication on the international level:

1. What changes does the individual undergo during his or her socialization in the foreign environment? How does the individual communicate with this environment and receive information?
2. How are the individual's perceptions about the foreign environment (its people, policies, etc.) changed in the communication process?
3. What is the impact of the individual's presence on the host country and the individuals in his/her environment or activities?
4. What are the contents of information flow between the individual and his/her environment?

It is clear from the above considerations that significant differences exist between the analysis of mass communication systems and that of person-to-person contacts. In the latter, the total communication system is actually at work, giving rise to different questions and modes of research. The human is the focus of inquiry in this setting. The area of international education exchange would seem to offer one of the most propitious fields of inquiry into how an individual's communication processes may or may not change when residing in another culture, and whether that change may affect information he/she receives on that country and the values, attitudes, and opinions that are based on that information. The sociology of international educational and cultural exchanges might offer a wealth of material and data on how the conduct of international relations might take place in the future.

Although much attention has been paid to the process of socialization of individuals on national and community levels, less attention has been directed to the study of socialization on the international level. Most of the analysis of international relations has been concerned with two traditional ideas: a theory of a mass society (mass public) and a theory of decision-making elites. The first theory, based on public opinion data and content analysis of the media, makes no distinction between groups and subgroups within national or international politics. Public opinion data or the content of the media will make little contribution to our understanding of how a given percentage of the population of country A favors closer relations with country B without considering such factors as ethnicity, professional and educational socialization, and the meaning of cooperation and coexistence between and among various classes of people. The second theory, by emphasizing the decision-making elite or the ruling class, takes a different view of international relations, seeing the public's impact as minimal and the formal decision makers of the time as the only group possessing policy influence. The decision-making elite theory ignores the two fundamental developments of the last fifty years: (1) that counter elites have been responsible for much of the development, change, revolution, and reform in the Third World, and (2) that the politics of the post-World War II period and the closing decades of the twentieth century are politics of instability.[45]

During the last three decades, this elitist view, coupled with insufficient attention paid to an excluded group of educated individuals who at the moment were not at the top of the power pyramid but later assumed political leadership in many countries, was responsible for much misperception of political decision makers as well as the embarrassing analysis of many writers. The crisis of post-World War II leadership in many new nations in Asia, Africa, and Latin America, such as Indonesia, Pakistan, Lebanon, Chile, Ghana, and Nigeria; the takeover of political leadership by the socialists in Greece and Spain; and, most dramatic of all, the Islamic revolution in Iran, rejecting alike the old-fashioned "nationalists," the contemporary "liberal social democrats," and the Marxist group, are all cases in point. Many of these new leaders, who attended universities in the United States, Britain, France, Germany and who more than ordinary citizens participated in many scientific, professional, cultural, and religious programs internationally, did not come from the traditional elite strata.

The revolution in Iran was perhaps the greatest imbroglio and embarrassment social science research and methodology has suffered in some time. With the exception of a few writers whose works were either unnoticed or unpublished, practically no one as late as 1977 could have guessed that Mohammed Reza Pahlavi would be overthrown by a man relatively unknown to the West, and by his many followers – some of whom had received their advanced education in the United States, France, Britain, and Germany – and would subsequently die in an ignominious exile. The failure to recognize the potential power of the ulama – the clergy – their historical and traditional role in education and the intellectual life in Iran, and the religio-political background of the many foreign-trained and educated professionals who stood in sharp contrast to a more "secular" and Western-oriented political/technological elite had had adverse consequences. Less attention was paid to the flow of information and power in the traditional and informal channels of communication. The dominant approach was to analyze the flow of information in an institutionalized "modern" political structure. The concept of "secularism" as it is used in the West had little practical application in Iran, because politics and religion have been fused in that country. The "experts" had realized the influence of the religious leader and were aware of the informal nature of information flow and the political process, but could not establish how vertically or horizontally encompassing they were. Others had written of the "uprooters," the "technocrats," and the "alienated" students, professionals, and intellectuals, but their uncritical methodology of interviews and survey research had produced little useful data and analysis on information flow and communication. The collapse of the Soviet Union was another reconfirmation of this trend in social science research.

It was precisely this exclusive concentration on the ruling elites on the one hand, and the monothetic thinking about the public and the middle echelon of the societies on the other, that made it almost impossible for those in charge of foreign relations to get an understanding of the process through which the publics and competing elites alike undermined the existing legitimacy of many institutions around the world. Today education and cultural relations are at the core of international relations. For international relations, after all, are relations between nations, and nations and communities are composed of human beings. Socialization and communication of individuals through this channel is indeed an important factor in international sociology. Although much of the international flow of information through these human channels is somewhat unstructured and unformalized, the unquantifiable nature of much of this type of research at present should not dissuade researchers, for the human dimension must be investigated more thoroughly if we are to gain a more truly balanced picture of international flow of information.

## Notes

1. Paul Pederson, "International Conferences: Significant Measures of Success," *International Journal of Intercultural Relations*, 5: 1 (1981), p. 51.

2. Eyvind Tew, *Yearbook of International Congress Proceedings* (Brussels: Union of International Associations, 1981).

3. E. Garfield, "ISI's New Index to Scientific and Technical Proceedings Lets You Know What Went On At a Conference Even If You Stayed At Home," *Essays of an Information Scientist*, 3: 40 (1978), p. 247.

4. US Department of State, Science and Foreign Relations *International Flow of Scientific and Technical Information* (Washington, DC: US Department of State, 1950), p. 34.

5. Union of International Associations and International Chamber of Commerce, *Yearbook of International Organizations*, 19th edn (Brussels: UIA and ICC, 1981).

6. Ibid. (1977 edition).

7. Victor S. Navasky, "Secrecy Strikes," *The Nation*, September 18, 1982, p. 227.

8. Ibid., p. 228.

9. Quoted in Ivars Peterson, "Controlling Technology Exports: Security vs. Knowledge," *Science News*, 121: 12 (March 12, 1982), p. 206.

10. Aucil Ahmad, "Flow of Science and Technology Information: The Cases of India and China," *Media Asia*, 6: 2 (1979), pp. 80–81.

11. Michael J. Flack, "International Educational, Cultural and Scientific Interchange," *Research on Exchanges: Proceedings of the German–American Conference at Wissenschaftszentrum*, DAAD, November 24–28, 1980, p. 1.

12. Ibid., p. 59.

13. Ibid., p. 61.

14. Quoted in Diether Breitenbach, "A Critique of Interchange Research," *Research on Exchanges: Proceedings of the German–American Conference at Wissenschaftszentrum*, DAAD, November 24–28, 1981, p. 8.

15. Ibid., p. 9.

16. Richard L. Merritt, "Effects of International Student Exchange," in Richard L. Merritt, ed., *Communication in International Politics* (Urbana, IL: University of Illinois Press, 1972), pp. 64–94.

17. Ithiel de Sola Pool, "Effects of Cross-National Contact on National and International Images," in Herbert C. Kelman, ed., *International Behavior: A Socio-psychological Analysis* (New York: Holt, Rinehart and Winston, 1965), pp. 104–129.

18. Frederick C. Barghoorn and Ellen Mickiewicz, "American Views of Soviet-American Exchange of Persons," in Merritt, ed., *Communication in International Politics*, pp. 146–167.

19. Herbert C. Kelman, "The Problem-Solving Workshop in Conflict Resolution," in ibid., pp. 168–206.

20. Leonard W. Doob, *Resolving Conflict in Africa: The Fermeda Workshop* (New Haven, CT: Yale University Press, 1970).

21. Richard W. Brislin, *Cross-Cultural Encounter* (New York: Pergamon Press, 1981).

22. John W. Bennett and Robert K. McKnight, "Misunderstanding in Communication Between Japanese Students and Americans," *Social Problems*, April 3, 1956, pp. 243–256.

23. Tamar Becker, "Patterns of Attitudinal Change Among Foreign Students," *American Journal of Sociology*, 73 (January 1968), pp. 431–442.

24. Hamid Mowlana and Gerald W. McLaughlin, "Some Variables Interacting with Media Exposure Among Foreign Students," *Sociology and Social Research*, 53: 4 (July 1969), pp. 511–522.

25. For example, see Deena R. Khatkhate, "The Brain Drain as a Social Safety Valve," *Finance and Development Quarterly*, 7: 1 (March 1970), pp. 32–36; George B. Baldwin, "Brain Drain or Overflow," *Foreign Affairs*, January 1970, pp. 358–365; Walter Adams, ed., *The Brain Drain* (New York: Macmillan, 1968).

26. S. Nagrajzn, "The Third World Brain Drain," *World Press Review*, September 1983, p. 46.

27. Ibid.

28. Ibid.

29. *UNESCO Statistical Yearbook 1982* (London: Computerprint, 1982, pp. 111, 479–481.

30. *International Youth Exchange: A Presidential Initiative*, The President's Council for International Youth Exchange and the Consortium of International Citizen Exchange, 1983–84, Washington, DC.

31. *Report of the United States Advisory Commission on Public Diplomacy*, Washington, DC, 1982, pp. 21–25.

32. Herbert C. Kelman, "International Interchange: Some Contributions from Theories of Attitude Change," International Studies Association Conference, St Louis, MO, March 22, 1974.

33. Merritt, ed., *Communication in International Politics*, pp. 79–83.

34. Anita L. Mishler, "Personal Contacts in International Exchanges," in Kelman, ed., *International Behavior*, p. 551.

35. Barghoorn and Mickiewicz, "American Views of Soviet–American Exchange of Persons," p. 159.

36. Barbara Burns, "Study Abroad and International Exchanges," *Annals of the American Academy of Political and Social Science*, 449 (May 1980), p. 130.

37. Ibid., p. 132.

38. Ibid., p. 132.

39. Ibid., p. 133.

40. Ibid., p. 133.

41. Ibid., p. 137.

42. Ibid., p. 138.

43. Quoted in Flack, "International Educational, Cultural and Scientific Interchange," p. 70.

44. Hamid Mowlana, "U.S.–Iranian Relations, 1954–78: A Case of Cultural Domination," paper presented at the Middle East Studies Association Conference, Salt Lake City, UT, November 8, 1979.

45. These points have been elaborated in Lewis Coser, "The Role of Groups: Contributions of Sociology," in Arthur S. Hoffman, ed., *International Communication and the New Diplomacy* (Bloomington, IN: Indiana University Press, 1968), pp. 106–123.

# 9

# Information Technology: Developing Communication Systems and Policies

While communication policy and planning in the past largely were sectorial and usually dealt with only one dimension of the development problem (i.e., communication vis-à-vis economic, political, or bureaucratic subjects), in the light of communication development, we have learned that this now entails a multistage type of analysis.

Communication policy and planning in any society or nation are influenced and shaped by real-world factors. Policy-making is the initial phase in which problems are recognized and specific governmental efforts are made to determine directions. The notion of communication policy and planning, however, as the integrative nature of developmental projects of all kinds is not well recognized. In general, the need for some control or regulation of the information- and communication-technology industries is acknowledged. There is, however, little agreement in most nations, on political and philosophical grounds, as to the best approaches to take in any given situation, resulting in policy that is usually fragmented and ineffective or altogether absent. Many less industrialized nations and regions lack cohesive and coherent communication policy to direct the effective incorporation of policy and planning into telecommunications as well as communication projects.

In many nations, information technology is a powerful resource, one that is not depleted with use. Further, this resource aids in the organization and allocation of other resources – economic, political, cultural, and legal. Control over the distribution of these resources positions nations strategically as well as operationally either inside or outside of the flow of international interactions determining power in the global system. Policy-making unavoidably is influenced by extranational forces. More significant than the obvious politico-economic and diplomatic influences is the impact of private corporations on government policy formulation, especially in the areas of technology transfer, know-how, and innovation.

Less industrially developed countries, without communication policy and planning infrastructures, for example, are in a weak position to control resource applications that are influenced heavily by private international businesses with agendas differing from their own national development objectives. On the other hand, such countries with high degrees of human and natural resources, through carefully designed national strategies for communication policy and planning, can effect powerful control over the economic, political, cultural, and technological and legal factors influencing development. For example, by setting a national policy mandating 51 percent local ownership of all foreign direct investment in India in computer-related technologies, India successfully maintained control over its communication policy and planning process and, at the same time, supported development of its national technological industries.

## The Communication Revolution

If the "communication revolutions" and the "explosion of information" are undeniable, their nature, causes, and consequences are much less certain.[1] Two opposing viewpoints have been prevalent during the last three decades. The first sees development of modern communication technology and the international flow of information as ordinary and evolutionary processes, similar to those processes through which Western society has frequently passed in the last four centuries.

Most of these experts view this stage as a unique form of acceleration of either economic, political, or technological growth. They see modern technology of communication as a "savior," having the capability, and indeed the power, to reduce conflict, poverty, and disintegration. If developed worldwide, they believe it can (and in many instances will) stimulate economic growth, helping to resolve such problems as population explosions and geographical, social, and psychological isolation.

The main issue is seen in a conflict of "democracy" and "totalitarianism." Further, some experts among these diagnosticians advance the theory of "strong men" and "wicked men," where conflicts between the "good fellow" leaders and the "lunatic" leaders are at the center of the issues. Through measures of *technology, information, and economic growth* they hope to correct the maladjustment, to eradicate the evil, and to keep the society and polity sane.

The second view has been more pessimistic. It sees the current crisis of the world not only as the death agony of the dominant industrial powers, but as that of the less industrialized world totally dominated and overtaken by the industrialized world. No remedy can avert this destiny; no cure can prevent the death of Western or Eastern or Southern culture unless basic structural *economic* and *political* transformations are made.

In the author's opinion, both of the foregoing diagnoses are incomplete and rather simplistic. Contrary to the optimistic view, the present world order is not ordinary but extraordinary. Unlike the second view, the present crisis is not merely an economic or political maladjustment, but simultaneously involves nearly the whole industrialized culture and society – both capitalist and socialist – in all their main sectors. The point is that the fundamental form of industrialized culture and society dominant for the last four centuries is now in a stage of transition, as much as it is a basically transitory force in the less industrialized societies where it has penetrated and dominated. What we are witnessing may be one of the turning points of human history: where one fundamental form of culture and society, that of industrialized nations and their modes of communication and information, is declining, and a different form is emerging.

Despite the terms used to describe this new era as "post-industrial" or the "information age," we still know little as to how the society and the international system might cope with the complexities of this new period. This means that the main issues of our time are not merely economic, political, and technological in nature, but are basically related to *culture* and *communication*. In the West – both capitalist and socialist – it is a crisis of sensate culture and communication in search of a new form and new pattern, being confronted with ever-increasing new technological and digitary information systems that contradict individual human needs and desires. In the less industrialized world, it is the confrontation between this collective sensate culture, economy, and policies, and an old ideational and idealistic form of native culture.

In the realm of technology and scientific discoveries, it is now clear that developments in communication technology such as satellites, computers, and video, during the last three decades, have far exceeded the ability of both policy makers and the academic community to deal effectively with such innovations. Numerous attempts have been made to label this new era, which differs significantly from the traditional telecommunications concept embodied in the work of several international organizations such as the International Telecommunications Union.[2] ITU, now over a century old, has dealt primarily with telephony, telegraphy, radio, and cable, and its inability to cope with issues evolving from new technology is evidenced in the somewhat unproductive bickering that has characterized some of its meetings in recent years.

This new technology differs also from the "classic" notion of mass media, the twentieth-century term that has come to represent primarily print media, radio, television, and cinema. As a result of technological development, all these individual aspects of the information and communication industries have combined to forge a new product with enormous potential for expansion into all aspects of daily life and significant implications for the economic market. Thus, the search for new labels to deal with this area has begun. Some of the most popular and widely used terms these days include "informatics," "telematics," "telesatcomputers," and "digital technology."

Concepts, in a subtle way, help shape the boundaries within which we examine a given object or phenomenon. In the communications field, conceptualization has become important in contemporary global society, not only by creating the image we hold of communication technology, but also by influencing the context within which we view the world and form ideas and policies. In short, concepts form the parameters within which we can operate. Furthermore, they act as a cause for rationalization and, ultimately, legitimization. Over a period of two decades or so, these concepts have become so thoroughly ingrained that they act as defenders of their own territories, not allowing new and possibly conflicting concepts to encroach upon their established domain.

The concept of mass media illustrates this tendency. A product of Western thought, the development of mass media coincided with the emergence of mass society through the growth of organizations that served to unite diverse elements into what is now considered mass culture in the industrialized countries. The industrialization of the West led to the inevitability of mass production and mass consumption, setting the stage for the concept of "mass society," which was so popular during the first half of this century among American and British sociologists.

This "Triple-M theory" – mass society, mass media, and mass culture – influenced what emerged as one of the dominant paradigms of societal organization. Mass society, essentially, is an industrial society. The division of labor has made its members more interdependent than before. In the Triple-M Theory, the triangle–circle of mass culture, mass media, and mass society is closed; the media of mass communication are the parents of mass culture, mass culture is the child of mass communication, mass media were born out of mass society. In its early days, the growth of mass culture, or what has been termed commodity culture by the critics of capitalism, led to strong dissident movements and wide appeal in the industrialized West for discrimination and taste. Elsewhere, the author has shown how the Triple-M Theory was confronted and contested by the political economy and technological deterministic theories in later years, and has offered an integrated theory of media and culture as an alternative.[3] Suffice it to say that the Triple-M Theory fell into disfavor as developing countries began to reject the conceptualizations that accompanied imported industrialization and technology.

As developing nations examined the domestic impact of communication technologies such as radio and television, it became apparent that the concept of mass communications and mass media, which had been openly accepted as prevailing components of all societies, were in fact inappropriate in many of these countries. This realization occurred slowly, over a period of 20 to 30 years, during which time developing countries attempted to employ the mass media as a means of organizing their populations into Western-style mass societies. Only in the 1960s, when student revolutions and political upheaval revealed weaknesses in Western societies and their assumptions, did the developing world begin to seek alternatives to "mass" development.

## Technology versus Tradition

These alternatives, patterned after Gandhi's India, Julius Nyerere's Tanzania, Mao Zedong's China, and Ayatollah Khomeini's Islamic Republic of Iran, took advantage of communications infrastructure already in existence: traditional channels such as large-scale community meetings, market places, mosques and bazaars.[4] These traditional channels have historically been ignored as identifiable areas worthy of classification and study. They are generally termed "oral," but the many variations in oral communications have not been determined. For instance, there is person-to-person communication, but some countries have also developed a traditional form of public communication that resembles the mass media. Without benefit of technology, this channel can reach as many people as a given newspaper. In studying these traditional channels, important potential uses will be identified and coordination between modern technology and traditional channels can be achieved. An example resulting from such a study was the integration of modern communication technology with the mosque in Iran for the purpose of education, dissemination of religious teachings, and political mobilization.[5]

The decline of conventional mass media as we know them in the 1960s and 1970s should hasten our examination of alternatives. In the 1980s and early 1990s, both in the United States and certain other industrialized countries, we have seen a rise of what might be called "class media" – specialized and individually tailored publications, radio stations, and movie houses, which can no longer claim to reach vast portions of the population as the term "mass" would imply. With the exception of television, we do not really have a medium that can reach large segments of the population even if we consider the so-called national publications. The tendency has been toward decentralization, with increased power to regional management. This tendency means that mass media, as we know them, are rapidly disappearing.

It is in this context that new technology has been developed and institutions such as the Intergovernmental Bureau of Informatics (IBI) have been established. These institutions tend to make free use of the term "informatics" without establishing its precise definition. In general, informatics refers to the convergence of computer and telecommunication technology, and "the emergence of a new complex of scientific, technological, and engineering disciplines and management techniques which makes it possible to deal with data and information in a more systematic manner," while remaining aware of the wider social, economic, and cultural contexts of information.[6] Several other catchwords have been coined in an attempt to conceptualize this multidisciplinary field, but the English "communications" and the French "telematique" are considered too awkward for universal acceptance. Thus, "informatics," from the French "informatique," currently seems to be the front runner in the competition.

A variety of definitions of informatics have been proposed in different countries. In the context of the IBI, informatics encompasses "the design, construction, evaluation, use, and maintenance of systems of information processing, including the hardware, software, organizational and human aspects, and their impact on industry, commerce, administration, and social and political life."[7] The IBI's official definition, somewhat more simplified, is: "Informatics is the rational and systematic application of information to economic, social and political problems."[8]

This new field is being influenced by two very different developments. The first is the emergence of microelectronic technology. Rapid development of microprocessors, coupled with broad-band communications, fiber optics, and other advances, is generating a new information technology.

The second aspect of informatics that has had an impact on the field is the realization of the need for coherent policy-making in this area. The 1978 SPIN Conference (Intergovernmental Conference on Strategies and Policies for Informatics), held in Torremolinos, Spain and attended by delegates from 78 countries, concluded that universal access to and implementation of informatics was essential. This tenet was affirmed unanimously, against a background of recognition that financial, labor, and infrastructural limitations exist today, and form the development gap.

The conference called for an exchange of experiences and information among countries at similar stages of informatics development; planning of educational and training programs for, and by, the use of informatics; and encouragement of scientific and technical research in the field of informatics. In all these endeavors, social, economic, and cultural conditions had to dictate the types of programs to be implemented. The conference did not mention traditional communications channels, but perhaps consideration of this area can be inferred from the references to social and cultural determinants.

The IBI has outlined seven principles that form its recommendation for a national informatics policy: (1) consideration of informatics in formulation of strategies and policies for national development; (2) special informatics authorities and agencies to coordinate effects; (3) more education and training programs to produce a labor force capable of utilizing the latest technology; (4) endogenous informatics production capability; (5) development of policies for the appropriate use of computer and telecommunications systems and services; (6) recognition of the need to preserve cultural traditions and control technology for the benefit of society; and (7) regional and international cooperation and interaction.

These principles sound very much like those that have been expounded time and again in the New World Information Order debates, and echo some of the findings of the MacBride Commission report. They are, understandably, somewhat idealistic and concentrate on the use of technology in solving the problems of inequality between developed and developing nations. Moreover, the question of whether informatics is advocating a communications policy or an information policy remains unclear. According to an IBI document, "[i]nformatics is not a philosophy nor a doctrine, but a methodology and a means to apply information power to real problems."[9] The basis of methodology is technology – electronic information-processing by computers. The combination has an added component when new communication modes such as teletext and videodata are considered: the technology of the mass media. This trend has resulted in use of the term "mass informatics," referring to applications such as electronic mail, electronic transfer of funds, computer-assisted instruction, and domestic informatics that brings computerization into the home.

The relationship between informatics and what has been termed the post-industrial information society needs to be examined. Although "information society" emphasizes the service sectors of the economy and the current phenomenon where over 50 percent of the labor force is employed in the sale of "information" of various types, "informatics" might ultimately prove to be a more useful adjective. At any rate, those in the forefront of the industry, particularly those involved in digital technology, would say that we have already entered the informatics society, thus taking into account not only the product but the means of transmission.

Cybernetics, the science of communication and control, is also related to the field of informatics, and the distinction between the two needs to be clarified. In studying the relationship between humans, machine, and society, cybernetics appears to overlap informatics. Like informatics, cybernetics deals with this relationship not only at the technological level, such as in military radar, but also on the societal level, such as in environmental issues. As a theoretical discipline, cybernetics has transcended the rapid technological changes in communications in this century: informatics, currently a futuristic term, could easily become outmoded in a decade.

## Communication Technology and National Development

What, then, can we say about the relation between national development and modern communication technology? The common assumption is that there is much the communication media and technologies could do to help the processes of development if the rulers and leaders of nations choose to seek the growth of that technology. Yet difficulties must be faced when the choice before them is a complex one. There is no convincing argument or model that places the development of the most modern technological hardware or software in the order of priorities in developmental needs. There is, indeed, a tendency to generalize the problems and situations of developing and even developed nations at the cost of a careful consideration of their diversity. The stage theories and classifications of communication revolution and their historical contexts are good analytical exercises, but cannot be applied in their pure form to the realities of contemporary societies. It is one thing to divide history neatly into such categories as pre-speech, speech, writing, printing, mass media, and telematic; but it is completely another to observe the functioning of these societies along the line of the combination of two or three, or even all.

Technology and informatics could easily be the dominant integrative cultural and epistemological paradigms in some societies, but no one can deny the sweeping forces of science, ideology, or mythology in the same societies. Electronic communication networks, centralized databases, and decentralized electronic cottage industries may dominate, but there will still exist trade unions, voluntary associations, churches, and temples.

Here, an attempt will be made to demonstrate that some analytical–historical–evolutionary stage of communication technology can guide our thinking; but only a whole integrative schema or model can best illustrate the complexities and contradictions of communication technology and society, and might give us a better picture of the dialectics of technology and development.

Historically, we can identify three major technological breakthroughs that have had profound impact in social, political, and economic aspects of human civilization. These three "revolutions' – the agricultural (1000 BC to the 1800s), the industrial (1800 to 1950), and the information (1960 to the present) – are now being discussed as the major stages in technological history. Each period was or is marked by significant changes in the definition of property and work. In the agricultural period, *land* was the most important measure of property and work. *Capital*, in the form of machinery and money, characterized the period of industrial growth. Today, *information* is emerging as the dominant power factor in the information or "post-industrial" age.[10]

No further steps will be taken here to emphasize these three distinct periods and establish further subcategories for each domain. What has been neglected in the discussion of this type of stage analysis is the fact that of all three – land, capital, and information – the last has had the longest and most pervasive impact throughout human history. Information in the form of skill and knowledge preceded capital formation, and in many ways characterizes all three stages. If we accept this assumption, it simply means that information and knowledge are not the exclusive property of industrialized societies, unless information and knowledge are defined in terms of the Western epistemological and philosophical context. An example is the amount of scientific information and knowledge produced in the Islamic world in such fields as medicine, mathematics, and astronomy, prior to the Industrial Revolution, not to mention the importance of communication, transportation, military operations, literature, and philosophy during the early civilizations of the Egyptians, the Chinese, and the Greeks. Information is the only thing that can grow and evolve, and the concept is the most important to any evolutionary and stage theory. The terms "information" and "knowledge" are used quite interchangeably. There exist, however, a number of definitions of the two terms that are extremely crucial to our discussion. For example, economist Joseph Hirschleifer defines information as "changes in belief distribution,"[11] which is somewhat in contrast with the definition given by information scientists who define information as "a measure of the freedom of choice in selecting a message."

In cybernetics, of course, information theory is one of the most important areas of discussion. Norbert Wiener, often cited as the founder of cybernetics theory, defines information as "the content of what is exchanged with the outer world as we adjust to it, and make our adjustments felt upon it."[12] He writes, "Information is information, not matter or energy. No materialism which does not admit this can be survived at the present day."[13] To Colin Cherry, "information content is not a commodity but rather a potential of signals." Thus, "information communicated will depend upon the choice of signals in any particular channel of communication with relation to the receiver's expectancies."[14] Others have defined information as "power" and industrial information as industrial or economic power. Kenneth Boulding defines information and knowledge as "that which reduces uncertainty."[15]

In the realm of philosophy we can find such writers as E. Wasmuth, who views "information as a time-relationship" or "that of continuous time-flow, or as a product of the two time relationships."[16] Another writer, G. Gunther, asserts "that information and communication processes are not just not material processes but also not mental phenomena."[17] These philosophical views are rejected by Marxist-Leninist writers as "idealist accounts" of information, since from the viewpoint of dialectical materialism there is only matter and its properties and products; there is neither a spiritual component nor any other metaphysical component of reality.[18] In short, this divergent opinion about information is related to the different ways of viewing information.

Thus a useful way to view the "post-industrial age" or the so-called "information age" is to see it as a tangible or "material" infrastructure being built into contemporary society. If we employ the concept of *infrastructure* we can then say that, historically, the earliest known infrastructure was the transportation infrastructure (i.e., roads, seaports, and mail). Energy, in the form of water, dams, electricity, and oil, was the second infrastructure, followed by printing, machinery, and eventually telecommunications as a third major technological infrastructure. We can then say that modern communication and information technologies, in the form of satellites, computers, and radar (or telematic/informatic), comprise the new infrastructure.

I have argued that the notion of "information" has been prevalent and equally vital in all historical stages in the past, and will remain so in the future. Therefore, it cannot be compared to such things as "land" and "capital" in describing the agricultural, industrial, and post-industrial periods of history. A major characteristic of the new infrastructure, or the post-industrial age, is its ability to produce *data*, and not necessarily information, in large quantities. Data production, processing, and distribution best characterize the technological development of our time. Information is different from data in that information is defined as a patterned distribution, or a patterned relationship between events.[19]

Knowledge production is defined broadly as "any human (or human-induced) activity effectively designed to create, alter, or confirm in a human mind – one's own or anyone else's – a meaningful apperception, awareness, cognizance, or consciousness of whatever it may be."[20] Here, the two major conceptual contributions made by economist Fritz Machlup, namely the distinction between (1) procedural (know-how and technology enabling one to perform action in a prescribed series of steps in order to obtain a desired result) and propositional knowledge (knowledge related to stated propositions) and (2) the treatment of knowledge as a manifestation of capital in order to integrate it into the larger economic paradigm and derive insights therefrom, are of considerable value in examining and understanding the key issues of today's international relations. Machlup expresses reservation about singling out a class of knowledge "under the heading 'scientific knowledge' or 'science'"[21] because the terms have meant and continue to mean different things depending on one's cultural and academic background. The position Machlup adopts vis-à-vis "truth" or veracity of knowledge is that "for much of knowledge (in the weak and wide sense) produced (acquired, disseminated) in our society, the requirements of verifiability or falsifiability would be quite unmanageable."[22]

It is as unrealistic to describe the characteristics of a given society or system as a pure end product of the unilinear development of a single historical period of human civilization or technological innovation as it is to ignore that tradition entirely. Rather, one might conceive of the communication system of a given country as a hybrid born of multifarious scientific and technological, as well as social, traditions, at various times betraying the influence of one or the other, or a combination of the traditions. This point is especially crucial if we consider other layers of human infrastructure in the form of culture, religion, government, and bureaucracy, without which societal communication cannot take place.

## A Conceptual Framework for Theory and Policy

Although we have seen a progression of policy research and a rise in the number of national communication policies during the last two decades, writings on communication strategy and planning as they relate to development remain somewhat fragmented, simplistic, bureaucratic, and market-oriented. Upon examination of both the literature and institutions dealing with communication policy and planning, the following different research approaches have been identified:

1. long-range planning with policy goals toward equitable distribution of communication power in a society's future;
2. comprehensive planning examining all aspects of a communication system within the broader sociopolitical framework of society;
3. development support communication designed to encourage the participation of beneficiaries in a project and to ensure its execution and success;
4. technology transfer and assessment, especially innovations in such areas as satellite communication, cable television, and telecom–computer linkups;

5. control and regulations and their legal and institutional consequences;
6. normative and goal-oriented approaches in which the information program policy plays an active role in broadening the political and cultural views of the people through alternative and critical programs;
7. information economics, determining the information sector of the economy's contribution to overall economic growth; and
8. an integrated approach toward a unified comprehensive methodology.

Traditionally, technological and institutional approaches to communication policy and planning have predominated. In other words, most writings, research, and prescriptions on communication policy and planning focus on those areas that are technologically mediated or institutionally arranged. The two approaches overlap somewhat, despite their general and specific distinctions.

Both technological and institutional approaches require that development planners work with existing resources or with those that can be realistically created within financial and time constraints. The availability and assessment of resources naturally become critical components of the planning process and involve identification and evaluation as well as assessment of distribution and potential distribution or extension of resources. Communication resources available to both approaches can be grouped into three categories: (1) traditional communication and interpersonal interactions; (2) conventional mass media and telecommunications; and (3) high technology and space applications.

The technology-mediated focus contents that international telecommunications is vital to progress in the developing countries. It maintains that since the modern world's technical and scientific culture is global, any country that cuts itself off from the electronic flow of knowledge in that global enterprise risks incurring information isolation and economic underdevelopment. The institutionally arranged focus, on the other hand, acknowledges that research and planning in communication and development is indeed a complex task and that the analyst must maintain a broad view of communication as a part of the larger development system, while at the same time focusing on the communication system itself and the relationship of its component parts. The central assumption of the institutional approach, in other words, is that communication planning for development is initiated on the premise that change is needed. Thus, institutional frameworks are intended for the practical use of planners and decision makers.

Recently, new contributions in development planning have been significant, among these the application of planning and management to development efforts. It is important here to take note of some of the most recent diagnoses of communication policies and planning as they apply to the developing countries. It increasingly is recognized that there is a need first to link communication development with overall development, through the formulation of national communication policies that reflect demo-

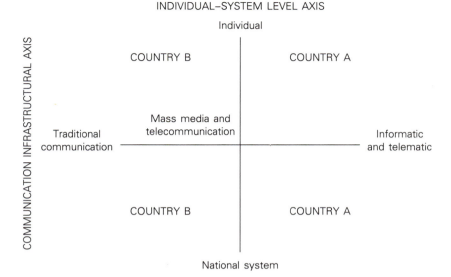

INDIVIDUAL–SYSTEM LEVEL AXIS

Individual

COUNTRY B    COUNTRY A

Mass media and
Traditional    telecommunication                    Informatic
communication                                        and telematic

COUNTRY B    COUNTRY A

National system

Figure 9.1 *Multidimensional and integrative approach to communication utility*

graphic imperatives, and, second, to develop an endogenous approach to development that simultaneously acknowledges opportunities as well as dangers in the extranational environment.

How and to what extent can technological and information media categories be "plugged into" contemporary theory and policy phenomena? So specific, multidimensional, and far reaching are these factors that to strictly relate the entire societal development, top to bottom, to the characterization of a country or a communication system will probably jeopardize the credibility of making the association in the first place. At the same time, it is valuable and necessary to employ a consideration of this body of stage theories as a backdrop for communications and media phenomena rather than viewing the latter as a complete crystallization of the former. The connection of different societies and different countries or systems to different aspects of communication technology is diffuse rather than direct. Thus, as illustrated in Figure 9.1, a given society or a country on both individual and nation-stage levels may reflect the feature of any combination of traditions of communication systems and technology, and some may be stronger and more dominant than others at any time and at any level (individual or nation-state), depending on social, cultural, political, and economic conditions.

These three stages of communication development – traditional, conventional mass media, and futuristic informatics – can be found in varying degrees in most societies today. Often in developing countries, however, the gap between the communications channels used by the society or nation-

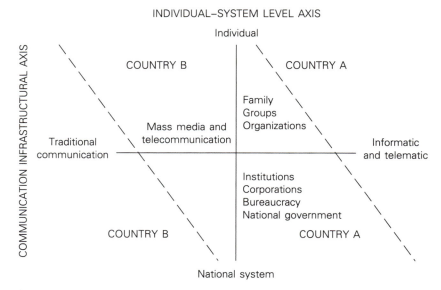

Figure 9.2     *Multidimensional and integrative approach to communication utility*

state and individuals within that society is enormous. For this reason, a continuum of stages is best depicted as four quadrants (see Figure 9.2) with a separation between individual and national (or established system) levels on the vertical, individual–system level axis, and between traditional communication, mass media and telecommunications, and informatic and telematic levels on the horizontal communication infrastructural axis.

Thus, American society, where individuals are generally as preoccupied with high information technology now readily available as the national system as a whole, would fit in the two right-hand quadrants. Even in the United States, however, isolated rural societies such as those found in Appalachia still rely on the local store and Sunday visiting as a source of news and information, despite widespread television ownership. Market places in rural Iowa or North Carolina and town meetings in New England are all examples of traditional channels of communication, as are the pubs in Britain, in spite of the use of advanced communications technologies at the national level. These individual cases could appear in the upper left quadrant somewhere between traditional and mass media. The significant aspect, in the case of both the United States and Britain, is that there is a level of homeostasis between the utilization of communication technologies on individual and national levels. In short, there is coordination and harmony between the system's adoption of information technologies and the individual's utilization of these technologies.

In many countries, such as oil-rich Nigeria, Venezuela, and Saudi Arabia, the polarity between individuals and the national system is, of course, much more striking as the national communication policies tend to move toward the direction of high technologies while the individuals remain in the realm of traditional or semi-traditional communication and information systems. In this example, the two points would be diagonally opposite on the graph, the individual's utility of information technology remaining in the traditional sector while the national system moves to the opposite sector, signifying the chasm between urban "sophistication" in major cities and the concerns of the average rural dweller. Thus, contradictions and polarity gaps in national communication policies become a major social, political, and economic problem.

The development of specific industries and services can be plotted along this graph as well. The airline industry, for instance, has moved steadily along the continuum from left to right, as has the banking system, a result of the computerization that now characterizes those enterprises.

The horizontal axis is the communication infrastructural system that a country utilizes. The vertical axis represents the actors. In Figure 9.2, a spectrum-like axis has been employed, as it is on the horizontal axis in Figure 9.1, to show the range of actors or users – from individuals to institutions and organizations to national systems.

Given these varying degrees of utilization, it would then be possible to consider a country like the United States on this diagram in a different manner. In this example, one can see that the further down the vertical axis an entity is, the more toward technological exposure of communication it will be. The lower portion of the vertical axis would be further to the right than the upper portion because the national systems are ahead of consumers with regard to technology use. The information flow in pre-revolutionary Iran clearly showed the conflict between the official communication and culture of the government and the traditional communication and culture of the masses rooted in Iranian national and religious tradition. Nowhere is this conflict better illustrated than in the structure and use of the means of communication at the disposal of both cultures. In contrast to the modern media and high technology were the traditional institutions by which the people obtained their information, and through which the revolution was accomplished. In this case, the individuals were to the far left of the diagram, while the national governmental system was at a much more distant right.

This is in contrast to the process in developing countries, in which a gap is created because the development of one sector, such as the national level, is conducted at the expense of the other institutional or individual sectors. For example, the introduction of personal computers (PCs) in the United States and Europe and the methods used in their rapid diffusion are classic examples of the integrative nature of the marketing techniques used by the multinational and other producers. Within a short span following the introduction of PCs in these areas, a high degree of diffusion of knowledge of and reliance on the systems was achieved, for example, among local and national bureaucracies, office workers, students, bank executives, and military personnel. Indeed, by providing, free of charge, hardware and software as well as time, especially to individuals and educational institutions, the producers and manufacturers of PCs were able to recruit as well as train enough "person power" to make their future market operative and more profitable. The cost of operations and maintenance of the communication hardware is facilitated once the public and institutional wealth of customers is recruited successfully into the system.

Thus the graph serves as a conceptual framework for communications development in which all channels of communication are represented and given equal weight. Abandoning the earlier assumptions that viewed development as necessarily industrial and Western, the traditional end of the continuum is given equal emphasis in realistic acknowledgement of its ongoing importance in most of the world. Here, we are not restricted to certain technology-driven conceptualizations. A given communication system in a given society may reflect the features of any combination of traditions, and some may be "stronger" than others at any given time, depending on social conditions.

**Implications for National and International Communication Policy**

Ideally, the first step in policy formation should be a precise definition of such concepts as "informatic" and "telematic." Although numerous definitions have been offered, a distinction must be made between informatics and the other areas which it overlaps. Only when informatics can stand alone as a separate field, or at least indicate specific stages of activities, will the terminology prove useful. As long as words like telematics, telecommunications, and cybernetics are widely used, there is bound to be confusion in the field.

The definition should also clarify exactly what is being transmitted electronically. Informatics implies that information is being transferred, and information differs significantly from the streams of uninterpreted data bits that travel from computer to computer via the telephone line. Only when information and communication policies are distinguished from informatics policy will the term be useful.

It is possible that informatics will replace other popular terminology if these preconditions are met. There is a serious need for standardization in the informatics field, not only in technical and engineering areas but in the theoretical area as well. Twenty years ago, telecommunications was an acceptable term to use, and most specialists in the field knew what was meant. In today's rapidly changing climate, however, precision in language is all important, as language shapes our ability to think and conceptualize. Therefore, it is imperative that terms not be created ad hoc, without deliberation. Once terminology comes into vogue, we become prisoners of that terminology, and our ability to move beyond is severely hampered. Images are created based on that name, especially as they relate to software, with all the political, cultural, and economic implications involved. Thus, even as the new informatics age is heralded as the latest technological achievement, some thoughtful consideration should be given to the ramifications of this achievement, and perhaps some planning for the future could benefit a world now inured to the constant assaults of technological revolution.

Such are the conditions without which the failure in designing a meaningful communication policy cannot be stopped and the tragedy of transition alleviated. There is no doubt that the realization of these factors is infinitely more difficult than the application of the superficial measures of economic, technological, or other "readjustments." Our remedy demands a fundamental transformation and change in our level of conceptualization and viewing communication and information flows as an integrative whole.

## Conclusion

Viewing the communication process as an integrated whole challenges the technological determinism that underlined much communication policy and planning of the 1970s. Aspects of this integrated approach have been emphasized by a number of scholars and planners in the 1980s and 1990s. This view considers the importance of modern technological innovation in terms of developmental objectives and communication needs and the distribution of political, cultural, and economic benefits to society. The process of aligning different societies, countries, or systems with various aspects of communication technology is a diffuse one.

Thus, a given society or country on both individual and national levels may reflect features of any combination of traditions of communication systems and technology, and some may be stronger and more dominant than others depending on social, cultural, political, and economic conditions. In this regard, this chapter, although general, hopefully can be a guideline for a much broader perspective on communication and policy with application to telecommunications or other communication-oriented projects. Such a remedy demands a fundamental transformation and change in our level of conceptualization toward viewing communication policy and planning as an integrative, holistic process.

## Notes

1. Some of the works in this area include: Jacques Ellul, *The Technological Society* (New York: Vintage Books, 1964); Oswald H. Ganley and Gladys D. Ganley, *To Inform or to Control: The New Communication Network* (New York: McGraw Hill, 1982); Alvin W. Gouldner, *Dialectic of Ideology and Technology* (New York: Macmillan, 1976); Youeji Masuda, *Information Society as Post-Industrial Society* (Tokyo: Institute for Information Society, 1980); Marc Porat, *The Information Economy* (Washington, DC: US Office of Telecommunications, 1977); Theodore Roszak, *Where the Wasteland Ends: Politics and Transcendence in Post-Industrial Society* (New York: Doubleday, 1972); Herbert Schiller, *Who*

*Knows: Information in the Age of the Fortune 500* (Norwood, NJ: Ablex Publishing Corporation, 1981); Wilson Dizard, *The Coming of the Information Age* (White Plains, NY: Longman, 1982); Norbert Wiener, *The Human use of Human Beings: Cybernetics and Society* (New York: Avon Books, 1967); Daniel Bell, *The Coming of Post-Industrial Society* (New York: Basic Books, 1973); Colin Cherry, *World Communication: Threat or Promise?* (London: John Wiley-Interscience, 1971), and *Technological Man: The Myth and the Reality* (New York: Mentor Books New American Library, 1969; and Kathleen Woodward, *The Myths of Information: Technology and Post-Industrial Culture* (Madison, WI: Coda Press, 1980).

2. An example is a symposium "The 'New Technology': Who Sells It? Who Needs It? Who Rules It?" published in *Journal of Communication*, 32: 4 (Autumn 1982), pp. 55–178.

3. Hamid Mowlana, "Mass Media and Culture: Toward An Integrated Theory" in William Gudykunst, ed., *Intercultural Communication Theory: Current Perspectives* (Beverly Hills, CA: Sage Publications, 1983), pp. 149–170.

4. See Julius K. Nyerere, *Ujamaa: Essays on Socialism* (Dar es Salaam: Oxford University Press, 1968). See also Kusum J. Singh, "Gandhi and Mao as Mass Communicators"; Asghar Fathi, "The Role of the Islamic Pulpit"; and Hamid Mowlana, "Technology versus Tradition: Communication in the Iranian Revolution"; all published in *Journal of Communication*, 29: 3 (Summer 1979), pp. 94–112.

5. Hamid Mowlana, "Technology Versus Tradition: Communication in the Iranian Revolution," *Journal of Communication*, 29: 3 (Summer 1979), pp. 107–112.

6. "Informatics and Development," *Intermedia*, 7: 1 (January 1979), p. 1.

7. Edward Ploman, "The Need for Informatics," *Intermedia*, 7: 1 (January 1979), p. 11.

8. F.A. Bernasconi, "Informatics, the IBI and SPIN," *Intermedia*, 7: 1 (January 1979), p. 12.

9. "Informatics and Development," *Intermedia*, 7: 1 (January 1979), p. 14.

10. See Bell, *The Coming of Post-Industrial Society*. For a discussion on information in the process of transfer of technology, see Hamid Mowlana, "The Multinational Corporations and the Diffusion of Technology," in Abdul A. Said and Luiz R. Simmons, eds, *The New Sovereigns: Multinational Corporations as World Powers* (Englewood Cliffs, NJ: Prentice Hall, 1975), pp. 77–90.

11. Joseph Hirshleifer, "Where Are We in the Theory of Information?" *American Economic Review*, 63: 2 (May 1973), p. 31.

12. Norbert Wiener, *The Human Use of Human Beings*, pp. 26–27.

13. Wiener, *Cybernetics, or Control and Communication in the Animal and the Machine*, new edn (Cambridge, MA: MIT Press, 1961), p. 132.

14. Colin Cherry, *On Human Communication* (Cambridge, MA: MIT Press, 1957), p. 13.

15. Kenneth Boulding, *The Image* (Ann Arbor, MI: University of Michigan Press, 1956), p. 1.

16. As quoted in Peter Paul Kirschenmann, *Information and Reflection: On Some Problems of Cybernetics and How Contemporary Dialectical Materialism Copes with Them* (Dordrecht: D. Reidel, 1970), p. 6. For the original work see E. Wasmuch, *Der Mensch und die Denkmaschine* (Man and the Thinking Machine) (Cologne: Olten, 1955).

17. Quoted in Wasmuth, *Der Mensch*, p. 7. For the original work see G. Gunther, *Das Bewusstsein der Maschinen – Eine Metaphysik der Kybernetik* (The Consciousness of Machines: The Metaphysics of Cybernetics) (Krefeld: Baden-Baden, 1963).

18. Wasmuth, *Der Mensch*, pp. 9–17, 94–105.

19. See, for example, Karl W. Deutsch, *The Nerves of Government: Models of Political Communication and Control* (New York: Free Press, 1963).

20. Fritz Machlup, *Knowledge: Its Creation, Distribution and Economic Significance*, Vol. I: *Knowledge and Knowledge Production* (Princeton, NJ: Princeton University Press, 1980), p. 186.

21. Ibid., p. 62.

22. Ibid., p. 117.

# 10
# Communication and Development: The Emerging Orders

Is there a communication of development? The term "development" as an all-encompassing concept referring to such widely different processes as "modernization," "Westernization," "Europeanization," "industrialization," "economic growth," "political change," "nation building," and a score of other economic, political, social and cultural activities and changes was not used extensively in the literature until the end of World War II. Yet, for over half a century prior to the outbreak of war, the relationship between communication as a social process and communications as a means and technology of the modern age was studied in the context of such specific phenomena as revolution, reform, economic growth, democracy, and political mobilization as well as education, literacy and cultural activities. Experiments and studies were implemented not only in the highly industrialized countries of the West but also in a number of less industrialized and agricultural economies such as the Soviet Union, Japan, Egypt, Iran, Turkey and Mexico. One important characteristic of this period was the clear-cut relation hypothesized between a given communication technology (and medium) and a specific "developmental" goal. Thus the role of the press as an organizer, an agitator, and propagandist was recognized, as was its place in the democratization, surveillance, and cultural transformations of societies and nations The central role of telecommunications – specifically the telephone, telegraph, and submarine cables – in economic growth and trade was recognized, and attention was given to the role of the press in urban development and the role of radio in agricultural and rural extension services.

The widespread use of "development" as a conceptual framework for a number of individual, institutional, national and international changes as well as for "progress," is a post-World War II phenomenon. In the 1940s and especially in the 1950s and 1960s, the term "development" became synonymous with growth, modernization, change, democracy, productivity, industrialization, and other related Western historical and evolutionary changes. Popularized first by (and among) the American scholars and policy makers, and soon introduced to Europe and especially the less industrialized countries of the world, the term "development" became a major issue in international organizations, despite its ill-defined and less than universally recognized meaning. The term was popular, especially among American scholars and policy makers, for several reasons.

1. The United States was the hegemonic world power at the end of World War II, and its government attempted to transform defeated countries as well as emerging non-Western and less industrialized countries of Asia, Latin America, and Africa into "Western-style" democracies through peaceful means and gradual reforms and reconstructions. Thus, "development" in both Western and non-Western societies was perceived as a gradual but multi-stage evolution rather than as a revolutionary process. In short, development meant the incorporation of less industrialized countries into the dominant model of the capitalist economic and social system.

2. Through the Marshall Plan to assist Western European reconstruction; the Truman Doctrine's Four Point program of economic and technical assistance to countries such as Greece, Iran and Turkey; the increase in the amount of US foreign aid to a number of countries on the path of "modernization" such as Pakistan, Thailand and South Korea; and the subsequent establishment of the US Agency for International Development (USAID), with its various programs and activities, the term development acquired a special meaning from the viewpoint of the United States as donor and a number of countries as recipients.

3. The establishment of the United Nations system and its affiliated agencies involved with aspects of national, regional and international activities of an economic, monetary, financial technical, educational, scientific, cultural and political nature further helped to enhance the concept of development, especially in the context of the political and economic modernization and growth of less industrialized countries and emerging nations. The 1950s and 1960s became known as the decades of development, when many countries in Africa, Asia, and Latin America, after years of struggle for independence and decolonization, were within reach of developmental models that they envisioned would improve their standards of living, establish economic and political infrastructure, and help them join the community of nations as participant and equal partners.

4. Finally, the keen interest of the United States and the Soviet Union during the Cold War and later of Europe in the study of non-Western societies under the rubric of "developing" countries was largely responsible not only for the further popularity of the term "development" but also for its conceptual and methodological growth.

Thus, development, both as a process and as a concept referring to several specific evolutionary phenomena, was used after World War II to describe two broad themes: (1) modernization, nationalism and political development; and (2) economic development and technological diffusion.

## Theoretical and Methodological Problems and Prospects

During the 1950s and 1960s, modernization, nationalism, and political development were the dominant approaches to development and nation building, especially among political scientists, sociologists, and social psychologists in the United States. The series initiated under the leadership of Gabriel Almond and sponsored by the Committee on Comparative Politics of the Social Science Research Council at Princeton University first began to compile cross-cultural data necessary for a discussion of modernization and political development.

Working within this paradigm, Lucian Pye, Ithiel de Sola Pool, Frederick Frey, and Richard Fagen perceived communications as a key function common to all political systems. Here the literature on political development and modernization tended to distinguish political from economic development. The writers emphasized the importance of Western democracy as well as institution building and citizen participation. The emphasis was on formal institutional channels of politics, mostly along the lines of parliamentary democracy. Multi-party systems, secularization, and the sovereignty of the nation-state system were strongly advocated and supported. Political development was viewed primarily as a process of national integration, as movement from less to more national unity.

Associated with this theory were two problems: the necessity to link previously autonomous units to each other and the requirements to bridge the gap between national elites and others in the same system. Political development also meant extending central and communication networks into and across previously isolated sectors of the society. Modernization, the political development process, involved increased structural differentiation in the political system, movement away from ascription criteria and toward achievement criteria in political recruitment and evaluation, a widening of the effective scope of political activity and increased secularization and "rationalizations."

However, by the end of the 1970s, these models of modernization and political development were being challenged not only on the theoretical but also on empirical and practical levels. The Islamic revolution in Iran and other developments in Asia, Africa and Latin America had sent shock waves through the regions and the world. Islam on the move became a worry for the West – that is, the United States and Europe. A decade later the disintegration of the Soviet Union and Yugoslavia, the developments in Eastern Europe and Germany's reunification were accompanied by Islam's return to the scene of history and its ability to mobilize its adherents from Algeria to Kashmir and Central Asia.

What went wrong with these development theories? Why did the theorists of modernization neither prophesy nor delineate the communication, political and cultural landscapes that prevail today? Was this because they paid too much heed to those elements in modern life which characterize formal institutions and formal ideologies? Or did they simply misconstrue the process of social change taking place in our time? Were they misled by their cultural bias and the pattern of discourse which had dominated their social interactions? How critical were their "critical" methodologies?

In the optimism of the development decades, it was believed that the increases in information made possible through broadcasting and print technologies would pull the "developing" countries up to the level of their neighbors to the north. Their theories rested on the hypothesis that individual behavior changes, brought about by the messages of the mass media, and mediated by opinion leaders and literacy, would produce a modern political and economic actor. This actor would plant the right types of seed, use credit efficiently, voice political views and demands through the appropriate channels, and organize the institutions needed to push traditional societies over the threshold of modernity and into the twentieth century.

During the post-World War II period and especially in the 1950s and 1960s, from an economic and technological perspective development was viewed as synonymous with economic growth measured in aggregate terms – a perspective that still has many adherents today. Here, the major deficit of national development or societal development is seen to be a deficit of economic resources. The "classical" school of development (Adam Smith, Thomas Malthus, John Stuart Mill, David Ricardo) focused its attention on economic growth. Total economic output was seen as dependent on the size of the labor force, the supply of land, the stock of capital, the proportions in which these factors of production were combined, and the level of technology.

The strategy of direct economic investment in developing countries to increase their rate of economic growth predominated in the years following the war. This thesis, which became the backbone of the Marshall Plan and related programs of the United States, was the basis of much of the economic aid flowing from developed to developing countries from the 1950s onwards.

One of the most influential views of development was Rostow's theory of economic growth, which identified five stages: (1) traditional society; (2) precondition for take-off, in which certain requisites were fulfilled; (3) take-off; (4) drive and climb to maturity; and finally, (5) high levels of mass consumption. This model was based on the belief that a steady increase in per capita income, especially during the take-off stage, through the mechanism of savings and investment and the emergence of a political and social framework capable of exploiting the impulses to expansion, would underline the drive to maturity, resulting in development.

The dominant liberal/capitalist model of development comprises the following four main elements: (1) economic growth through industrialization and accompanying urbanization; (2) capital-intensive technology mainly imported from the more developed nations; (3) centralized planning, mainly by economists and financial experts, to guide and speed up the process of development; and (4) assertion that the causes of underdevelopment are mainly within developing countries themselves. The implication for the role of communications in this model was obvious: to transfer technological innovations from industrially developed countries and agencies to their clients and to create an appetite for change by raising a "climate for modernization" among the public in the industrially less developed nations. The classical diffusion models of communication as well as the orthodox theories of communication and modernization were compatible with this development model.

However, as we entered the last decades of the twentieth century the core areas of that liberal/capitalist model, mainly the United States and a number of European countries, were in deep financial and economic crises. According to the US Labor Department, nearly a generation after US technology companies unleashed a new wave of computers, telecommunications gear and electronic equipment, high-tech communication machines were cutting productivity in the US service industry.[1]

Indeed, during the 1980s, the average rate of growth in the productivity information and service industries was far below what it was before the advent of the computer technology in the early 1970s. By the early 1990s, unemployment and a major economic recession were in full swing in the USA – witness 1991's unprecedented bank mergers, deregulations, airline failures and consolidations in retailing, advertising, and telecommunications. The burden of recession had shifted to the white-collar workforce, mainly the 60 percent of the workforce employed in information and service industries. Blue-collar workers were also hurt, but they had been accustomed to harsh economic reversals since the 1950s.

The economic and development communication models in the socialist countries of Eastern Europe and the Soviet Union were even more disastrous. The centrally, state-run economic and communication sectors, combined with inefficient bureaucracy and heavy investment in the defense sector, had produced a largely corrupt elite hierarchy with little legitimacy for survival. In short, the dominant capitalist and socialist models were no longer the "ideals" by the end of the 1980s.

## From Modernization to Postmodernity and Beyond

Three categories of writing or approaches have dominated the paradigm of communication and development since the 1950s. The first approach is to view communication and development as a cause–effect relationship. The second approach deals primarily with what might be called cost–benefit analysis or utilitarianism. The third approach deals primarily with infrastructural analysis. Here, political economy, cultural identity, and value system are linked with communication and development by examining the structure of existing communication, economic, political, and cultural systems at all levels: national, international, and global.

Classical and neo-classical economic thinkers saw communication as a necessary factor for economic development and growth. In the United States various causal models correspond roughly to this theoretical perspective, including the works of Daniel Lerner,[2] and theoreticians associated with the school of modernization. Often, these models were stage theories such as those proposed by Walter Rostow.

Lerner's causal model suggested a sequence of institutional developments leading to self-sustaining growth and modernization: urbanization, literacy, extension of the mass media, higher per capita income and political participation. Lerner contended that growth in one of these areas listed sequentially stimulates growth in the others, and that the process moves society toward modernization. He maintained that a society must develop empathy – the ability of a person to imagine significant positive change in his or her own status – in order to proceed to modernity. In explaining an individual's progression from traditional, to transitional, to a modern way of life, Lerner advanced the notion that modernization in developing societies will follow the historical model of Western development. The key factors to modernization are physical, social, and psychological mobilities, which express themselves in the concept of empathy. The entire process is facilitated by the mass media, which act as an agent and index of change.

Lerner used a communication framework to characterize the traditional/modern difference. Modern society to him was the "media system." Within the media system, the channel of communication is the "broadcast," the audience is "heterogeneous" (mass), the content of the message is "descriptive" (news), and the source is "professional" (skilled). In the oral system, the channel is the person, the audience is "primary" (small group), the content is "prescriptive" (rules), and the source is "hierarchical" (status-oriented).

According to the model of modernization, the change from traditional to transitional and then to modern society was always accompanied by a change from oral communication systems to mass communication systems. The change was always unidirectional. The difference between the two systems, according to Lerner, was that traditional interpersonal communication enforces traditional attitudes and mores, whereas mass communication teaches new skills, attitudes, and behavior. Mass media are therefore a "mobility multiplier" that has the capacity to communicate both the character and the possibility of change to a growing audience. Lerner asserts that an interactive relationship exists between the media index of modernization and other social institutions. The closest correlational growth of organization and literacy happens after take-off at 10 percent urbanization and ends at 25 percent urbanization. After this point, literacy growth correlates most highly with mass media growth.

Lerner's proposition that access to mass media is a precondition for participation in modern society and that mass media directly affect personal attitudes and behavior has been questioned not only by critics of the orthodox models of development but also by the proponents of communications and development. For example, Lucian Pye[3] asserted that all aspects of communication rather than the mass media by themselves are important agents of political participation, while Ithiel de Sola Pool[4] was skeptical about whether the media have the same direct effect on changes in attitudes and skills.

Another area of contention was Lerner's correlation growth hypothesis. Seymour Martin Lipset,[5] who used a similar model in his study of political participation, was among the early writers of modernization who cautioned that the functional interdependence of urbanization, literacy, media exposure, and political participation may not be as well established as Lerner's data showed.

Some studies on mass media exposure and modernization partially confirmed Lerner's correlation hypothesis. Others could not verify the basic chain of interaction in which urbanization, literacy, media participation and political participation increased in direct relationship to one another. For example, Wilbur, Schramm and W. Lee Ruggles[6] concluded that by 1961 urbanization was no longer as basic to the growth of literacy and mass media as Lerner had assumed several years earlier. Their suggestion was that the spread of modern electronic technology (especially radio), coupled with rods and rapid transportation into villages, had made urbanization less essential to the process of development and the general growth in education. It was found that the monotonic relationship of growth stopped at substantially lower levels of urbanization than those proposed by Lerner.

Examples of causal models dealing with communication and development on the individual level include those of David C. McClelland.[7] McClelland's work examined the relationship between personality and innovational activity. McClelland measured the degree of achievement motivation present in various countries at various periods in history and correlated it with economic advances in those countries. He concluded that the need for achievement, which he equated with entrepreneurial activity, is key to economic growth not only in Western capitalist countries but also in economies controlled and fostered largely by the state. Socialization and communication in the early stage of life play a crucial role in the formation of a need for achievement.

This second set of approaches to communication and development contains divergent themes that can be classified as: diffusion models; mobilization theories; technological assessments and transfer theories; development communication approaches; and general systems approaches and analyses.

The communication-development models such as those of Lerner – founded primarily in economic realization – found their social realization counterpart in the work of Everett Rogers.[8] Rogers defined the role of communication as providing the channels for passage of development information, and he proposed that since mass communication exists in advanced societies, developing countries should consider these same infrastructural ideas in their societies.

The diffusion model, one of the dominant approaches to the role of communication in development, reached the pinnacle of its popularity in the 1960s partially through the publication of the work of Rogers and his associates and the execution of numerous projects by the US Agency for International Development, testing diffusion models in Latin America, Asia, and Africa. These theories are still prevalent today in much of the communications and development programs in areas like health promotion. At the most abstract level diffusion research is an approach to understanding the process of social change. Social change, the process by which alternation occurs in the structure and function of a social system, may, in Rogers' view, be either immanent change – stimulated from within a social system – or contact change – the result of external stimulus. Change can be understood as a process of three sequential stages: invention, the process by which new ideas are increased or developed; diffusion, the process by which these new ideas are communicated to the members of a given social system; and consequences, the changes that occur within the social system as a result of the adoption or rejection of the innovation. Social change is seen as an effect of communications, and diffusion research is regarded as a subset of communication research dealing with the transfer of ideas.

The emergence of diffusion research since the 1950s as a single integrated body of concepts and generalizations was facilitated by its application to a variety of developmental ideas. The earliest of these traditions of diffusion research was rooted in anthropology, where diffusion explained change in one society as a result of the introduction of ideas and technologies from another. Sociologists were also concerned with diffusion. The French sociologist Gabriel Torde, for example, at the beginning of this century, suggested that the adoption of new ideas can be a S-shaped curve. A small number of individuals initially adopt the innovation, followed by a rapid rate of adoption, and then a diminution as the last member of the system finally adopts. Some of the classic studies were conducted in the field of rural sociology, dating from the study conducted by the US Department of Agriculture in the 1920s of campaigns to introduce new agricultural practices. In the 1940s, studies, for example, of the diffusion of hybrid seed corn, investigating the social characteristics of innovators and the functions of various communication channels in the innovation-decision-making process, were common. The fields of education, marketing, journalism, and medical sociology have produced diffusion research that seeks to understand the pattern and pace by which new ideas are diffused within and among the different strata of society.

There are hidden assumptions in the communication and diffusion model: the idea that communication by itself can generate development regardless of socio-economic and political conditions; the idea that increased production and consumption of goods and services represents the essence of development and that a fair distribution will follow in time; and the idea that the key to increased productivity is technological innovation, no matter who benefits or who is harmed.

New diffusionists, who are now among the critics of the orthodox theories of diffusion, have admitted flaws in diffusion theory, modernization theory, and the traditional communication models that carry their imprint. Yet, a close scrutiny of recent writings shows that, although critical of the pitfalls of past experience, they are basically loyal to the underlying tenets of the dominant paradigm of both communication and development. In the last two decades, the research and interest in the area of development communication and the use of different communication strategies and technologies for developmental programs have increased considerably. Countries and communities throughout the world face the interrelated problems of deciding how best to use modern technology while minimizing any negative impact on indigenous cultures. Although it has been demonstrated that the various forms of mass media have considerable potential for use in developing countries, traditional forms and channels of communication and their integration with modern communication systems have been found to be most effective in generating desired results with minimal negative impacts.

Communication and diffusion research in the United States had found mass media channels to be relatively more important in the information and "knowledge" function, whereas interpersonal channels were relatively more important in the persuasion function of the decision-making process in general and in the innovation–decision-making process in particular.[9] Two "important" concepts were identified by these studies: the "two-step flow" of mass communication ideas and the "opinion leadership" notion, in which the flow of information in the first step was from source to opinion leaders and in the second step from opinion leaders to their followers.[10] This discovery, though negating some of the earlier notions of direct influence of mass media messages on the public, was hardly a new finding for non-Western and less industrially developed countries, where modern mass media systems were not yet dominant. Nevertheless, because the development of these societies along prescribed Western lines required the spread of modern mass media technologies, for some time, especially in the 1950s and 1960s, the two-step flow notion was replicated in the developmental projects in the poorer countries, with emphasis given to the spread of centralized communication technologies. It was only in the 1970s as a result of changes in the political, economic and social systems of many developing countries, that the function and role of traditional communication systems (such as religious meeting places and marketplaces) as independent and fully integrated systems of their own were realized.

The structural approach to development and communication examines the infrastructure of the world communication system to determine whether it impedes or promotes development on all levels. Positions taken by countries of Asia, Africa, and Latin America in the debate over a New World Information/Communication Order are based on this approach. The structural approach or infrastructural analysis of communication and development is relatively new compared with the literature on causal and utilitarian approaches. It covers the traditional political economy approach to communication as well as works dealing with the social and cultural dimensions of communication systems, on both national and international levels. The area is grounded in economics, political science, and sociology, and contributors to it come from a variety of epistemological and methodological schools. Although many studies in the area are primarily oriented toward political economy theories, a substantial portion of the work, especially in the 1980s and 1990s, has been carried out by structural/ cultural theorists whose views of development most approximate monistic/ emancipatory models.

Examples of research and writings in this area include: Dallas Smythe's[11] work on communication, capitalism, and dependency; Herbert Schiller's[12] critical examination of the structure of the American communication system from political and economic perspectives; Armand Matellart's[13] research on the role of transnational actors and culture industries, my[14] analysis of the international flow of information and my integrative approach to communication and developmental processes; Cees Hamelink's[15] writings on self-reliance, cultural autonomy, and national and international communication policies; and Luis Ramiro Beltrán and Elizabeth Fox de Cardona's structural perspectives on communication and development in Latin America.[16]

The structural analysis of communication and development deals not only with the questions of the political economy of information but also with a set of cultural and social indicators relevant to communication and society in general. For example, an integrated framework for comparative communication systems has been proposed in which emphasis is given to the process of both message production, distribution, and intent rather than to the atomistic notion of content and effects.[17]

The distribution stage of communication systems, long neglected, has been singled out and emphasized, and a number of indicators have been identified that focus on the linkages among society's cultural, economic, political, and communication institutions. This integrative approach to communication and development policies and planning not only considers such variables as ownership, production, and distribution, but equally takes into account the perceived and actual control in communication systems and capital, income distribution, bureaucracy, and message use.

The structural approach rejects the argument of the communication and development paradigm that communication brings about structural change by first creating socio-demographic conditions or by changing individual psychological characteristics. Acknowledging the importance of the individual level of communication and change, it takes the position that structural change is a precondition for any successful developmental objectives.

The liberal/capitalist model was centered on concepts of industrialization, individual freedom of choice, a high level of consumption, and a laissez-faire economy. The second model – that of socialism à la Marxism/Leninism –

ostensibly challenged the first one, but basically it too emphasized the genesis of modernization, which meant material growth, large bureaucracies, and technological growth. However, it kept these dimensions within the systems of state control. Pluralism, in a real sense, meant little to this model and the emphasis was put on the creation of a superstate which was supposed to deliver the world community of proletariat and workers.

The Third World response to these two models was a critique of them rather than a well-defined, coherently identified, and clearly mapped approach constituting a model in its own right. More specifically, such discourses as dependency theories, self-sufficiency, and cultural autonomy and disassociation were all responses to the dysfunctioning of the two dominant approaches rather than a coherent set of alternative proposals for development and communication.

The approaches of the past, focusing either on individual psychological characteristics or on structural conditions, fail to encompass the changes that have occurred as a result of the expansion of communication processes and products in post-industrial societies. The economic and political crisis in the north – low growth, high unemployment, inadequate social services and education, national disarticulation, political apathy, and breakdown of representative organizations – no longer provides a "model" for the "underdeveloped" countries to follow or presents the corresponding psychological characteristics of modernity.

In many ways, communication now is development. The revolutions of post-industrial society are revolutions in information and communication processes and services affecting social, political, and economic structures. Communication and development studies become fused in a common search not for the impact of one on the other – communication does not cause development – but the concomitant evolution of the two toward new social, political, and economic organizations.

With the demise of the Soviet Union and a number of other socialist regimes, the dominant paradigm of communication and development has taken a new name but remained loyal to its basic principles. This neo-modernization model of development is now referred to as "post modernity," "information-society" and "globalization." Its major premises are outlined in such international forums as the "Big Seven," the OECD, United Nations Security Council, and, of course, the discussion of such items as the New World Order proposed by the United States and a number of European countries, including the new state of Russia. However, voices searching for alternative models are also being heard, mainly from the Islamic culture. The newly emerging states of Eastern Europe may be looking for a new "civil society," but they have no blueprint of their own for an alternative model of development.

Illustrations of the confusing new development paradigm can be seen in some of the apparent paradoxes of the latest communications developments. For example, after struggling for decades to maintain a public sector in telecommunication services and to maintain national sovereignty over communication resources, many countries of Latin America are actively seeking or have found buyers for their national telephone services. By selling traditional telecommunication monopolies, Chile, Venezuela, Argentina, and Mexico hope to lower the cost of communication services for national and foreign investors, upgrade technology and services, and eliminate costly government subsidies for domestic services. But whether this will resolve their development problems is a major question. The countries of central Europe, for example, emerging from decades of communist rule, are attempting to formulate communication policies for their domestic media that balance freedom of expression and commercial exploitation, but have yet to come up with a blueprint.

Clearly, communication has become everyone's problem. The challenge to communication theorists worldwide is to look at the field comprehensively in a way that would include:

- a perspective of communication and the transformation of society, focusing on the centrality of different world views;
- a breakdown of the general and stereotypical notions of the "developing" countries into more specific and concrete functional and geopolitical areas with socio-cultural elements as a common ground for description and designation rather than a narrow economic criterion;
- a framework of analysis with its focus on the central world view that underpins culture as an integrating element in the process of change, emphasizing values and belief systems that permeate the process and help to proceed to the parameters of both individual and societal change in a more systematic and coherent way;
- a view that development, in all its complexity, is communication and that communication is development. Communication development, if fused as an area of inquiry and research, should be referred to as a single term, encouraging the construction of development programs to fit the society, rather than orienting society to fit development programs;
- a perspective that encompasses the decline of nationalism and secular national ideologies patterned on European and Western schools of thought, and the concurrent discourse and revival of notions of community along sociocultural lines;
- development and developmental projects that can be discussed in comparative ways and on horizontal levels so that the study of any given phenomenon related to social change can examine the problem not only in the "Third World" or the less developed world's laboratory, but in the industrialized world as well;
- a perspective that rejects setting goals for the final completion of the processes of change in societies. Whereas project and plans may have specific goals and objectives, change in a society is continual movement in time and space – and never ends. Transformation is not an external object. It lies deep within the individual.

## Knowledge Affluence and Information Hunger

Today, many of the development statistics from Latin America, for example income, are actually behind what they were 10 or even 20 years ago. Yet, communication and development theorists by and large continue to work within the dominant paradigm of the 1950s and 1960s, postulating that the increase in information flow and media use in the region is beneficial to objectives of economic growth and political democracy.

Although development was not necessarily among them, enormous changes did occur throughout the world, especially since World War II, as a result of communications. Many of these changes have shaken the timbers of political and economic development theories. The changes generally were not noticed by development communication scholars, however, who were more concerned with measuring attitudes and behaviors of peasants and farmers, tracing information flows to outlying areas, and counting the newspapers and radio sets in remote villages. The field of communication and development, by focusing primarily on the ordained modernization of what was called the Third World, ignored transformations taking place in the Second and First Worlds as a result of new communication technologies and the regimes and institutions that formed around them. The theories and methods used in the traditional field of communication and development were, in this respect, stillborn. By the time most of the research took place, the development model that the "First World" and the "research world" hoped the Third World would follow was no longer alive in their own backyards.

The paradigm of the communication and development theorists was unprepared for the global transformations of post-industrial society, for example: the paramount economic role of information products and services; the imbrication of supply and demand brought about by the culture industries; and the displacement of traditional political institutions and parties by mass media-led campaigns and candidates.

Mainstream development communication theorists were not alone in their blindness to these larger changes. During the same period, the so-called radical/left theorists of communication and development were equally shortsighted. Although their models recognized the larger structural conditions that limited economic progress, and identified the dependent technological and financial relations between the center and the periphery, they failed to address the wider changes occurring worldwide as a result of the information and communication "revolutions" and sociocultural developments. For them, culture or communication remained a dependent variable to economic and political forces, mechanically determined by the interests and the conflict of the two major super forces and the powers of imperialist countries. Furthermore, as their object of analysis was largely the poorer countries, the left and the "new left" theorists ignored the changes occurring elsewhere, for example in the countries under communist regimes. In part for this reason, most theorists were unable to explain the key role played by communications in the rapid and momentous changes of the Soviet Union and the countries of Eastern Europe in the last few years except with liberal theories of communication and democracy.

Scholars and communication theorists from Asia, Latin America, and Africa, for the most part products of the educational institutions and training of Europe and the United States, initially shared the paradigm of the communication and development field as it evolved in the North. Scholars of those regions that were the objects of development, however, were in a unique position to capture the paradoxes of a model that anticipated a development role for a communications industry that was rapidly expanding as a global market for goods and services. Radio and television industries pushed into the further village and the poorest slum, yet did not produce a modern society but heightened the polarization of rich and poor and the disparities within the economy. Mexico found itself able to flood the world with soap operas, for example, but watched as its traditional cultural wealth and diversity was packaged and sold by commercial television monopolies without the concomitant and hypothesized formation of community organizations or institutions for political representation.

Communication and development is no longer a North–South issue or an issue of wealth and poverty. The problems initially posed as exclusive to the "developing" regions of the world – poverty, disease, illiteracy, lack of basic economic skills, and information – are now problems of large population groups within the "developed" countries. A shrinking public sector and the lack of democratically formulated policies for communication institutions are problems that face the member of the European Union, the United States, the new countries of the former Soviet Union, and the emerging democracies of Africa. Problems of nation building, political apathy, lack of voter participation, and political manipulation plague new and old democracies throughout the world. The importance of information products and services at all levels of the post-industrial economy pose new challenges to economic growth and distribution worldwide.

Today the disparity between information-poor and information-rich societies can be observed in the development of national, regional, and global communication infrastructure. Two dominant trends, the so-called "information superhighway" and the complex networks of digital data and information images, are illustrative of the development of communication infrastructure as we enter the twenty-first century, yet the question remains: to what degree can these new infrastructures reinforce the problems of information hunger or the prospects of knowledge affluence?

## Networking as Communication

The concepts "networks" and "networking" have become fashionable over the last several years to describe what is seen as a new phenomenon related to the formation of individual and institutional ties for communication applied toward achieving specific ends. The concepts also have been used in reference to a type of telecommunications expansion encompassing sizable numbers of corporate clientele and institutions, mostly in the private sector but also in the public sector and the educational institutions. Here we approach the phenomenon of networking from the perspective of the types of communication processes that take advantage of the new human and technological infrastructures to transfer social messages in terms of attitudes, values, and ideas. The focus is on the social and economic structures that give birth to networks as well as the values and ideas they propagate. The creation of so-called "networking" is nothing new; it is simply the upshot of the marriage between changing social structures and technological infrastructure. The impact and values around which these networks operate, however, are new, for example environmental protection, human rights, cultural identity, and corporate responsibility, as well as the globalization of production and the standardization of cultural formats.

Networks and networking consist of many separate entities and a system of interconnection that ties them together through any means: word of mouth, the mail, the telephone line, the computer modem; and within any institutional context: a religious movement, a political party, a large corporation, a grassroots public interest group. Are existing and emerging international networks compatible with the existing social and cultural order? If not, in what directions are changes occurring? Has the marriage of changing social structures and technological advances worked to the benefit of the status quo? Who has won and who has lost in the mediation between new technologies and the demands of social, political, and cultural movements? In short, we assume that emerging networks at the international communications level have the ability and the capacity to challenge as well as to reinforce the existing social, cultural, economic, and political systems. What dimensions should we analyze in order to assess the impact of this challenge?

Many of the international communication networks are created as a result of the convergence of modern technologies for the processing, storing, and sharing of information and the needs of emerging socio-economic groups. In a number of cases, at both a macro- and micro-level, these international networks undermine existing structures of social communication, some of which are supportive of the status quo. In other cases, international communication networks debilitate traditional systems of solidarity and community which in the past have supported objectives of social justice and equality. International communication networking can be an obstacle to the existing national and international powers as well as to the forces that oppose these powers. In the former case networks are a kind of "nomadic" sniper force, clipping the ability of existing elite infrastructures and piercing the conventional networks of international communication. In the latter, networks strengthen the power over users of existing organizations, for example the case of international networks of financial institutions for sharing credit and financial histories of individuals.

Networks are mediators; they are used by and arise from individuals and institutions in order to achieve certain ends, although, at times, the consequences of networks can escape the control of their organizers and, at others, networks can organize spontaneously without an apparent direction or objective in mind. International communication networking is basically a potential resource for power and its redistribution. It is through networks, especially in the history of advanced communication technologies, that the new transformations of power are taking place. International communication networking generates power infrastructure through mobilization and assimilation and transfers these resources and mechanisms of control to groups and individuals.

## Sociocultural Dimensions of Networking

Development, once described as mainly a "Third World" problem in the decades after World War II, has now demonstrated itself as a worldwide problem. A cursory look at both the emerging communication networks and the economic, social, and political problems associated with them demonstrates the multidimensional aspect of communication and development.

What are the dimensions along which sociocultural change can occur as a result of networks and networking? Four broad areas of dimensional change can be cited here. One of the most obvious dimensions of change is in the degree of *centralization of decision-making and control*. Concentrated power structures of information and management mediated through international communication networks can serve to consolidate much of the policy and planning of organizations and institutions, hence contributing to the centralization of decision-making and control. This dimension, however, can work in both directions now that the formation of an efficient international communication network can also allow for a greater participation of separate entities in the decisions and direction of the organization. In other words, networks can also work in the direction of decentralization.

Another dimension is *homogeneity*. The ability to connect simultaneously a large number of entities around a specific purpose or movement necessarily involves a certain degree of homogenization. On the simplest technological level, all members of the network must be able to connect into the information web with some sort of standardized interface. They must use some form of common terminology and codes in order to share information. These processes, and the resulting cultural impact of working toward common objectives or products, can result in a decrease in the diversity of codes, values and "cultures" of the separate entities. The scope of the network and the fact that it can include a large number of very disparate entities from different contexts and cultures, however, can also mean that the diversity of the network and therefore of the objectives it works for is increased, for example in the case of some of the library networks. Herein lies another paradox of networking: it can work both for and against homogeneity.

Yet another dimension of change is in the operation of *hegemony*. Networks formed around specific interest areas can work effectively to increase the power of those interests. It would be counter-intuitive to think of a successful network formed to achieve a certain end that does not increase the power and control of its authors. Yet, if the objective of the network is empowerment and democratization, as for example could be the case in voter registration and public awareness or the mobilization of public opinion around global environmental concerns, overall hegemony may in fact be decreased by increasing the number of informed participants in the decision-making process.

Finally, there is a dimension of change in the connection between networks and networking and the present *global system of nation-states*. International communication networks are often created parallel to the state's existing communication infrastructure and are often of a non-governmental nature. This can mean both citizen or public ownership and control as well as private, commercial ownership and control. In either case the network operates outside traditional lines of state power and administration, thereby potentially weakening the national state and the public sector. When the state is acting to redistribute power and wealth and protect minority and disadvantaged interests, the decrease of state power can be cause for concern. In cases of non-representative, authoritarian states, on the other hand, a decrease of state power is cause for celebration.

Some of the most important types of international communication networks that have potential impact on sociocultural and politico-economic levels are: (1) religio-political networking; (2) eco-cultural networking; (3) inter-governmental/non-governmental networking in areas like international tourism, science, technology, education; (4) corporate networking in terms of expansion of marketing values, corporate efficiency, the maximization of profit and commercialism; (5) cultural industry and mass media networking. For example, one of the most important sociocultural changes accompanying the processes of networking is the worldwide religio-political movements that have manifested themselves during the last two decades. Islamic resurgence in various parts around the world is the most visible manifestation of these sociocultural changes involving an integrated system of networking of both traditional and technological communication.

## Networks in the Islamic Societies

From the Islamic revolution in Iran to the Muslim mobilization in Algeria, from the "Intifada" in Palestine to sociocultural assimilation and awareness in such places as Tajikistan, Uzbekistan, and Bosnia, Islamic parties and communities have used the rich and traditional infrastructures of mosques, madrasah, hey'at, and so on, along with modern communication infrastructures such as telecommunication, tapes, fax, satellites and related technologies, to form new integrated systems of networking in an attempt to achieve their social and cultural goals.[18]

Within the cultural and educational realms, the creation and utilization of emerging networks of communication are having a profound impact on the sociology of knowledge within Islamic societies. For example, conventionally, the power of the religious scholars in Muslim societies has been based on their role as the depositories of knowledge, as data banks, as individuals who could instantly quote the Qur'an and hadith as well as comments, criticism, and opinions of classical jurists. New information technologies and networks, however, have the potential of making this knowledge available to a wider population. It is in the use of distributive and decentralized networks that their greatest potential lies for Muslim societies and cultures. The use of personal computers has already become widespread in such Muslim countries as Malaysia, Pakistan, and Egypt. The basic sources of Islam are readily available on floppy disks and are being used for study and criticism by many intellectuals and students of Islamic culture who otherwise would have had difficulty in having access to these materials. A plethora of data bases on the Qur'an and hadith now open up these texts and make them accessible to average, non-expert users.[19] The existing databases on the Qur'an and hadith make available only the basic sources of Islam; moreover, they do not, as the ulama have been quick to argue, furnish the user with knowledge or expertise required for the interpretation of text. A database does not equip the non-expert to undertake the independent reasoning that leads to a new understanding or interpretation of fundamental texts. For that, one would still have to fulfil the stringent criteria laid down in the later classical period by religious authorities. However, a network of combined traditional and modern data banks using compact discs may indeed assist the young students of Islamic culture and theology to achieve what may have taken the earlier ulama many years.

The compact disc with appropriate text and expert systems will be available in many Islamic societies in about a decade. Initially. it will be used by intellectuals and professionals working on specific problems, lawyers defending difficult cases from Islamic viewpoints, medical doctors facing ethical dilemmas, and scientists looking for public support for their projects. But eventually, just as computers and current religious databases, CD-based expert systems will find their way into universities and colleges.[20] And it is here, in the preparation of the next generation of critically aware Muslims, that the most profound impact of the new communication networks will be felt. Given the vast geographical diversity of Islamic ummah (community), the international communication implications of such networks in bringing the large number of Islamic countries under a unified system of information are indeed profound.

*Telecommunications and Finance*

One of the most important areas of growth in international networking is in the fields of intergovernmental and nongovernmental organizations, particularly in the sphere of economic, corporate, and business activities. For example, the increasing involvement and prominence of mixed sector alliances and coalitions in the international system, particularly those in the tourism infrastructure, illustrate shifts occurring in the international economic power base. Corresponding formal and informal arrangements have formed on national and international levels within the private sector and between public and private institutions. These arrangements are arising to accommodate contending interests in the international tourism infrastructure over division of labor in the industry. Those centering on the allocation of strategic international financial and telecommunications resources in international tourism are prime examples.

The convergence of telecommunications technologies with transnational banking and investment is contributing to the genesis of new supernational economies of scale in the tourism infrastructure and to the formation of oligopolies in the transnational trade of information capital. This convergence has the potential for increasing the dependence of the information capital-poor – no longer always the underdeveloped or lesser industrialized nations or regions – on the information capital-rich. The joint impact of telecommunications and tourism on the international division of labor is evident in trends toward coalitions, regionalism, and informal and formal international dependency and "welfare" systems in which telecommunication is the core. These trends are altering the conduct of international relations and are contributing to the integration, disintegration, and transformation of power in the international system.

Multinational corporations were the first to take advantage of the flows of trade information through complex telecommunication networks. Use of these networks can result in increased trade efficiency, but there is uncertainty as to who will be connected to which network, at what costs and with what benefits and risk. (These questions are being considered by international bodies such as UNCTAD, the OECD, WTO, and the European Union.) The development of these networks depends on the technical and regulatory conditions which apply to the public telecommunication networks. These conditions often are administered by institutions resting on a false assertion – namely that technical infrastructures are separate from the political, economic, and social ones. Furthermore, private service providers are increasingly extending their value-added services beyond the national borders. They want to serve their customers, mostly multinationals, who do not want to deal with other, different public telecom operators every time they cross a border. Equally, the public telecom operators, partially set free by liberalization and confronted with a squeeze on their national telephone profits, are desperately looking beyond their nest for the more lucrative international markets.

The growth of private and pseudo-private telecommunications networks, driven by goals of economic efficiency and profit, are becoming the norm in today's world of communications. As technology and deregulation make it possible for these networks to spread to developed and underdeveloped countries alike, a number of questions arise regarding the shrinking public space of telecommunications and the philosophies of subsidy that have traditionally reigned in the provision of communication services. While the commercial origins of the networks are clear, their impact on such areas as local telephone rates and services is not. By directing scarce resources to modern telephone switching computers instead of the expansion of basic urban and rural networks, a private, corporate community building is being privileged at the expense of citizens' participation. As a small minority of customers (mainly international firms) generate most profits, will the telephone companies leave residential or poorer customers outside their networks?

The last two decades have witnessed an exponential increase in the volume of information and data flow. It seems that time and distance no longer are constraining elements upon communication. However, social and cultural factors continue to play even more crucial roles in the so-called "international" networks than before. We are indeed witnessing a decrease in the "time cushion" between sociocultural changes, their impact and consequences, and an increase in dependence upon information and communication services. The growth of complex human and technologically linked systems is fragmenting basic societal services, resulting in abrupt changes in perception of the sociocultural environment. These radical conceptual changes are being introduced in national, regional, and international systems by increased volumes of information and communication. A new power structure is emerging based on information, data, and knowledge and leaving behind it leveling effects on traditional and existing social strata. Many decisions affecting the global sociocultural environment are now largely occurring outside local and even national political and economic systems. Not only are communication networks as cultural ecology affecting the sociocultural environment, but information and cultural relations are becoming ever more central to the conduct of international and global systems.

## Development in Eastern Europe and Russia

What are the implications of these growing networks of international communication and new communications ecology for the new emerging systems of Eastern Europe and Russia?

The downfall of communism and the ensuing collapse of the proletarian dictatorships which characterized the governments of Eastern Europe and the Soviet Union for many decades were initially greeted with great euphoria by all Eastern Europeans. It was hoped that with the yoke of communism lifted, freedom, accompanied by economic prosperity, would quickly flourish throughout the region. However, this optimistic scenario has not materialized as many hoped that it would, and the fledgling governments of Eastern Europe have rapidly been overwhelmed by seemingly insurmountable problems. These difficulties have given rise to a wave of pessimism throughout the region as people realize that the Western world which they once so greatly longed for has its own "dark side," and that living in a world dominated by Western capitalists may not be as appetizing as it once had seemed. In fact, some have concluded that the system of Western capitalism has as great a need for reform as did the system of Stalinist communism.

Although there may be many who deny it, the current situation in Eastern Europe – and to a great extent Russia and other republics of the former Soviet Union – has a striking and rather frightening resemblance to the situation which was faced by many Third World countries 40 years ago after the Western colonial powers withdrew. This situation is most similar with regard to three specific areas. First, both groups are the product of colonialism. Although the details of such colonialism may differ in some respects, it is undeniable that each situation has come into being precisely because of the colonial domination which was once so characteristic of the respective groups. Second, both groups gained their "independence" only within the context of an established set of rules which dealt with economic and commercial behavior. Third, each group is completely marginalized from the dominant forces which wield all of the political, economic, technological and cultural power. Indeed, the only major difference that can be found between the Third World and the countries of Eastern Europe is that Eastern European countries do share a common civilization and culture with the West.[21]

With these facts in mind one comes to realize that the course of development in Eastern Europe will very likely be dominated by the following characteristics. The International Monetary Fund (IMF) and the World Bank will enforce the top-down, capitalist model of development on Eastern European states; Eastern European states will be trapped in the debt syndrome, their only advantage being their large pool of cheap and abundant labor; and, finally, industrialization will take priority over agricultural development, with the result of a deformed economy. It is also likely that Eastern Europe will fall prey to the "hopeful syndrome," whereby it increases its dependence on the West by complying with all of its demands, yet will still be denied many of the economic benefits it so desperately seeks.

While this scenario is pessimistic, it cannot be denied that such parallels do exist between the Third World and Eastern Europe. Only time will tell whether or not the newly independent countries of Eastern Europe will indeed follow the path of the Third World. Rather, it must be hoped that they will find a new course to the ultimate goal of self-determination and self-sufficiency – a course that will allow them to avoid the unfortunate experiences of the Third World.

## Notes

1. Keith Schneider, "High Tech Actually Cuts Productivity in U.S. Service Industry," *International Herald Tribune*, June 19, 1987, p. 9.

2. Daniel Lerner, *The Passing of Traditional Society: Modernizing the Middle East* (Glencoe, IL: Free Press, 1958), pp. 1–102.

3. Lucian W. Pye, ed., *Communication and Political Development* (Princeton, NJ: Princeton University Press, 1963).

4. Ithiel de Sola Pool, "The Mass Media and Politics in the Modernization Process," in ibid., pp. 234–253.

5. Seymour Martin Lipset, "Some Social Requisites of Democracy: Economic Development and Political Legitimacy," *American Political Science Review*, LII (March 1959), pp. 69–105.

6. Wilbur Schramm and W. Lee Ruggles, "How Mass Media Systems Grow," in Daniel Lerner and Wilbur Schramm, eds, *Communication and Change in Developing Countries* (Honolulu: University of Hawaii Press, 1967), pp. 57–75.

7. David C. McClelland, *The Achieving Society* (Princeton, NJ: Van Nostrand, 1961).

8. Everett Rogers and F.F. Shoemaker, *Communication of Innovations: A Cross-Cultural Approach* (New York: Free Press, 1971).

9. Ibid.

10. Elihu Katz, "The Two-Step Flow of Communication," *Public Opinion Quarterly*, XXI (Spring 1957), pp. 61–78.

11. Dallas W. Smythe, *Dependency Road: Communications, Capitalism, Consciousness, and Canada* (Norwood, NJ: Ablex Publishing Corporation, 1981).

12. Herbert Schiller, *Mass Communication and the American Empire*, updated 2nd edn (Boulder, CO: Westview Press, 1992).

13. Armand Matellart, *Multinational Corporations and the Control of Culture* (Brighton: Harvester Press, 1979), and *Transnationals and the Third World: The Struggle for Culture* (South Hadley, MA: Bergin and Garvey Publishers, 1983).

14. Hamid Mowlana, *International Flow of Information: A Global Report and Analysis*, Reports and Papers on Mass Communication No. 99 (Paris: UNESCO, 1985).

15. Cees J. Hamelink, *Cultural Autonomy in Global Communication* (White Plains, NY: Longman, 1983).

16. Luis Ramiro Beltrán and Elizabeth Fox de Cardona, "Latin America and the United States: Flaws in the Free Flow of Information," in Kaarle Nordenstreng and Herbert Schiller, eds, *National Sovereignty and International Communication* (Norwood, NJ: Ablex Publishing Corporation, 1979).

17. Hamid Mowlana and Laurie J. Wilson, *The Passing of Modernity: Communication and the Transformation of Society* (White Plains, NY: Longman, 1990), Chapter 1.

18. Hamid Mowlana, "Technology versus Tradition: Communication in the Iranian Revolution," *Journal of Communication*, 29: 3 (Summer 1979), pp. 107–112.

19. The most popular packages are "el-Qur'an and al-Hadith Database" produced by the Islamic Computing Centre, London; the multi-lingual data based on the Qur'an, hadith and Islamic history produced by Institute Alif, Paris; and "The Hafiz," produced by ISL Software, San Antonio, Texas.

20. See Ziauddin Sardar, "Paper, Printing and Compact Discs: The Making and Unmaking of Islamic Culture," *Culture, Media and Society* (Special issue on Communication and Islam, edited by Philip Schlesinger and Hamid Mowlana), 15 (January 1993), pp. 43–60.

21. Ziauddin Sardar and Merryl Wyn Davies, "The Future of Eastern Europe," *Futures*, March 1992, pp. 150–157.

# 11

# International Communication Research: From Functionalism to Postmodernism and Beyond

As we near the end of the twentieth century, there seems to be growing interest in two fundamental areas of communication arts and sciences: a resurgence in the study of the philosophy of communication, as evidenced by the number of publications and conference panels in this area; and a keen interest in new epistemological schools of thought and research methodologies beyond the "ferment in the field"[1] in which positive empiricism and critical theory were the only positions debated among the students of communication studies. Whereas the philosophy of communication is replacing transcendental philosophy as the prime concern of philosophical reflection, there is also a new interest in exploring new conduits of inquiries and fresh approaches to methodologies.[2]

I have defined international communication as a field of inquiry and research that consists of the transfer of values, attitudes, opinion, and information through individuals, groups, governments, and technologies, as well as the study of the structure of institutions responsible for promoting or inhibiting such messages among and between nations and cultures. It is a field of study and research which entails an analysis of the channels and institutions of communication. More important, it involves examination of the mutually shared meanings that make communication possible.

In an attempt to discern the substance of international communication as a field of inquiry, many controversial theoretical questions are raised. Both explicitly and implicitly, the new literature portrays the quest for a substantial, and more elaborated, theory, one that will take into account the "high stakes" enterprise of communication in an era of technological and industrial change. Communication research, like any scientific study, depends essentially on the quality of theory or conceptualization to give it direction and focus. Specifying the conditions under which predictions can be hypothesized is the function of a well-integrated theory of communication research. The basis for achieving this is still an unresolved issue of debate among communication researchers.

This question is not merely a scholarly controversy, but also a highly politicized debate that is fundamentally based on the notion of power and its implications for communication. The fact that communication research does not function in a political vacuum makes the concept of power a very relevant issue indeed. Hence, many of the scholarly debates in the social sciences are, in fact, political controversies, poorly disguised.

The role of theory and the areas of research priority need to be clarified. To know the important questions, the way they should be approached, and the scholar's role in society are issues of crucial importance. The crux of the matter is whether theory should emanate out of reality to explicate it or whether it should construct another vision of reality. In short, should it perpetuate, modify, or eradicate the existing order? Assuming that a universal paradigm of communication behavior is attainable, the political biases hinder the prospect of achieving this hypothetical endeavor. Perhaps the reason is that much of what passes for metatheoretical debate in actuality fixates on pseudo problems instead of illuminating substantive issues. In other words, the current disputes within the realm of communication research are often fueled by ideological preferences and not substantive intellectual issues.

**Communication Research in Transition**

In general, there seem to have been four kinds of communication models underpinning the research carried out during the last four decades: (1) mathematical, (2) social psychological, (3) linguistic, and (4) political economy and cultural analysis. The mathematical models of information and communication seem to represent a growing field and the low-level mathematical theories have come from empirical and theoretical research done on information flow, military strategy, and even politics and nationalism. The social psychological tradition has had tremendous influence on politics and mass media research. The linguistic tradition, meanwhile, has led to such areas as symbol analysis. Finally, political economy and cultural analysis have often acted as alternatives and challenging perspectives to the first three.

Can communication research attain the knowledge through which to understand and to change social reality? This is the persistent and troublesome question for international communication research in the twenty-first century. This question presumes the necessity and feasibility of social change: the evolutionary or revolutionary – relative to historical circumstances – transition from a present society to a projected society. Yet, the prevalent theoretical monomania and methodological exclusivity of communication research cannot meet the challenge of designing concrete images of situations that can be realized. Comprehending the reasons for the failure to meet this "normative" challenge is a very bewildering task. It has been said that work by communication researchers, particularly within the domain of mass communication, demonstrates a heightened concern for the practical implications and social relevance of communication issues. Although the tightly controlled laboratory study that dominated early research efforts is still much employed, a heartening move toward naturalistic studies and more reliance on field experimentation has considerably evolved. Diversity in research strategies is the order of the day, and the restless urge for social relevance has served as one powerful stimulus for such diversity.[3]

A new perspective on the effects of media emerged when the notion of the "unlimited capacity" of media to directly affect behavior in itself proved invalid. It has been argued that media have come to be viewed not as an active agent of change in isolation, but as having influence through a complex set of cultural, economic, and sociopolitical factors.[4] Thus, there is a need for a radical departure from the premises of the old perspective about the role and effect of media. A review of the work of key theorists concerned with the relation of media and cultures suggests that a more elaborate theory for the interaction of change in social structure, change in communication patterns, and change in culture is needed in communication research. Implied in this assertion is a new research perspective in which the focus is shifted from communication as social control to communication as integral to sociocultural change. Therefore, a different set of disciplinary methodologies must be formulated to operationalize this type of research.

The old framework was challenged on the basis of its preoccupation with effects of mass media messages on audiences perceived as potential customers. This type of research displaced the focus of inquiry away from the media (the object) to the audience (the subject). In addition, the methodology adopted revealed its pro-status quo bias in that it never considered the alternative of creating a new system but rather presented a functional adjustment of the old. A transition toward a new paradigm is evident, but there is no general unanimity on the direction of the paradigmatic shift.

The new rhetoric for a more comprehensive theory was stipulated by the realization of the ever-increasing importance of research in the high-stakes enterprise of communication for an era of "information production." The significance of studying communications is becoming a self-evident fact, more obvious every day. The long-term, deep structural forces and the dynamics of the power relations are making communication the central process in global, national, and local social organizations. The most powerful national and transnational decision-making groups are employing compelling new information technologies to consolidate and extend their positions. The maintenance of power systems nationally and transnationally is in the balance. Thus, communication study is largely the outcome of global and national forces that have propelled the communication process and information to the center of domestic as well as international attention and concern.[5]

The emerging crisis within the philosophy of science and the growing political cynicism among the general public has given rise to a widespread questioning of the prevalent modes behind the established legitimacy of both knowledge and power. This questioning, within communication studies, has generated an interest in the critical social theory initially advocated by Max Horkheimer, Friedrich Pollock, Theodor Adorno, and their associates at the Institut für Soziale Forschung (the Frankfurt School) in the 1930s. The critical approach to communication research has subsequently been articulated and enriched by Herbert Marcuse and Jürgen Habermas in their respective endeavors to secure a basis for emancipating communication in industrial societies.[6] The preoccupation of researchers with the power structure came as a result of this realization. Hence, there is no safe harbor in which researchers can avoid established power relations, even if they declare their neutrality. Neutrality itself is not apolitical because of the unavoidable alignment of the research process with economic and political factors.

The central characteristic of this historical era makes international communication a significant field of inquiry. Five major factors contribute to this phenomenon. First, the transformation of the world political scene from a handful of commanding states to the threshold of a potentially genuine international community promotes the vitality of international communication as an area of study. Second, the reactions of 180 or more nations to their pre-independence and post-liberation communication experiences have crystallized the particular importance of this field. The once seemingly silenced periphery is now a multitude of independent actors voicing their own interests and reflecting their own creativity. The other side of the coin is the importance of international communication to the system-maintenance of the major powers, a third critical element. The fourth contributing factor to the prevalent significance of international communication is the gigantic expansion of the transnational corporations. Indeed, the most revolutionary dimension of these corporations is not their size, but their world view. Fifth, and finally, the concept of the sovereign nation-state as a force controlling the economic life of its citizens has been eroded and the role of international communication has become central to this process.

**Challenge to Theoretical Orthodoxy**

Communication research has been based upon the conceptual and methodological orientations established by researchers in the West and particularly in the United States. This fact has led to the inappropriate application of culture-bound research methods to survey studies in less developed countries. That communication studies have subscribed indiscriminately and markedly to theoretical models mostly imported from the United States is not the main issue. The crucial matter is that the "made-in-the-USA" type of communication research suffers from insensitivity to contextual and social-structural factors in different societies. Thus, the style of communication research appropriate for US conditions has proved to be quite inappropriate in other socio-economic and political contexts. The failure of the so-called "development-oriented communication campaigns" has become self-evident when applied to the Third World countries.

Review of the communication literature reveals that the most serious theoretical problem stems from the premise that communication plays an independent role in affecting social changes and behavior. Consequently, two preoccupations were paramount from the early days of Harold Lasswell and Robert Merton: one was with the effects of mass media on individuals' behavior, and the other was with the function of these media in society. Stated differently, researchers examined what media do to people and how messages can use people, rather than studying ways in which people use or can use messages. The joint and systematic comprehension of channel-message capabilities and audience-response mechanisms was to produce a behavior-controlling rhetoric serving the interest of the communicator. Accordingly, research methods appropriate to these main conceptual requirements were devised whereby content analysis and the sample survey through structured interviews came to form the basic methodological arsenal of most communicologists.[7] This method restricted the researcher's attention to the receiver's possible reactions to specific manifest contents of communications, while keeping covert the motivations and intentions of the communicator. Emphasis has been placed on the development of increasingly formal theory and methodology in the hope that a body of scientific rules will provide the key to conduct future research. Unfortunately, this process has resulted in models that are hardly recognizable as representations of behavior in the real world. Furthermore, if ideally there is no bias inherent in the scientific method, such a bias exists in reality, for results clearly find their way into ideological, economic, and political practice. The abstract analytical categories of idealist thought have become substantive descriptions and have taken habitual priority over the whole social process of which, as analytical categories, they were attempting to speak.

The belief in one-way mechanistic causation rather than mutual causation is the underlying epistemological error that characterizes the linear models. The basic problems with the linear models emanate from the epistemological assumptions about the nature of the individual and the nature of information, how we seek it, and what kind of quality it is. Information is treated as if it were purely a physical entity which can be moved around like billiard balls on a table.[8] Hence, mainstream communication researchers perceive the concept of causality in simple linear terms, in which the sender, message, and receiver are isolated as units in an unmediated simple causal chain. Often what have been proposed as alternatives to the hypodermic model have been merely elaborations.

In the final analysis, all empirical results are conditioned by a theoretical base, even when that base remains unexposed. It has been asserted that the epistemological differences besetting the world of communication scholars lie in the notion of science as emancipation or as domestication, that underlying this dichotomy is the ontological definition of reality, either as including yet to be realized potentialities or as confined to factual manifestations.

The definition of reality as potentiality is fundamental to the choice of science as a tool of emancipation. Therefore, on the one hand, science can be a tool for the liberation of people from those forces that keep them from being free to think about what they want to do. On the other hand, science can be a tool for the overt or subtle domestication of people into a dependency upon those forces that prescribe social reality as an objective part to which they must adapt.

The ever-increasing production of communication technologies will give rise to a new wave of exciting research on communications. Communication research will most likely be directed toward new questions made salient by drastic changes in the communications situations. New technologies raise different questions than do the mass media. An information retrieval system is not the sole format for the coming age, yet it is the prototype of what is becoming increasingly important. The chief characteristic of the new electronic media is that they provide diverse material on demand to individuals.[9] They also allow for fragmentation of the mass audience and even for silent individualized communication. In this case, the relevant research question will focus on the way the new media are institutionalized and modified to meet what society demands rather than what the electronic media are technically capable of delivering.

In an effort to critically assess the contributions and limitations of critical theory, one can ask whether the emancipatory project of critical theorists have offered any practical plan for resistance or a program for translating criticism into action. Thus, much critical analysis tends simply to assume that existing institutional structures are the problem and must be changed. Unfortunately it usually does not provide a clear idea of how these structures should, could, or would be realistically changed to alternative institutional structures that research has shown are better.

Today the apparent diversity of critical approaches and the range of sources for critical positions that cut across all of the human sciences account for the difficulty in identifying common premises.[10] With the advent of new information technologies, the established powers are strengthened, new dependencies are created, and new social discrepancies are brought about. The situation is worsening day by day, and the price of fitting into the establishment is higher than ever. This is because the *ethical* questions have been subsumed under the banner of science, progress, and development.

Here a brief historical note is in order. In the 1960s there was a convergence of external social events and epistemological currents which necessitated reevaluation of positive empiricism as the post-World War II mainstream paradigm of international communication research and literature. At least two epistemological currents were at work during this postwar period. In the face of the dominant empirical framework, there arose a revival of critical theory led by the students and followers of the founding fathers of the Frankfurt School in Germany and later in the United States. Combined with this resurgence of critical theory was the underlying apologist posture of the positive empiricists in their self-critical examination of their roots in behavioralism and of the limitation of the behavioral science movement as an epistemological base. United States communication research, under the influence of positive empiricism, was characterized by its preoccupation with effects of mass media messages on audiences perceived as potential consumers. This type of research displaced the focus of inquiry away from the media (the object) to the audience (the subject). The major aim was to learn about persuasion and adjustment for conformity. Science was neutral and causality was perceived in simple linear terms. Communication was viewed as a contentless process. What distinguished critical approaches from other communication research was the redefinition of the notion of causality and the concern with the means in which the control of knowledge is fundamental to the exercise of social power. Critical researchers addressed the production of information outputs, instead of focusing on individual consumption and media products. They tried to comprehend the sources and exercise of power, particularly in relation to communication processes and information flow.

Superordinant to the empirical and critical theory frameworks was that of so-called *postmodernism* (or *poststructuralism*) which coexisted as a silent partner in the literature of philosophy, epistemology, and literary criticism from the 1940s forward.[11] The genesis of postmodernist thought derived from a reevaluation of the limits of existentialism and a disenchantment with the structuralist phenomenology of critical theory and the objectively quantitative restrictions of empiricism. The postmodernists and poststructuralists attacked the authority of reason. Not only did they criticize the rationality of the natural world and the methodological difficulties of conquering it but they also questioned the concept of self as living. Their discourse circles around *becoming*. They were concerned not with the study of structures such as laws, regularities, patterns, but with the practical historical forces that would impose or resist structure. Mostly an intellectual exercise in the French social science tradition, this postmodernist writing was based in the esoteric realm of philosophy, language, and literature. Its appeal to and acceptance by Western social scientists was to come much later, in the 1980s, when its tenets appear to offer possible explanations for the unconventionality of contemporary communication issues and events.

From the 1960s through the 1970s all three epistemological currents were at work in the West; however, the manifestations of these lines of thought in the communication literature of this period were summarized, quite interestingly, only in terms of the critical theory versus empiricism debate. The revivalism of critical theory was well documented in the literature but acknowledgement of the influence of postmodernist conceptions was blatantly absent. In retrospect, the Western non-recognition of the postmodernist contribution is all the more remarkable when considered in the context of the late 1960s. What will be the ultimate postmodernist contribution to the 1980s and beyond has its roots in a given social milieu, of which a number of events in 1968 are quintessential examples.

In 1968 in the United States, a general social discontent was manifested in the student rebellions against the Vietnam War. This dissent was reflected in communication research in the criticism of behavioralism and empiricism which dominated the social sciences. In Europe there was evidence of other social movements in the 1968 student rebellion in France and the liberalization movement in Prague. Beyond the West, and ignored by it, there was evidence of the roots of the Islamic movement in Iran and elsewhere professing a different epistemological view.

In developing a history of the development of communication discourse, the omissions in the field of inquiry and research can be of great import. The lack of inclusion of other perspectives, except that of positivism and critical theories, into the literature of communication of the early post-World War II period falls into this category. It was only in the late 1970s and 1980s that students of communication and of the other social sciences slowly became interested in the study of contemporary social phenomena, employing different typology and world views beyond that of empirical positivism and critical perspectives.

Attempts were being made to develop a different approach to communication in which linearity was replaced by circularity, causality by catalysis, syntax by semantic-pragmatics, the rationality of Western norms by the irrationality of desiring production, hierarchical relations by heterarchical relations, and the centered subject by the decentered web of relations and difference.

For example, one perspective outlined viewed communication on the principle of connection, heterogeneity, and multiplicity. There are no discrete boxes of sender, receiver, media, and message, no homogeneous set of ready-made signifying messages as an information theory, no subjective linear choices which may prevent the entry of heterogeneous substances of expression into the process. As noted by Deleuze and Guattari, "There is no longer a tripartite division between a field of reality (the world) and a field of representation (the book) and a field of subjectivity."[12]

In the linear sender-receiver model of communication, and in the tradition of Western social, cultural, and political discourse, the component of the media took a royal if not a despotic position. With the rise of mass media theory and urban sociology, coupled with the tremendous attention paid to industrial and technological growth, communication research in both empirical/administrative and critical/dialectic circles was transformed into the royal position of media status. This media-centered research, ranging from studies of popular culture (cultural identity in the terms of the Frankfurt School) to audience analysis and totalitarianism, culminated in the work of Marshall McLuhan – "the medium is the message."

If the deterministic image of society that the "Triple-M" (mass society, mass media, mass culture) theorists portray is drawn from the laissez-faire doctrine of economics (if not totally from the Protestant view of society), the political economy theorists draw most of their ideas from the Marxist view of production.

By and large the Triple-M Theory of the media and culture is a theory of social control from above even though it is premised on the necessity for making concessions to mass tastes in order that the masses be controlled most effectively. The political economy theorists view the process from below, where, through an elaborate feedback of political and economic machinery, the masses can participate in the production and distribution of cultural messages. Both theories of social communication, however, tend to be media-centered, linear, and structural.

The process of deconstruction or restructuring begins when the black box of the media is removed from the communication model and discourse, all the while recognizing media's traces everywhere and in every point in the process. *This is communication without media.* We are watching television as much as it watches us. Instead of focusing our attention on a single element, we pay attention to an assemblage in its multiplicities.

Here we can think of communication not as a tree with roots and branches, but as a rhizome, a network, where any point can be connected to any other with roots everyplace. As Deleuze and Guattari point out: "A rhizome ceaselessly establishes connections between semiotic chains. Organization of power, and circumstances relative to the arts, sciences, and social struggle. . . . There is no ideal speaker-listener, any more than there is a homogeneous linguistic community."[13]

**What We Have Learned**

The purpose of the present study has been to synthesize the relevant research already undertaken by different institutions and organizations in all aspects of the international flow of information, in both its human and its technological dimensions. Close examination of these salient areas may aid us in analyzing political, cultural, economic, technological, and professional practices affecting the international flow of information.

It has been argued here that examination of the international functional implications of communication – in both human and technological terms – is another way of studying the complex phenomenon of international relations. After an examination of the range and definition of the phenomenon, an attempt has been made to lay a foundation for an identification and critical evaluation of major approaches, theories, concepts, and propositions, with particular attention focused on problems of analytical integration within the field of study and problems of interdisciplinary contribution and coherence. Toward this end, a framework of analysis has been proposed with the hope that it might provide a guideline for a methodology to follow in future evaluations of related development.

Research on the international flow of information has grown enormously over the last 10 years, but we do not know the extent of growth in international communication itself. A major contention of this analysis is that because of the tendency to focus on a few actors and factors, and because of a paucity of systematic research, the present state of knowledge on the international flow of information is rather fragmented. No full-scale investigation has shown the possible effects of international information systems on international policies, politics, and economics.

Despite these shortcomings, we are in a much better position today to draw a rough skeleton of the global information flow than we were a decade ago. In summarizing, integrating, and evaluating the vast and diverse amount of research on the international flow of information, we can only hope that such an exercise will provide us with a concise statement of what we know and what we have yet to learn.

The demand for a New International Economic Order (NIEO) is familiar as the main basis of disputations in the North–South dialogue between the developed and the developing nations. A similar demand for a New World Information/Communication Order (NWICO) is less known among the general public in many countries, primarily because of erroneous perceptions that it is less important, and partially because the public media have presented the importance of the international flow of information in an extremely narrow sense. Thus, people generally tend to perceive the issues of the economic debate – trade figures, gross national product, energy prices, etc. – as concrete aspects directly affecting their lives. Information is seen as a comparatively abstract or non-material good, rather low in developmental priorities.

Over the last 10 years, however, the calls to reexamine the international flow of information and to reevaluate the existing structure of global communication have snowballed, first among the information specialists in non-aligned group meetings, and subsequently as part of Third World demands for a comprehensive set of new world orders. Consequently, the study of the international flow of information has occupied the most prominent position among the students of international communication, as well as among policy makers dealing with national and international development issues. This upsurge of research, writings, and debates came about as a result of the increasing realization that the imbalances perceived in the economic field were also present in the information and communication field, and in equal need of redress. Some of the imbalances are painfully obvious, as documented in this study, and research conducted during the past several years has demonstrated an imbalance of the world's communication and information resources that now is widely accepted.

It is precisely here that a more daring historical analysis of real processes and conceptual development outlined in this study would facilitate understanding as to how information flow has become one of the major issues of our time. Although this study is not meant to be an historical analysis of international flow of information processes, it is hoped that the combined presentation of the synchronic and diachronic elements in the preceding chapters has demonstrated the crucial role played by information and communication in our global environment. Thus, the once-debated issue of information and communication, which was perceived a decade ago as another disputation between the industrialized and less industrialized countries of the world, has now become a global issue.

Viewing analyses of the international flow of information historically and as a whole, we see that the study of information flow has gone through two distinct but interrelated phases, and that third phase is just beginning to emerge. The first period characterizing the analyses of the flow of information in the 1950s and the 1960s emphasized the message and production aspects of communication media, with little or no concern given to the broader aspects of international flow of information that could transcend the boundaries of conventional media and telecommunications to include the human-oriented types of information channels. The main characteristics of this period, as evidenced in the present study, are the fragmentary nature of the analysis of content, as well as emphasis on the processes of message production in terms of both techniques and socio-economic factors. A few studies attempting to examine the cultural, educational, scientific, and related aspects of international information flow were conducted in isolation.

The second phase of international flow of information research is characterized by the studies carried out in the 1970s, especially in the latter part of that decade. The analyses of this period are recognized as being critical of the first phase just mentioned, and emphasize both the production and distribution aspects of the message as well as the possible or probable impacts of the content. In short, research in the second period took a comparatively broader view of the international flow of information, extending it beyond conventional journalistic and media studies and relating it to the process of political economy and structure of the system itself.

The development of research during these two periods can be better understood if we consider historical processes of the last two decades, such as the birth of new nation-states, the greater demands of citizens to participate in political and economic decision-making, the increasing number and power of transnational actors, the increase of mobility and human movements across national boundaries, the worldwide development of electronic communication technologies, the unsuccessful trials for establishing an international network for distributing television and other programs and documentaries, the transfer and growth of earlier sporadic news and information to a now-massive data and information flow, the neglect of and failure to cope with inequality and problems arising from the electromagnetic spectrum and the computer satellite systems, and, last but not least, the development of political debate around the New World Information/Communication Order.

We are at present on the threshold of a third phase, that of the so-called "post-industrialized" or "information age" now closely associated with the post-traditional telecommunication technologies such as videotext, computerized communication technologies, telematics, and scores of other technological auxiliaries often combined under the rubric of "informatics," implying complex communication and information systems and their interrelationships with the "information age." It is also a phase in which international communication and the flow of information are becoming viewed not only as hardware and software development but as behavioral and social development also. In short, there is an urgent need to view the phenomenon of information flow in its human–technological dimension and in the context of individual, national, international, and global issues and ramifications.

The communications revolution has meant the spread of technology, systems innovation, and the speed and quantity at which messages travel. But the real evolution is the *communication* revolution – explained in terms of a quest for satisfactory human interaction – rather than a *communications* revolution viewed through the lens of technological and institutional spread and growth. One characteristic of this third phase is that the interpretation of communication policies is no longer restricted; it realizes the possibility of and need for integrating the hitherto distinct spheres of information and communication policies.

In the preceding chapters, some tentative conclusions were drawn by examining the data and the research literature in specific aspects of international flow of information. Here follows an identification of the general trends and the emerging picture of the world information flow as one views the landscape of accumulated empirical evidence.

*Directionality of the Flow*

Inherent in the term "flow" is a vector quality. Three directional patterns have been hypothesized: center–periphery, vertical North–South flow, and triangular flow (a variation of North–South flow). In fact, the verticality of the North–South flow downward from the information-rich North to the information-poor South has come to be a common assumption lending itself to a foundation for further study. Researchers have generally set out to show that flows have been from North to South, and more often than not, in terms of the media selected and comparisons made, it has been demonstrated that such a directional trend exists.

The term "imbalance," however, has not been clearly defined by researchers. It has had quantitative and qualitative meanings to both researchers and policy makers. Whatever its meaning, "imbalance" in information and communication flows and structures is often regarded in isolation, rather than being seen as another manifestation of much deeper economic and political imbalances. Interestingly, the nature, pattern, and direction of the world economy are more or less parallel and depict the directionality of world information flow. In almost all kinds of information flow, whether it is news or data, educational, scientific, or human flow, the pattern is the same. The cycles are quite similar to cycles in other trade areas where industrially less developed countries export raw materials to industrialized countries for processing and then purchase back the more costly finished products. Notably lacking is the exchange of data, news, information, cultural programs and products, and persons among developing countries.

On the other hand, there exists a much better balance in terms of both quantity and quality of information among the industrially developed countries (see Figure 6.1 p. 112 above). This is not to say that proximity of cultural factors is not important in determining the flow direction, but merely to indicate the undeniably strong and important relations between the economic and political control of human and material resources, on the one hand, and communication, information, and cultural control on the other.

*Quality Versus Quantity*

Although there has been some quantitative improvement in the amount of information and news exchanges internationally during the last several years, the qualitative improvement is either incomplete or totally lacking. Indeed, such research evidence supports the hypothesis that in the areas of news flow, cultural and ideological distortion and biases have been predominant during the last several years, particularly in relation to several unfolding international, regional, and national events and development.

*Communication Technologies and International Policies*

There is a broadly shared perception of a growing overall gap between industrially developed and developing countries in the way they are able to create, process, and apply the needed information for economic, political, and cultural development. While such development, as convergence between telecommunication and computing, underlines a trend in the industrialized countries, the increasing needs and determination of developing countries to provide telecommunications in support of their national and international policies remain basic. Research supports the fact that the growth of technology is not necessarily increasing the access of all peoples to information, nationally or internationally. On the contrary, there is a disparity between the poor and the rich. At the same time, competition within and between the industrialized countries in the area of implementation and services is growing. Yet, during the last five years, there has been a remarkable global consensus regarding the needs for and value of structural change and development in the world communication system.

There is also a growing need for and realization of an international regulatory/standard-setting process and institutional modification of the present international communication system. The future need for increased tasks and responsibilities of the system will not be realized unless equitable legal, structural, and international steps are taken now. Otherwise, not only will the continuation of the current design of international communication enhance rather than diminish the dominance of certain industrialized countries, but the result of other industrialized nations' challenge to American dominance in the global market will disrupt the fragile new information economy.

## Trends in National Policies

The debate and writings on communication and information issues during the last 10 years have stimulated governments in both industrialized and developing countries to adopt national policies, and in some cases comprehensive plans, to respond to problems brought about by advances in computer and telecommunications technologies and to protect vital national interests. Developing countries particularly view their dependence on foreign firms and transnational actors as evidence that the important basis for national decision-making is now located outside their national boundaries.

These national policies are being designed in order to preserve national sovereignty; to ensure national security; to assure access to information held in data banks; to preserve cultural identity; to design appropriate educational, scientific, and artistic policies; and, in some cases, to protect individual privacy. While these measures are observable in some geographical areas in the direction of public interest, there are also cases in which national and local policies are directed toward a greater restriction of the individual citizenry and groups, in the direction of political and economic control. There is also a tendency in some industrialized countries toward commercialization and privatization of public communication.

## Imbalance in Communication Research

As research on the international flow of information has expanded during the last 10 years with most dramatic growth registered in the beginning of the 1980s, it has been accompanied by several new lines of inquiry. In fact, the last five years can be characterized as the most active period of international communication research in history. There is no doubt that the debate on the New World Information/Communication Order in various international forums, including UNESCO's declarations and activities, has been primarily responsible for this growth. The numerous conferences, symposia, and workshops held in many parts of the world; the increased number of periodicals and journals devoted to various aspects of information and communication; and a somewhat inflated amount of publishing in this area are all illustrative of this phenomenon.[14]

One of the findings of this study is that a substantial number of these studies have been carried out by the Third World scholars, a development that was almost absent in the early years of communication research. Yet, there exists a communication imbalance between field and subjects, between the issues and different geographical areas, and between epistemological and philosophical orientations. If there is to be a correction in communication imbalance, we need no less than a new order in communication research.[15]

For example, a survey for this study showed that there is no major textbook in the field of international relations either in North American or in Europe that has devoted a chapter to international communication and international flow of information. Little attempt has been made to incorporate the international implications of communication and information technology in the broader area of international affairs. Equally, the authors of communication textbooks have failed to place the findings of communication research in the context of international relations.

Furthermore, most studies on information flow have focused on only a few regions of the world, namely North America, Western Europe, and, to a lesser degree, Latin America and Asia. Thus, the contributions on the study of flow in Africa, the Middle East, and the socialist countries in the East have been less representative. When research is available, such things as language, translation, and distribution have become factors impeding the flow of information.

It should also be emphasized that the study of international communication in general, and the flow of information in particular, have been on the centrality of the North. Little attention has been given to South–South relations as a phenomenon in international communication and international relations. The study of the international flow of information as it relates to the southern half of the globe is usually cast in terms of "Third World development," and in the field of international politics as a case of "regional conflict management."

Among many writers on Third World development and communication there is not only no deep consciousness about the nature of change independent from big-power politics, but there is little consensus as to the nature and direction of indigenous cultural revolution or evolution now taking place. Thus the literature in this area fails to explain and predict the characteristics of the social process. This is particularly true when writings and research are dominated by a certain epistemological orientation. Unfortunately, to a great extent, the field has been the victim of either pure positivism or crude ideological orientations and biases. The failure of many students of international relations and international communication who have had this orientation, both in the West and in the East, to predict the social, cultural, and political development of many parts of the world in the last 10 years is a case in point. In short, there has been a high level of advocacy and a low level of analysis.

Therefore, the final global generalizations made in many past research findings are already flawed. Fortunately, one positive result of the ongoing and current discussion/controversy on the structure of world information is that it has stimulated debates on the nature and direction of communication research.[16] It is hoped that such debates will have a profound impact on the quality of research, and bring about a kind of pluralism that is badly needed.

There have been serious flaws in the study of information flow during the last three decades. Specifically, the analyses were inadequate in six major ways.

First, they were concerned primarily with the examination of channels and content, leaving either end of the process – the source and the destination– untouched. There have been no serious efforts to study precisely who makes what use of which kind of information on the destination level. Equally little attempt has been made to carry the research beyond the framework of the media to examine the primary sources of the message.

Furthermore, both traditions of international flow of information research in the 1950s–1960s and the 1970s–1980s proceeded with the assumption that distribution, consumption, and exposure to outside messages would have the desired impact. The literature on the flow emphasized the exposure, but could only make inferences on probable effect or impact. Less emphasis was placed on exactly what would happen to the recipients of information once they were exposed to internal and external messages. Less attention was paid to the dynamics of internal human and societal communication, and to the complexity of culture, in relation to mass media or other technologically mediated messages. Unless these factors are taken into account in a variety of cultural, political, and economic settings, we will have no more at our disposal than the "conventional wisdom" and guesswork as to the impact and effects of information on individuals, groups, and the international system as a whole.

Second, both phases and traditions of research were inherently biased toward the study of only that type of flow that was technologically oriented and developed, and that would fit the predetermined definitions of "mass media," "communications media," and "information media." Thus, the research of the past not only deemphasized but, to a large extent, ignored the role played by traditional, personal, and group channels in the process of information flow.

Third, the analysis of the flow of communication media was not externally related to the input and output of information in such areas as education, tourism, migration, science, and the arts. Consequently, the fragmentary nature of the studies, coupled with each discipline's traditional resistance to loss of autonomy, prevented both scholars and policy makers from having access to a wider framework of the international flow of information including both human and technological, economic and political, and cultural as well as social spheres.

Fourth, researchers almost totally ignored examination of the role of non-readers, non-viewers, and non-listeners who for a variety of reasons were not in the center of modern media exposure in the international flow of information, and concentrated only on those targets that were mediated through modern media technologies. Equally little attention was paid to the nature and patterns of information among the different socio-demographic strata, such as its international business and political leaders, or children and other specific age groups.

Fifth, the first period of the flow studies in the 1950s and 1960s emphasized the East–West relationship; the second phase characterizing the 1970s was tailored to the North–South axis, with emphasis being placed on the West–South aspect of that flow. Less attention was given to the international flow of information among the socialist nations, on the one hand, and the less industrialized countries of the Third World, on the other. The underlying assumptions of many scholars and policy makers, which divided the world into a monolithic pattern of First, Second, and Third Worlds, obviously hampered the analysis in light of diversification and pluralism, and contributed much to the stereotyping and the homogeneity of the Third World.

Sixth, most of these studies, using power paradigms either in their political or economic forms, paid less explicit and implicit attention to cultural analysis and methods. Therefore, the question of culture, though popular and controversial, remained subservient either to political or economic analyses, or to technological discourses, both in theory and methods.

**What Needs to be Learned**

This study began with the notion that to understand the international flow of information, and, thus, the role of communication in international relations, it is important that both the stages of production and distribution of messages be analyzed in terms of hardware and software. In light of preceding chapters and the conclusions drawn from the analysis of different dimensions of international flow of information, it is now appropriate to suggest that any future study of the flow of information must include two additional dimensions within the production–distribution process outlined previously. In the production stage these are the analysis of the source or sources that initially feed the stream of information through institutions, groups, transnational actors, and other channels. This will carry the process of the creation of symbols and messages beyond the present levels of analysis to the political, economic, and cultural groups, both national and international, that initially provide the information.

In the distribution stage, studies must be carried beyond conventional exposure to information, to analyses of the process of absorption, internalization, and utilization of messages in a given population nationally or internationally. It is only by paying close attention to the latter stage that we can learn something about the function or dysfunction and manifest or latent aspects of message transmission. Thus, the international flow of information, if it is studied comprehensively, must include a careful consideration of the factors in four distinct but related stages of the communication process: the source, the process of production, the process of distribution, and the process of utilization.

One important trend underlying most of the studies of flow is that, from its beginning right after World War II and continuing until the late 1970s, it was primarily, if not totally, an inter-nation- or "international"-oriented analysis rather than being world or global in context. That is to say, nation-states were most often the units of analysis in the traditional international relations framework, rather than communities, cultures, or regions in their anthropological, cultural, and historical contexts. In short, the division of the world into many units called nation-states, the desire of each nation-state to gain full political, economic, and cultural autonomy, and the articulation of the concept of power in terms of security, military, and economic capabilities of governments created a unique framework in which international flow of information analyses took place. More attention was paid to the sovereignty of nation-states than to the welfare of individuals. More emphasis was put on preservation and retention of national culture than individual identity. Yet, as we approach the end of the century, not only has the number of world actors in terms of nation-states increased, but a large number of transnational and supranational organizations have been created that are alternately in conflict or cooperation with nation-states.

Additionally, it is now clear that as a result of many social, political, economic, and cultural factors, there is a greater demand by transnational actors and individuals outside the nation-state for the articulation, formulation, and implementation of different policies. It is clear that a comprehensive analysis of the international flow of information must account for these factors, and research projects designed to examine the various facets of international information flow should include all these varied dimensions in their most complex forms.

Most current books, articles, and monographs barely scratch the surface of the problem. They view information and communication problems as a mere maladjustment of a purely economic, political, technological, or biological nature. In terms of the East–West conflict, communication and information problems are seen as incidental or ideological. In terms of the North–South debate, they are presumed to be economic. What is not understood is that communication problems are inherent in the nature of the modern industrialized and information culture. Accordingly, for the elimination of problems, the solutions prescribed with perfect confidence are either economic–technological readjustment – in money, banking, transportation, training and communication technology, computers, satellites, video, teletext, and other media auxiliaries – or a modification of political systems; a new bureaucracy, a new infrastructure, a new management, or a new form of disassociation. There is no doubt that some of these measures, where properly applied, can result in some improvements. But there is also no doubt that none of them can reach the source of the problem.

It is now clear that the development of modern communication technology and the continuous stream of information flow have increased consciousness of national sovereignty and have made proliferation of states and transnational actors possible. This has generated important functional demands on the international system well beyond its capacity to handle sufficiently with the existing machinery. This in turn raises important questions about the viability of the prevailing model and order of international information system to cope with the rapidly changing environment of international relations in general, and international communication in particular.

The fact that "the vessel of sovereignty" is leaking, and in some instances may even be sinking, is now beyond doubt. Nations may act as though they are in control of their full national rights, but the erosion of sovereignty through communication technology and new transnational actors is paralleled by the growing constraints on freedom of national action and the increasing responsibility seen for international organizations. As the locus of decision-making is continuously transferred from national to international and transnational levels, an increasing number of issues will have to be settled in an international environment. Otherwise the conflict is inevitable. It is here that international organizations, particularly those dealing with communication and information issues, are likely to become a more central force in international relations.

The problem of national policies versus international policies and considerations becomes crucial not only in the sphere of communication technology but also in the set of related global issues connected directly with the nature of information flow and the quality of communication. Such issues as environmental alteration as a result of human activity; weather and climate modification; large-scale experimental and weaponry actions with substantial and potential environmental effects; pollution; mineral and organic resources of the seabed; living resources of the sea; congestion in ocean uses; forestry; agriculture; geography; resource mapping; data gathering and distribution; navigation and traffic control; food and population – accompanied by increased public interest in protecting the environment – will result in a growing recognition that governments, a group of powerful nation-states, or a number of profit-motivated transnational actors do not have the right to act unilaterally in communication and technological areas when the effects may spread beyond national borders. The existing legal regime and the institutional structure of the global communication system with the entire complex of intergovernmental organizations will have even more difficulty in the future in meeting the needs and responsibilities of the new systems that will be developed in a few years unless serious and conscious attempts are made to prepare them for a new order.

A list of several (not exhaustive) functional elements and implications of the international flow of information as it relates to the international system can be cited here with the purpose of illustrating the kind of functional international requirement needed for many of the information flow systems examined in this volume.

1. *Management*. This is a crucial aspect of the international information system. As experience has shown in at least some cases, national ownership

and operation are not an adequate permanent arrangement for a variety of political, technical, and social reasons. If nationally owned, information systems are at the mercy of extreme international and regional cooperatives. Here, international bodies – both old and new – can contribute to the smooth operation of newly established information resources by having management responsibility and even legal ownership. Resource and technology operation, technical assistance, conduct of research, and financing of projects can certainly fall in this category.

Information exchange, data gathering and analysis, monitoring of physical phenomena, and facilitating national, regional, and international programs are among the elements related to the management function. Here, information and equal access to it are seen as factors for reducing dependency in economic, political, and cultural relations. An important issue here is that information and access to information are often viewed as power. The measure of the distribution of access, for example, can be seen in terms of global distribution of national focal points (NFPs). Focal points refer to "offices in appropriate national ministries, designed to serve as the liaison centers within an international information system." NFPs are particularly important for the developing countries because they bring the system and user close to one another. A study by Ernst Haas and John Gerard Ruggie found that "[i]n 1980, 17 major global information systems maintained 1039 NFPs; UN regional commissions maintained an additional 160."[17] Unfortunately, there appears to be concentration of NFPs among the richer countries, indicating, according to Haas and Ruggie, that developing countries have not had a significant input in the information provided.

Another implication is the potential role of international information systems to provide conceptual guidance in policy-making. A final consequence is the power of information systems to generate new forms of social organization. These consequences of the current state of information systems are, of course, speculative because of the incomplete state of knowledge about international information systems, but Haas and Ruggie conclude that research effort in this area is both justified and worthwhile. Their preliminary conclusion emphasizes that "[i]nformation systems can also affect the dependency of poorer countries on the industrialized North by compensating for the lack of material power within the developing world." In reference to cultural dependency, they conclude that "in the short run at least, the internationalization of Northern designs and products are enhanced rather than diminished by the prevailing structure of information flow."[18]

2. *Legal and regulatory aspects.* In the last three decades, communication policy and regulations have emerged as important issues in international relations and conflict resolution, and are expected to remain dominant issues into the twenty-first century. The lack of consistency and coherence in legal concepts and applications has been conditioned not only by historical circumstances but also by the development of new technologies.

Today in international law there is simply no generally recognized category under the heading of "information law." In many cases "information law" has been associated only with human rights. In other instances, it has referred to telecommunication law, space law, postal law, intellectual property rights, or a set of ad hoc rules and regulations developed through institutional and historical circumstances. Such salient areas as culture and education, trade and customs regulations, transborder flow of broadcast signals, terrestrial transmission, television signals via cable systems, and the host of related social, political, and technological elements are left open to different interpretations and national considerations. At the same time, international organizations serve as forums in the entire process of establishing international rules and norms. As a direct consequence of this norm allocation and establishment of international rules and regulations, international and intergovernmental organizations must deal with the disagreements arising from the interpretation and operation of new communication systems. Thus adjudication, mediation, and enforcement of standards and regulations are the functional areas within the realm of legal matters that the international community must consider at present and in the near future.

3. *Economic and strategic consequences*. Economic and strategic consequences are at the heart of the functional elements of international flow of information and modern communication technologies. Some of the systems being developed may involve differential costs of application for some geographical areas, as well as considerable differential benefits. Aside from purely economic consequences, there are security, political, and military factors that must be considered once the new systems are in operation. It is said that in such cases there will be strong pressure for these new systems to be internationally operated, with the users assured a voice in management and ownership. The profit potential of some of these systems cannot be ignored, nor can the equity principle involved in procurement and other related activities. It is here that these functional implications will have to accompany either the creation of new institutions or the modifications of existing infrastructure. Since information is a resource convertible to all kinds of power, there is, and in all probability will be, intensive competition and conflict over its production and utilization. In short, many questions are debatable, among them: Who pays and who profits? What will be the ecology of national and international systems in the future? What will be the stratification of the information elite nationally and globally? What will be the relationship between the knowers and users? Will it reduce the amount of armed conflict or will it lead directly to the ruinization of the Cold War? What about alienation, mental isolation, withdrawal, and cultural acceptability of individuals, groups, institutions, and even nation-states?

4. *Reliability and quality*. Finally, there remain the elements of reliability and quality of information, especially as they apply to human–machine

communication. The barriers to the quality and reliability of information arise not so much from the information transfer process, but rather from the translation required to accommodate the highly different and distinct characteristics of receivers and sources. Whereas humans, though noisy and narrow-banded, have simultaneous active channels such as facial expression and other intelligent and flexible sensory organs, machines are single-minded and highly restrained by programming. Machines can produce and generate text much faster than can be assimilated by humans, but information other than text can be assimilated much more rapidly by humans. Thus, forecasting human–machine technology is much more difficult than predicting hardware technology. Yet the information flow resulting from machine and from human–machine interaction is increasing at an enormous rate.

For example, the NASA Task Group in forecasting space technology between 1980 and 2000, predicted that:

> by the year 2000, imaging experiments in Earth applications satellites will be capable of returning $10^{13}$–$10^{15}$ bits per day, in comparison to the present rate of $10^{10}$–$10^{11}$ bits per day. The lower value of $10^{13}$ bits will encode approximately one million 300-page books; that much data per day corresponds to 30 Libraries of Congress per year.[19]

Comparable increases in data can be expected from other missions or technologies. Yet, the same report acknowledges "that reliability has not received attention in the individual forecasts in proportion to importance."[20] At the same time, the introduction of robots is no longer a science fiction. The NASA forecast in 1976 indicated that:

> During the last decade of this century the technological and economic developments of the preceding 15 years in information science and in computer hardware, combined with advances in problem-solving, learning, decision-making, sensory analysis, and other fields of artificial intelligence, will permit the introduction of simple robots to society at large.[21]

This has now become a reality.

Here lie the questions of reliability, quality, and utility, as well as individual, social, and global utility of information. This increase in the volume of information is not limited to space and satellite technologies. The elements and problems are equally applicable to all kinds of information channels outlined in this study. The increase in the amount of information will require increasing the amount of selectivity and absorption. It is also here that not the amount and quantity of information but its selectivity and quality will be crucial for communication.

There might indeed be a consensus on a now popular and somewhat orthodox view that the industrialized countries of the North have entered the information age, that many others are on the threshold, and that sooner or later the less industrialized societies and nations will enter the circle. There is, in fact, a broader view that regardless of the level of development, all nations are already in the midst of the information age – internationally if not globally. Although we might accept these views and propositions as natural or inevitable phenomena, the important question remains: Will we handle the Information Revolution better than we handled the Industrial Revolution?

## Research Questions for the Twenty-First Century

The international communication critiques of the last decade or so, noble and persuasive as they were in their presentation, did not go beyond political and economic debates. Whose version of the New World Information and Communication order are we supposed to construct? Should there be a new single world structure based on a nation-state system as we have now? Or would that constitute too many orders in the field of free play? Can we equate universal agreement with universal good? Whose idea of international peace and world community are we talking about? In the tree-shaped and linear model of communication, we have examined ground, roots, branches and we have analyzed the gatekeepers through channels; but have we located the gate-makers and gate-producers whose roots cannot be detected from our model? Will the progressive replacement of the mechanical and energy-based mode by yet more powerful linear models, inspired by current information/communication paradigms, serve to transform rational self-perception and to give individuals a new image of themselves? Would a new rationalism created as a result of the modern technologies be likely to impose a policy of radical instrumentalism, under which social problems would be treated as technical problems? These questions and the many others that inevitably will follow are pressing international communication research into new, uncharted territories in the twenty-first century. And this will be for the better.

As we approach the twenty-first century, I believe that the most wide-ranging questions regarding communication research will be seen at the international level. The increasing internationalization of domestic policies and its domestication of international politics should provide new challenges for international communication scholars. Here are examples of the main problem areas and themes as well as a few research questions raised by the new communication technologies and new development in international and intercultural communication:

1. In what ways are relationships between modern nation-states likely to be affected during emerging communication technologies and their political, economic, and cultural impacts? At the center of this question are the economic and strategic aspects of international communication for the wealthy and powerful states as well as the inevitability of technological dependency for the so-called developing countries and the Third World. The fact that existing instructional and regulatory structures of international systems have proven incapable of dealing with all the technological and political questions makes the international legal

regime somewhat problematic at the present time. This also raises further questions as to whether past and present strategies of self-reliance and self-sufficiency handled by a few developing countries will be applicable to new realities in the twenty-first century. The question remains: How possible will it be in the future for developing countries to maintain a capacity for independent technology assessment? To what degree will the decline of the superpowers make them abandon the strategy of status quo and help lure some fundamental changes into the structure of international communication as we know it?

2. To what extent do the new international communication technologies increase the erosion of cultural vitality and how will the modern nation-state systems with their secular-oriented national sovereign signifier cope with emerging religious political ideologies such as Islam which is based on universal community or *ummah*? This will require a thorough examination and understanding of communication systems of non-Western societies in both their traditional and modern forms as well as research into the world views, theories, and assumptions underlying the modes of both interpersonal and social communication in most geographical areas of the world. Especially important is the question of whether our orthodox and traditional methods of research will be enlisted to reinforce obstacles to our understanding of intercultural communication, or whether we will be able to improve and create methodologies that may assist us to expand our knowledge in understanding and respect for other forms of communication.

3. How much do we really know about the relationships between international communication and international peace and conflict resolutions? At the core of this question is the growing importance of modern communication technologies for the expansion and maintenance of the existing military–industrial complex of modern states, especially the great powers. At the same time, the last part of the twentieth century has seen nationalism, anti-imperialism, and revolution in many parts of the world and diverse nations and cultures in quest for self-determination and a new world order, as militarily weak powers confront the major powers with increasing success. Will the new century bring about a new course of action for reconciliation and cooperation or will it increase the amount of disinformation and deception through modern channels of communication thus leading the world into a greater stage of entropy?

4. What should (or would) the role of mass media be in helping to articulate and give identity to the various biological (age group), psychological, and aesthetic groupings that have begun to emerge as a result of the decline of traditional groupings and the increase of the so-called "postmodern" or "hypermodern" environments? Traditional communication research, especially in the field of mass media, emphasized the flow of information and content analysis, the gatekeeper process, and audience investigation but paid little attention to the sources generating information as well as the ultimate utilizers who

absorbed the information for a variety of decision-making purposes. Consequently, our knowledge about the role of communicators, political leaders, economic elites, religious and spiritual personalities, and new actors who have gained legitimacy remains sketchy. We also know very little about how information is handled by those who are exposed to it. Communication research in the twenty-first century must go beyond the simple production and distribution stages and must direct its attention to both the initial sources of the message and its absorption and utilization. To do this, international communication research needs to go beyond the existing political, economic, and sociological models to incorporate anthropological, linguistic, and sociocultural frameworks into its well-established domain.

5. What is the evolution of linguistic form and specialized languages under the impact of modern international communication technologies and the development of science and arts? The relationship between language and international communication, though very obvious to any student in the field, has been very much neglected in both textbooks and research journals. The relationships between world languages and international flow of goods and services as well as cultural industries will, in my estimate, be of even greater importance in the future as we move toward adopting a single language as a means of technical and instrumental transfer of know-how and at the same time are faced with the ever-growing interests in national languages and educational policies.

6. Has communication research a role to play in understanding the dynamics of modern world systems in terms of studying the transnational actors, international division of labor, immigrants, refugees, and individual economic, political, cultural, and military elites whose actions and reactions bypass national boundaries and in themselves formally and informally constitute new leases of power, bargaining, and negotiations?

7. What role can communication research play in ecological and environmental issues in the twenty-first century? What about the impact of communication technologies in such areas as disaster prevention, public health, hunger, and other international, regional, and national crisis issues?

8. And last, but not least, would information society of the twenty-first century also be primarily a material society as was the case with the Industrial Revolution? Where are the spiritual and ethical or moral sources of the new era we are talking about? What would be the role of communication researchers in handling these critical questions?

## Notes

1. Gerald R. Miller, "Taking Stock of a Discipline," *Journal of Communication* (Ferment in the Field – Special Issue), 33 (1983), pp. 31–41.

2. John Rajchman, *Michel Foucault: The Freedom of Philosophy* (New York: Columbia University Press, 1985); Ken Wilbur, *Up from Eden: A Transpersonal View of Human Evolution* (Boulder, CO: Anchor Press, 1983); A. Katherine N. Hayles, *The Cosmic Web: Scientific Field Models and Literary Strategies in the 20th Century* (Ithaca, NY: Cornell University Press, 1983); Erick Jantsch, *The Self Organization Universe* (New York: Perryman Press, 1980); Lawrance Grossberg, "Does Communication Theory Need Intersubjectivity? Toward an Immanent Philosophy of Interpersonal Relations," in Michael Burgoon, ed., *Communication Yearbook*, 6 (1982), pp. 171–205; Ihah Hassam, *The Postmodern Turn: Essays in Postmodern Theory and Culture* (Columbus, OH: Ohio University Press, 1982); Michel Foucault, *Discipline and Punish: The Birth of the Prison* (New York: Vintage Books, 1979); and Hamid Mowlana, *Global Communication in Transition: The End of Diversity?* (Beverly Hills, CA: Sage Publications, 1996).

3. Miller, "Taking Stock of a Discipline."

4. Robert H. White, "Mass Communication and Culture: Transition to a New Paradigm," *Journal of Communication*, 33 (1983), pp. 279–301.

5. Herbert I. Schiller, "Critical Research in the Information Age," *Journal of Communication*, 33 (1983), p. 256.

6. Jennifer Daryl Slack, "The Political and Epistemological Constituents of Critical Communication Research," *Journal of Communication*, 33 (1983), pp. 208–219.

7. Luis Ramiro Beltrán, "Alien Promises, Objects, and Methods in Latin American Communication Research," in Everett Rogers, ed., *Communication and Development: Critical Perspective* (Beverly Hills, CA: Sage Publications, 1976), pp. 15–42.

8. Lawrence D. Kincaid, *The Convergence Model of Communication* (Honolulu: East–West Communication Institute, 1979), p. 4.

9. Ithiel de Sola Pool, "What Ferment?" *Journal of Communication*, 33 (1983), pp. 260–261.

10. Cary Nelson and Lawrence Grossberg, *Marxism and Interpretation of Culture* (Urbana, IL: University of Illinois Press, 1987).

11. Jean-François Lyotard, *The Postmodern Condition: A Report on Knowledge* (Minneapolis, MN: University of Minnesota Press, 1984); Jean Baudrillard, "The Implosion of Meaning in the Media and the Implosion of the Social in the Masses," in Kathleen Woodward, ed., *The Myths of Information: Technology and Postindustrial Culture* (Madison, WI: Coda Press, 1980), pp. 137–150; Jürgen Habermas, "Modernity – An Incomplete Project," in Hal Foster, ed., *The Anti-Aesthetic. Essays on Postmodern Culture* (Port Townsend, WA: Bay Press, 1983); Hal Foster, ed., *The Anti-Aesthetic: Essays on Postmodernism Culture* (Port Townsend, WA: Bay Press, 1983; Foucault, *Discipline and Punish*.

12. Gilles Deleuze and Felix Guattari, *A Thousand Plateaus: Capitalism and Schizophrenia* (Minneapolis, MN: University of Minnesota Press, 1987), p. 23.

13. Ibid., p. 7.

14. To cite the various symposia held on international communication will take many pages. For a list of periodicals in the field of mass communication alone see Sylvester Dziki, *World Directory of Mass Communication Periodicals*, Cracow (Poland), Bibliographical Section of IAMCR and Press Research Centre, Cracow, Poland, 1980.

15. This point has also been emphasized by K.E. Eapen, "Reshaping Training and Research for the NIIO," *Media Development*, XXVII: 4 (1980), pp. 16–19.

16. For example see: International Association for Mass Communication Research, New Structure of International Communication: The Role of Research (Main papers from the 1980 Caracas Conference), Leicester, International Association for Mass Communication Research, 1982: UNESCO and International Association for Mass Communication Research Consultation Meeting Report of July 1982, "Communication in the Eighties: The Nature of the Problem and Some Proposals for an International Research Strategy," prepared by Annabelle Sreberny-Mohammadi, Leicester, Centre for Mass Communication Research, University of Leicester, January 1983; E.M. Rogers and F. Balle, eds, *Mass Communication Research in the United States and Europe* (Norwood, NJ: Ablex Publishing Corporation, 1983);

James D. Holleran, "Warning Schools or Complementary Perspectives?: A Case of Critical Eclecticism," Leicester, Centre for Mass Communication Research, Leicester University, 1983; Hamid Mowlana, "Mass Media and Culture: Toward an Integrated Theory," in William B. Gudykunst, ed., *Intercultural Communication Theory: Current Perspectives* (Beverly Hills, CA: Sage Publications, 1983); Tamas Szecsko, "The Grammar of Global Communication," *Intermedia*, 10: 2 (March 1982); Alex Edelstein, *Comparative Communication Research* (Beverly Hills, CA: Sage Publications, 1982); G. Melisoek, K.E. Rosengren, and J. Stappers, eds, *Cultural Indicators: An International Symposium* (Vienna: Akademie der Eisenschaften, 1983); and George Gerbner and Marsha Siefert, eds, *World Communications: A Handbook* (White Plains, NY: Longman, 1983). See also *Journal of Communication*, 33 (1983; the entire issue is devoted to communication research). For a more general and epistemological debate on communication and society see Jürgen Habermas, *Communication and the Evolution of Society* (Boston, MA: Beacon Press, 1979); Ali Shari'ati, *Marxism and Other Western Fallacies* (Berkeley, CA: Mizan Press, 1980); and I.V. Blauberg, V.N. Sadovsky, and E.G. Yudin, *Systems Theory: Philosophical and Methodological Problems* (Moscow: Progress Publishers, 1977).

17. Ernst B. Haas and John Gerard Ruggie, "What Message in the Medium of Information System?" *International Studies Quarterly*, 26: 2 (June 1982), p. 205.

18. Ibid., p. 218.

19. National Aeronautics and Space Administration (NASA), *A Forecast of Space Technology: 1900–2000* (Washington, DC: Government Printing Office, 1976), p. 3-117.

20. Ibid., pp. 3-119.

21. Ibid., p. 3-105.

# 12

# The Unfinished Revolution:
# The Crisis Of Our Age

It is ironic that for at least the last three decades both the idealist-humanist and the strategist (this term would encompass the latter three approaches mentioned earlier) have emphasized the so-called "communication revolution" as a focus of analysis for their respective schools of thought. The communications revolution has meant the spread of technology, systems innovation, and the speed and quantity of messages. However, as we noted in the previous chapter the real revolution has been the *communication* revolution, explained in terms of a quest for satisfactory human interaction, rather than a *communications* revolution viewed through the lens of technological and institutional spread and growth. In other words, the cultural components of international and human relations have been overshadowed by the political, economic, and technological aspects of the field. This is unfortunate, for modern political development, social rebellion, religious resurgence, and contemporary revolutionary movements in both the industrially developed and the less industrialized societies can be better understood if we look at them from the perspective of human interaction (i.e., from a communication analysis), rather than from a purely politico-economic or technological perspective.

Western theories of human development, both Marxist and liberal democratic, proceed from a shared assumption that the development of societies requires that modern economic and social organization replace traditional structures. Widely accepted in the West and diffused among the elites of the less industrialized countries, this assumption encompasses, among other things, industrialization in the economy; secularization in thought, personality, and communication; the development of a "cosmopolitan attitude"; integration into the "world culture"; and rejection of traditional thoughts and technologies simply because they dominated the past and thus are not "modern." But contemporary movements around the world, whether in groups, communities, or nations, all share an alternative vision of human and societal development. This "third way" eschews both Marxism and liberal democracy. It has its roots in more humane, ethical, traditionalist, anti-bloc, self-reliance theories of societal development. In short, the "third way" seeks not to promote itself or its ideology; it seeks dignity through dialogue. It is the quest for dialogue that underlies the current revolutionary movements around the world.

The French Revolution, for all of its noble ideas and promises, in the end did not further this quest for dialogue among individuals. On the contrary, it marked the watershed in the rise of the individual *vis-à-vis* the nation-state. The concepts of freedom, equality, and fraternity that came to the forefront – in terms of political and economic aspirations by the individual making demands on the state – have played a major role in revolutions ever since and led to the rise of modern nationalism. But this juncture can be identified as the point of departure of individuals from their communities. No longer was interpersonal communication the main mode of communication. Bureaucracies arose to take care of human needs. Humans communicated with each other more as roles than as individuals. Mass *media* began to *mediate* government–citizen communication. People became alienated from one another as cultures moved inexorably from association (*Gemeinschaft*) into abstraction (*Gesellschaft*). The growth of "instrumental" and "functional" communication became paramount in the decline of genuine inter/intrapersonal dialogue.

This preliminary exploration of the area of inquiry of human communication, of course, appears to present few or no points of controversy. The detrimental effect of modern technological society and its monstrous institutions on the capacity for inter-intrapersonal communication has been well documented, analyzed, and accepted as a fait accompli by countless sociologists, anthropologists, and psychologists. What still begs analysis is the possibility of reversing this trend, of reviving the capacity for human communication among already alienated individuals. Two steps are required. First, we must shift our attention and our emphasis from *communications* (as means) to *communication* (as sharing and trust). Intellectually, this will require a reorientation in communication studies: from sole concern with the roles, effects, and impacts of communication media to the study and discovery of a communication theory of society. Second, we must create an environment in the form of a restraining influence that can stop this deterioration in relations, can protect humanity from self-destruction, and can eventually direct the machinery of communication to explore human growth and potential.

## Communication as Cultural Ecology

Ecology as a concept offers a useful framework not only for the well-being or deterioration of our planet and physical environment but for principles that can be applied to our cultural as well as media environment. The ecological perspective argues for sustainable development and a communication system that satisfies our needs without diminishing the prospects of future utilization.

It now seems more imperative than ever to discuss global tension, not only in terms of explicitly economic, geopolitical, and military structures, but also equally in the context of cultural communication and information struggles. To suggest that culture and communication are crucial for analyses of international relations is not to view these areas as exclusive territories of the idealist approach to world politics that so often characterized the Wilsonian era of international politics and the more normative discourse of war and peace literature which followed the years immediately after World Wars I and II. The post-Cold War era, I believe, will bring the cultural dimensions of world politics to center-stage.

For one, the reductionism of the conservative school of realpolitik, and that of radical political economy, which dominated the scholarly and policy fields for over four decades, proved incomplete in answering the many questions regarding developments around the world. Furthermore, the epistemological tradition of research, in which the realm of ideas was separated from that of matter, was not only historically specific to the tradition of Western philosophy and science but also created a dualism which impeded the formulation of concepts and theories of a practical nature. Most important of all, the erosion of state legitimacy, and the political development that followed the events of Eastern Europe and the Soviet Union, combined with the economic crisis in the West and challenges emanating from non-Western culture, made the "inevitable" conduct of human affairs by the Western powers more problematic.

Today, as the West moves toward the Information Society Paradigm, the conceptions of justice, derived from civil society by the intellectual elites of the nineteenth and twentieth centuries, have run into trouble. On the international level, the conventional argument was popularized that, if one wanted peace, one should prepare for war. The systems of autonomous nation-states had little sense of community but strove for power and divergent interests under pluralism. For much of humankind, on national and international levels, culture became increasingly something that arrived in cans. Indeed, a contradiction developed between nationalism of the small powers and integration of the big powers. Thus, hegemony in the name of universalism was asserted by the big powers as small nations struggled against domination. Both realism and historical materialism directed attention to conflict. On the national and societal level, the line between civil rights and state rights became blurred.

Elsewhere, I have argued that the process of information and technological innovations, as it relates to communication between human beings and their environment and among peoples and nations, can be explained under what could be termed *the unitary theory of communication as ecology*.[1] I use the term *ecology* here in a broad sense to include all the symbolic environments in which human and technological communication takes place.

Thus, the major dimensions of this ecological terrain include the following: (1) ecology of goods and commodities, such as industrial and manufacturing items; (2) ecology of services, which includes banking, insurance, and education; (3) ecology of warfare, meaning all the military and security

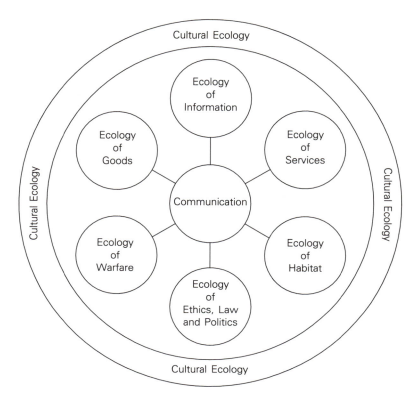

Figure 12.1 *Unitary model of communication as cultural ecology. The order in which the six ecological dimensions are shown is not fixed and static, but rather dynamic and interchangeable*

hardware, software, and the infrastructure therein; (4) ecology of information, encompassing such processes as cultural industries and mass media; (5) ecology of habitat, comprising such areas as demography, housing, physical environment, and pollution; and (6) ecology of ethics and morality, referring to specific normative discourse such as religion, mores, laws, and social contracts (see Figure 12.1).

These six terrains are not spatial but relational and integrative – that is, not only do we interact with these environments as separate and one-to-one bases, but also the interactions of all these six with each other and with human beings in an integrative form characterize the unique aspect of our civilization. Hence, our cultural, economic, and political environments cannot be understood completely unless we turn our attention to this unitary phenomenon in terms of communication and culture. Thus, our notion of self, society, and universe is very much shaped by this ecological view and the way we perceive language, literacy, arts, sciences, and in short reality.

## Communication and the Human Potential

Today many scientists in the United States, Europe, Japan, and Russia are in agreement that human beings are using a very small fraction – between 6 percent and 10 percent – of their capacities. For example, the capacity to experience our environment more freely through our olfactory organs remains a potential. Ever since the air became an overcrowded garbage dump for industrial wastes and the internal combustion engine, it has become easier for us to turn off our sense of smell than to keep it functioning. We have experienced similar closures with other senses as well. By closing ourselves off from both our physical and interpersonal environment, we have reduced our capacity to communicate. Consequently, we perceive less clearly and, as a result, we feel less.

Not only do we shut off awareness of our own feelings, but we are becoming desensitized as to how other people feel. Today, in many industrialized societies, the media (especially television), peer groups and bureaucracies (same-age groups and working cliques), and loneliness accompanied with boredom have replaced parents, relatives, neighbors, and other caring adults. Research in at least half a dozen human-potential centers across the United States supports the hypothesis that our capacities are almost infinite. But the question remains: how can we learn to use them when "negative conditioning" limits our confidence and approach to life?

Take, for example, the media system and the educational system – two of the most powerful channels of communications. The excessive focus on violence in television programs and motion pictures, and the emphasis on sensationalism in much of today's radio and television news, are the result of a narrow, almost brutal attitude toward life that is inimical to the development of the human potential. The world is increasingly perceived as a threat, and viewers and readers become anxious and lose their reservoir of trust. In many people there slowly grows a conviction that it is safer to withdraw from such a world, to isolate oneself from its struggle, and to let others make decisions. As our self-concept erodes, our "trust factor" – a fundamental element in harmonious social life – diminishes.

Many commentators around the world have argued that our modern educational system damages creative minds and limits experiences with problem solving rather than effectively teaching necessary skills and fostering diverse abilities. Compartmentalizing information not only makes it more difficult to learn and to retain but also ignores the necessary perspective and practical aspects that a more comprehensive approach would include. Each student has unique needs and abilities which must be taken into consideration when planning a course of study.

The general tendency now is to emphasize the vocational aspect of education, using a hard-headed, businesslike tone. Higher education is represented as an industry engaged in manufacturing socially needed commodities such as secretaries, engineers, economists, and even communicators. As usual, the central claim is efficiency, and the logic is that mass education requires mass-production methods. To some critics, the result is already clear: "technication," meaning standardization. In the age of cybernetics and our highly technological society, the process of personal orientation and self-discovery is becoming not a luxury but a necessity. On most of our college campuses few students, apart from those who have a vocation and know exactly where they are going, know enough either of themselves or of the world to make effective choices. Although we are limited by our culture, we must seek alternatives that best suit our political, social, and economic needs. Education is the mainstay of culture, for how one learns is culturally determined; but flexibility and creativity are the keys to positive change and growth.

## Toward a New Perspective of Global Communication

Classical theories of social change and social processes did not consider communication as an independent dimension of human activity. At the same time, the science of humanity tended to classify itself with the natural sciences. Consequently, knowledge of historical change and social evolution made possible the control of social processes in a manner analogous to the control learned in the natural sciences.[2] A reductionist tendency was generated, in which the communication act was incorporated into production and work.[3] Communication and culture became subservient to the mode of production rather than being a superstructure itself. This conceptualization made it impossible to separate some of society's most distinguished activities that were not in simple feedback relations to work and production.

Elsewhere, I have described how the old theories of communication and culture – drawn from the laissez-faire doctrine of economics, technological determinism school of thought, and the political economy paradigm – have usually taken a one-way view of the process, that of the impact of the technology and the media on work and culture, and have suggested an integrative framework in which culture and value systems are in central position in the process with significant impact on the media and work.[4] Here, in the interest of time and space, I would only add that we might consider a communication theory of society in which cultural traditions are the basis of the rationalization of action and in which the organizational principles of communication determine the range of possibilities within which economic, political, and technological development might evolve. In short, it is the mode of communication – not in its technical and instrumental forms but in its human-interaction form – that determines the outcome of social processes.

Extending this to international relations, or, to use a better term, world society, it justifies and encourages new approaches to cross-cultural relations. The limitations of the traditional approaches to communicating across and between cultures are too apparent when one looks at recent, less-than-successful policies of the great or small powers toward each other. The discontents and revolutions in many parts of the world have been efforts by individuals to communicate their needs for dialogue, and for respect and dignity.[5] In short, there is more at stake in recent revolutions and protests than the traditional fight for nationalism and material goods. Transcending these limits would benefit not only individuals and institutions interested in the humanistic sharing of values but also those with political, economic, and technological concerns.

Today, the process of intercultural relations has become more complex and multidimensional. Aside from the development of technological hardware, we can observe the emergence of a universal superculture based on science and technology, development of world economy and population, revival of cultural identity and ethnicity, appearance of transnational actors, and the role played by nation-states in national development. While these latter activities are more difficult to quantify and categorize than most conventionally directed activities of governmental and nongovernmental actors, there is an increasing realization of their importance in the overall intercultural as well as international communication processes.

Based on the propositions just outlined, I feel that the prospect for future intercultural relations will be shaped by three realizations:

1. True democracy will not occur without the development of communication at a dualistic level: the technical means of communications and communication itself.
2. Future intercultural cooperation and conflict will be determined by the relationship of communications (technological development) and communication (traditional classical channels for satisfactory human interaction).
3. The new international relations will emphasize more than relations among nation-states or transnational actors: they will emphasize relations among individuals along social and psychological channels.

Analysis of these three points may provide us with a better understanding of the future relations between cultures and peoples.

A definition of international communication (a term used here to include both international and intercultural communication) combines both a national and international dimension. It is a term used to describe a field of inquiry and research that consists of the transfer of values, attitudes, opinion, and information through individuals, groups, governments, and technologies, as well as the study of the structure of institutions responsible for promoting or inhibiting such messages among nations and cultures. It entails an analysis of the channels and institutions of communication, but, more important, it involves examination of the mutually shared meanings that make communication possible. These meanings might take the form of information, opinions, and values, and an examination of their native origin might well be necessary for their international and cross-cultural comprehension. For many, international communication also involves a normative element: the idea that the multiplication of communication channels and international contacts will automatically bring great international understanding. However, both the theories of major contribution to the field and the weight of empirical findings refute this notion. Advances in communication technology, without an accompanying transformation of values, will not result in the mutually shared images and meanings that form the basis of any international consensus.

The meaning of any message is the change it produces in the subjective knowledge structure, or in the image, of communicators. Accordingly, the value systems of communicators are the single most important element in determining the effect of the message on images. Similarly, the question of primary significance is whether the communicator and recipient see common meaning in the message. While many scholars appear to put more emphasis on this acquisition of common meanings, all stress the significance of this dynamism in the communication process. While recognizing the dual nature of human language as both social and personal, we might even put more emphasis on the concept of mutual human involvement in the communication process, for communication consists of a sharing of mutually recognized signs. Thus, for communication to have meaning it requires a change in the image of the recipient. However, new meanings or the reinforcement of previously held meanings must take place if the process is to be termed communication.

We should also give further consideration to the implications of nationality, ethnicity, and group difference, because in some cases loyalties toward one group mean to some extent antagonism toward other groups. As a result, resistance to the process of international communication is frequently perceived as a positive act in promoting the coherence of the smaller group and its cultural identity.

While the notions of cultural pluralism or multiculturalism are recent, the phenomenon they express is not. The birth of nations during the last four decades or so and the upheavals and changes occurring in the old nations across cultural and social lines are not simply the result of political and economic changes. They also represent an important communication, cultural, and intellectual development. Advances in communication and transportation, when coupled with social and psychological elements, have helped to lessen cultural isolationism. These advances also tend to increase the cultural awareness of minorities by making them more aware of the distinction between themselves and others. Individuals become more aware of alien groups as well as those who share their own identities. Thus communication plays a pervasive role not only in social mobility and nation building, but also in strengthening group consciousness.[6] It is here that the symbolic environment created along the lines of mutually shared images and meanings by non-technical aspects of communication plays a crucial role in coping with possible dysfunctioning processes of communication technology.

Greater international understanding, therefore, is not a direct or automatic result of the rapid expansion of international communication. At least one writer has made the important distinction between "knowledge by reporting" and "knowledge by encounter."[7] The former has proliferated on a grand scale, but has merely led in most cases to perception of the affairs of other peoples in abstract clichés. The proliferation of communication through the international media, for example, may in fact desensitize those on the receiving end, as in many cases during wars and international crises. "Knowledge by encounter" has expanded at a greatly reduced pace, and, consequently, effective international and intercultural communication has been handicapped by the dearth of mutually recognized signs. Even the increase in exchange of individuals fails substantially to promote this "knowledge by encounter," because most of this flow, like tourism, involves the movement of richer people to the poorer and more antiquated areas of other countries in order to confirm what the visitors already believe. While this view seems to contain an element of exaggeration, there is much evidence to support the conclusion that the "whole world communication network may drive us apart emotionally."[8] Unless a reorientation of value systems takes place to bring about a corresponding change in the images and perceptions of communicators, the technological revolution in the machinery of international communication will be unlikely to result in an enhanced sharing of mutually recognized signs and meanings. Modern communication technology does not guarantee improved international understanding, but it does allow more possibility for it.

**An Ethical Framework**

It has been suggested in this study that the quest for dialogue and the transcendence of alienation through interpersonal communication is an ongoing revolution in society, and that this must be recognized and examined. The point here is to note a social phenomenon, not to lament the lack of good conversation. This is both a human and societal problem. The suggestion is that the way *people* relate to each other in a world of "internationalized" culture and consciousness may be more important than how *nation-states* relate. On this human level, we must distinguish between the politically "sexy" right to communicate and the more homely need, or even yearning, to communicate.

This is not to suggest that we should abandon our efforts to improve our communication technology; nor is it proposed that organizational, technical, or even politically organized communication should be limited. In an extension of Shakespeare's observation that the world is a stage where all humans are the players nestles one of the most powerful tributes to the utility of international communication forums. The United Nations with all its shortcomings, UNESCO, and many other intergovernmental and non-governmental organizations and institutions have served as theaters where nation-actors might play out their roles, communicating frustrations that, if left unexpressed, might lead to violence. The value of this cannot be underestimated in view of the recurrent scenario in world history, in which comparatively small countries that feel neglected or unheard can set in motion chains of events that climax in catastrophic conflagrations. Another advantage of international forums has been the fact that they have at least partially compelled a farewell to that long chapter of human history where the strong agreed to divide the rest of the world between themselves, literally and figuratively, or set the rules that the weak would follow.

The world scope of the media and communication must ultimately be viewed as a whole. While nations will always retain characteristics of lifestyle to maintain separate distinction, it is important to consider the kind of impact a hypothetical global ethical framework might have. After all, the whole idea behind a media entity, both technological and traditional, lies in the effectiveness of its communication. Communication can only function on interpersonal, local, and national levels for so long. Eventually it transcends national boundaries to blanket other countries' operations and gain insight into new and different cultural schemes. It also creates an international or global symbolic environment in which the conduct of international political and economic behavior must take place. It is at this juncture, when the nature of the media coverage crosses cultural lines, that an ethical framework, one that hovers above all nations, must be considered. Recent studies in the United States and in Europe show dramatic changes in public opinion on such issues as arms, defense expenditure, nuclear war, and allocation of world resources as a result of the demise of the Cold War. In the United States, although the threat of war has become less, the military spending has remained constant. The American public in general, have supported their government's military involvements in such places as the Persian Gulf, Haiti, Bosnia, etc. Yet, the same population feels that such expenditures are a waste of available resources. It is perhaps difficult at this juncture to prove that the media coverage is in major part responsible for this shift of attitude, but the long history of media coverage of the arms race, and perpetuation of the so-called "threat" and arms "gap" notions cannot be denied; nor can we dispute any longer the inability of the media to cover the current religious resurgence and political upheaval around the world.

This in itself supports the argument that what is needed now is a shift from a manipulative, technology-oriented communication to more interaction, human dialogue, and exchange of ideas. To achieve this we must move to create and promote a set of principles or considerations that is not culture-bound but universal, strives for the dignity and potential of human beings, and saves the world from a catastrophic war and destruction. Present narrowly defined ethical or professional codes of ethics are irrelevant, inconsistent, and ineffective as tools in creating such an atmosphere of understanding simply because they do not challenge the technological determinist view of communication, are acquiescent to the centralized system of management, and put too much hope in the hands of nation-states and actors to deliver the goods. A confluence of historical factors has produced this disorder in the moral dimension of our communication process. The utilitarianism that pervades the world and marks various political economies generates a stream of dissenters who consider social choices unjust. Until some synthesis of the moral system is achieved, our conduct at home and abroad will continue to be indecisive. But before we can begin to suggest a better future we have to engage in a dialogue and national debate about the cycle of desire in our own institutions. Prevention of war, respect for human dignity, and recognition of diverse cultural values, religions, and traditions different from our own are the areas that must be promoted and publicized internationally.

The kinds of principles that an international code of consideration might propose should be designed to apply to a form of behavior that engenders moral, ethical, and thoughtful issue-coverage, whether or not there is fertile ground present in a given country for it to flourish. Part of the idea of a code of ethics is that it be exactly that: ethical. The concept of ethics does not imply force. It is the study of what ought to be, so far as this depends upon the voluntary action of individuals. While it is still too utopian to hope for countries to feel an ethical duty and obligation in mass media communication, the only way for such a proposition to be sustained would be for professional organizations, and not governments, to decide on these principles. It is impossible to create a universal code of ethical and professional media conduct, but it is not impossible to draw a set of broad considerations and principles on which the human resources can be mobilized. The ultimate ethical power the communication institutions have within themselves is to serve the public, and the zenith of serving that public is reached when a communication entity succeeds in raising a group, a public, or a world, whatever its size, to a higher level of understanding and insight.

In this spirit I would propose four basic principles, or what one might call a set of considerations:

1. *Prevention of war and promotion of peace.* If, as so often demonstrated, international media can mobilize for war and exacerbate tensions, why can they not do the reverse? International media and all communication institutions should:

- increase the amount of information available on peaceful solutions to conflict;
- break down stereotypes that dehumanize opposing populations;
- be aware of hidden biases of coverage on controversial issues;
- serve as early warning devices to bring attention to potential flash points;
- remind opponents of peaceful solutions to conflicts;
- confer prestige on the peacemaker;

- help create a public mood conducive to the spirit of reconciliation; and
- put peacemakers on opposite sides in touch with one another.

2. *Respect for culture, tradition, and values.* No one culture or value system has ownership of the truth. Only in the dialogue of adversaries will the truth emerge. International media and communication institutions should:

- promote respect and tolerance for the world's manifold cultures;
- uphold tradition in the face of unchallenged outside intrusion;
- facilitate the often difficult and distorted communication between cultures;
- help diverse value systems arrive at common definitions for such universal goals as peace, integrity, and national sovereignty;
- point out that deeply ingrained cultural values determine in part a nation's political behavior; and
- strengthen and preserve cultural identities and support cultures in the face of outside domination.

3. *Promotion of human rights and dignity.* Communication institutions must provide a voice to the dissenter and the downtrodden. Freedom of speech, of the press, and of information are vital for the realization of human rights. Communication should:

- publicize violations of human rights and international conventions;
- promote access of individuals and groups to media outlets in the face of domination by elites or majorities; and
- promote the democratization of communication, which means removing the obstacles to the free interchange of ideas, information, and experience among equals.

4. *Preservation of the home, human association, family, and community.* International media and communication institutions must attempt to reverse the trend toward alienation, de-individuation, atomization, and anonymity. They should, for example:

- promote interpersonal communication by facilitating more interaction among people rather than narcotizing them through mass-distributed programming; and
- facilitate self-reliance and interdependence by publicizing local, decentralized solutions to common problems.

I would be the first to acknowledge that these principles are general, culturally relative, and will at times have different meanings in the context of prevailing ideologies and belief systems. The point, however, is to place them in the main agenda of the day as we normally do with political, military, technological, economic, and business issues, with the hope that a social, ethical, and moral ecological balance can be created and a genuine learning process take place in the international system. Our knowledge of the "real" or "true" international system is incomplete, since we do not have a coherent theory or scientific data on the image-creating processes of the international system. The images of the international system in the minds of decision makers and the public alike are derived not from a systematic and scientific study of day-to-day events, but from a mélange of contradictory and ill-designed "literary" information. Today, the road to a stable peace in the world requires a learning process on the part of not only the national decision makers but the public as a whole. Its roots can be traced to three general but interrelated areas. First is the common maturity and civility of all types of international societies that could outgrow the adolescent disease of nationalism and ethnocentrism; second is the learning process accompanied by the high cost of human and material alienation – showing that "bad behavior" does not pay off in the long run; and third is the communication and symbolic environment and climate, in the form of restraining influences that can keep nation-states from devouring each other. It is to this last point that this epilogue is addressed.

## Notes

1. See Hamid Mowlana, *Global Communication in Transition: The End of Diversity?* (Thousand Oaks, CA: Sage Publications, 1996).

2. For a non-Western view of this process, see Ali Shari'ati, *Marxism and Other Western Fallacies* (Berkeley, CA: Mizan Press, 1980).

3. For a Western view along the line of critical theory see Jürgen Habermas, *Communication and the Evolution of Society* (Boston: MA: Beacon Press, 1979).

4. Hamid Mowlana, "Mass Media and Culture: Toward an Integrated Theory," in William Gudykunst, ed., *Intercultural Communication Theory: Current Perspectives* (Beverly Hills, CA: Sage Publications, 1983), pp. 149–170.

5. Hamid Mowlana, "Technology versus Tradition: Communication in the Iranian Revolution," *Journal of Communication*, 29: 3 (1979), pp. 107–112.

6. See Hamid Mowlana and Ann Elizabeth Robinson, "Ethnic Mobilization and Communication Theory," in Abdul A. Said and Luiz R. Simmons, eds, *Ethnicity in an International Context* (New Brunswick, NJ: Transaction Books, 1976), pp. 48–63.

7. Colin Cherry, *World Communication: Threat or Promise?* (London: John Wiley-Interscience, 1971), p. 8.

8. Ibid., p. 175.

# Bibliography

This is a selected bibliography representing the different dimensions of international flow of information. For additional references see the text.

Adams, William C., ed., *Television Coverage of International Affairs* (Norwood, NJ: Ablex Publishing Corporation, 1982).

Adams, William C., ed., *Television Coverage of the Middle East* (Norwood, NJ: Ablex Publishing Corporation, 1981).

Alcalay, Ammiel, *After Jews and Arabs: Remaking Levantine Culture* (Minneapolis, MN: University of Minnesota Press, 1992).

Alger, Chadwick F., "Foreign Policies of the United States Public," *International Studies Quarterly*, XXI: 2 (June 1977), pp. 277–317.

Altbach, Philip G. and Eva-Maria Rathberger, *Publishing in the Third World: Trend Report and Bibliography* (New York: Praeger, 1980).

Anand, R.P., ed., *Cultural Factors in International Relations* (New Delhi: Abhinav Publications, 1981).

Arbatov, Georgi, *The War of Ideas in Contemporary International Relations* (Moscow: Progress Publishers, 1973).

Arno, Andrew and Wimal Dissanakaye, eds, *The News Media in National and International Conflict* (Boulder, CO: Westview Press, 1984).

Barnet, Richard J. and John Cavanagh, *Global Dreams: Imperial Corporations and the New World Order* (New York: Simon and Schuster, 1994).

Bell, Daniel, *The Coming of Post-Industrial Society* (New York: Basic Books, 1973).

Beltrán, Luis Ramiro, "TV Etchings in the Minds of Latin Americans: Conservatism, Materialism and Conformism," *Gazette* 24: 1 (1978), pp. 61–65.

Beltrán, Luis Ramiro and Elizabeth Fox de Cardona, *Comunicación Dominada: Estados Unidos en los Medios de America Latina* (Nueva Imagen, Mexico: ILET, Ed., 1980).

Bickley, Verner and Puthenraramril John Philir, eds, *Cultural Relations in the Global Community* (New Delhi: Abhinav Publications, 1981).

Blanchard, Margaret *Exporting the First Amendment* (White Plains, NY: Longman, 1987).

Board of Governors of the National Inquiry, *Scholarly Communication: The Report of the National Inquiry* (Baltimore, MD: Johns Hopkins University Press, 1979).

Bortnick, Jane, "International Information Flow: The Developing World Perspective," *Cornell International Law Journal*, Summer 1981, pp. 333–354.

Botkin, James, Dan Dimancescu and Ray Stata, *Global Stakes: The Future of High Technology in America* (Cambridge, MA: Harper and Row, 1982).

Boulding, Kenneth, *The Image* (Ann Arbor, MI: University of Michigan Press, 1956).

Bourgault, Louise M., *Mass Media in Sub-Saharan Africa* (Bloomington, IN: Indiana University Press, 1995).

Boyd, Douglas A., *Broadcasting in the Arab World: A Survey of Radio and Television in the Middle East* (Philadelphia, PA: Temple University Press, 1982).

Boyd-Barrett, Oliver, *The International News Agencies* (Beverly Hills, CA: Sage Publications, 1980).

Boyd-Barrett, Oliver and Daya Kishan Thussu, *Contra Flow in Global News: International and Regional News Exchange Mechanisms* (London: John Libbey [in association with UNESCO], 1992).

Brislin, Richard W., *Cross-Cultural Encounter* (New York: Pergamon Press, 1981).

Browne, Donald R., *International Radio Broadcasting: The Limits of the Limitless Medium* (New York: Praeger, 1982).

Burgess, Philip M. and Raymond W. Lawton, *Indicators of International Behavior: An Assessment of Events Data Research* (International Studies Series) (Beverly Hills, CA: Sage Publications, 1972).

Burns, Barbara, "Study Abroad and International Exchanges." *Annals of the American Academy of Political and Social Science*, 449 (May 1980), pp. 130–138.

Burton, John W., *Conflict and Communication* (London: Macmillan, 1969).

Bushkin, Arthur A., "Information Exchange: An International Trade Issue?" *Satellite Communications*, January 1983, pp. 42–43.

Charles, Whitney D. and Allen Wartella, eds, *World Radio TV Handbook* (New York: Billboard A.G., Volume 35, 1981).

Chay, John, "Communication and International Relations," in John Chay, ed., *Culture and International Relations* (New York: Praeger, 1990), pp. 223–237.

Cherry, Colin, *World Communication: Threat or Promise?* (London: John Wiley-Interscience, 1971).

Christol, Carl Q., *The Modern International Law of Outer Space* (New York: Pergamon Press, 1982).

Cioffi-Revilla, Claudio, Richard Merrit, and Dina A. Zinnes, *Communication and Interaction in Global Politics* (Urbana, IL: University of Illinois Press, 1987).

Clark, Peter M. and Hamid Mowlana, "Iran's Perception of Western Europe: A Study in National and Foreign Policy Articulation," *International Interactions* 4: 2 (1978), pp. 99–123.

Cleverdon, Robert and Anthony Edwards, *International Tourism to 1900* (Cambridge, MA: Abt Books, 1982).

Codding, George and Anthony Rutkowski, *The International Telecommunication Union in a Changing World* (Dedham, MA: Artech House 1982).

Cohen, Bernard C., *The Press and Foreign Policy* (Princeton, NJ: Princeton University Press, 1963).

Cohen, Erik, "Nomads from Influence: Notes on the Phenomenon of Drifter Tourism," *International Journal of Comparative Sociology*, 14, (March–June 1973), pp. 89–103.

Comor, Edward A., ed., *The Global Political Economy of Communication* (New York: St Martin's Press, 1994).

Conference Board, Inc., *Information Technology: Some Critical Implications for Decision Makers* (New York: Conference Board, 1972).

Cooper, Thomas W. with Clifford G. Christians, Frances Forde Plude and Robert A. White, eds, *Communication Ethics and Global Change* (White Plains, NY: Longman, 1989).

Cooper Chen, Anne, *Games in the Global Village: A 50 Nation Study of Entertainment Television* (Bowling Green, OH: Bowling Green State University Popular Press, 1994).

Coser, Lewis A., Charles Kadushin and Walter W. Powell, *Books: The Culture and Commerce of Publishing* (New York: Basic Books, 1982).

Crane, Rhonda J., *The Politics of International Standards: France and the Color TV War* (Norwood, NJ: Ablex Publishing Corporation, 1979).

Cruise O'Brien, Rita, *Domination and Dependence in Mass Communications* (University of Sussex, 1976).

Davison, W. Phillips, *International Political Communication* (New York: Praeger, 1965).

Davison, W. Phillips, *Mass Communication and Conflict Resolution* (New York: Praeger, 1984).

de Kadt, Emanuel, *Tourism: Passport to Development* (New York: Praeger, 1979).

de la Haye, Yves, *Marx and Engels on the Means of Communication* (New York: International General, 1979).

Dertouzos, Michael L. and Joel Moses, eds, *The Computer Age: A Twenty-Year View* (Cambridge, MA: MIT Press, 1981).

Deutsch, Karl W., *Nationalism and Social Communication* (Cambridge, MA: MIT Press, 1966).

Deutsch, Karl W., *The Nerves of Government: Models of Political Communication and Control* (New York: Free Press, 1963).

Dizard, Wilson, *The Coming Information Age* (White Plains, NY: Longman, 1982).

Duke, Judith S., ed., *The Knowledge Industry 200: America's Two Hundred Largest Media Companies* (White Plains, NY: Knowledge Industry Publications, 1993).

Dunn, Hopeton S., ed., *Globalization, Communications and Caribbean Identity* (Jamaica: Tan Randle Publishers, 1995).

Dziki, Sylwester, *World Directory Mass Communication Periodicals* (Cracow: Press Research Center and Bibliographical Section of the International Association for Mass Communication Research, 1980).

Eapen, Eapen K., "Reshaping Training and Research for the NIIO," *Media Development*, XXVII: 4 (1980), pp. 16–19.

Edelstein, Alex, *Comparative Communication Research* (Beverly Hills, CA: Sage Publications, 1982).

Edelstein, Alex, J.E. Bowes and S.M. Hersel, eds, *Information Societies: Comparing the Japanese and American Experiences* (Seattle: University of Washington Press, 1978).

Ellul, Jacques, *Propaganda: The Formation of Men's Attitudes* (New York: Alfred Knopf, 1965).

Eugster, Ernest, *Television Programming Across National Boundaries: The EBU and OIRT Experience* (Dedham, MA: Artech House, 1983).

Fanon, F., *The Wretched of the Earth* (Harmondsworth: Penguin, 1967).

Faraone, Roque, "El Poder Económico y la Función Ideolóigica de Control Social que Ejerce la Prensa en el Uruguay," *Comunicación y Cambio Social*, Colección Intiyán, CIESPAL, 2nd edn (Quito: CIESPAL, 1981), pp. 191–202.

Farrell, John C. and Asa P. Smith, eds, *Image and Reality in World Politics* (New York: Columbia University Press, 1967).

Fascell, Dante, ed., *International News: Freedom Under Attack* (Beverly Hills, CA: Sage Publications, 1979).

Featherstone, M., ed., *Global Culture: Nationalism, Globalization and Modernity* (London: Sage Publications, 1988).

Feketekuty, Geza, *International Trade in Services: An Overview and Blueprint for Services* (Cambridge, MA: Ballinger, 1988).

Feldman, Mark B. and David B. Garcia, "National Regulation of Transborder Data Flows," *North Carolina Journal of International Law and Commercial Regulations*, 7: 1 (Winter 1982), pp. 1–25.

Feldstein, M., ed., *The United States in the World Economy* (Chicago: University of Chicago Press, 1988).

Fischer, Heinz-Dietrich and John C. Merrill, eds, *International and Intercultural Communication* (New York: Hastings House, 1976).

Fisher, Glen H., *American Communication in a Global Society* (Norwood, NJ: Ablex Publishing Corporation, 1979).

Fisher, Glen H., *Public Diplomacy and the Behavioral Sciences* (Bloomington, IN: University of Indiana Press, 1972).

Fortner, Robert S., *International Communication: History, Conflict and Control of the Global Metropolis* (Belmont, CA: Wadsworth, 1993).

Frederick, Howard H, *Global Communication and International Relations* (Belmont, CA: Wadsworth, 1993).

Freire, Paulo, *Pedagogy of the Oppressed* (New York: Seabury Press, 1970).

Galtung, Johan, "A Structural Theory of Imperialism," *Journal of Peace Research*, 8: 2 (1971), pp. 81–118.

Galtung, Johan, *The True World: A Transnational Perspective* (New York: Free Press, 1980).

Galtung, Johan and Vincent C. Richard, *Global Glasnost: Toward a New International Information/Communication Order?* (Cresskill, NJ: Hampton Press, 1992).

Ganley, Oswald H. and Gladys D. Ganley, *To Inform or To Control: The New Communication Network* (New York: McGraw-Hill, 1982).

Gans, Herbert J., *Deciding What's News* (New York: Vintage Books, 1979).

Gerbner, George, ed., *Mass Media Policies in Changing Cultures* (New York: John Wiley, 1977).

Gerbner, George and George Marvanyi, "The Many Worlds of the World's Press," *Journal of Communication*, 27: 1 (Winter 1977), pp. 52–66.

Gerbner, George and Marsha Siefert, eds, *World Communications: A Handbook* (White Plains, NY: Longman, 1984).

Gerbner, George, Hamid Mowlana, and Kaarle Nordenstreng, eds, *The Global Media Debate: Its Rise, Fall and Renewal* (Norwood, NJ: Ablex Publishing Corporation, 1993).

Gerbner, George, Hamid Mowlana and Herbert Schiller, eds, *Invisible Crises: What Conglomerate Control of Media Means for America and the World* (Boulder, CO:Westview Press, 1996).

Giddens, Anthony, *The Consequences of Modernity* (Cambridge: Polity, 1990)

Gidengil, E.L., "Centers and Peripheries: An Empirical Test of Galtung's Theory of Imperialism," *Journal of Peace Research*, 15: 2 (1978), pp. 51–66.

Glenn, Edmund S. with Christian Glenn, *Man and Mankind: Conflict and Communication Between Cultures* (Norwood, NJ: Ablex Publishing Corporation, 1981).

Golding, Peter and Phillip Elliot, *Making the News* (London: Longman, 1979).

Gonzalez Manet, Enrique, "Medios de Difusión, Cultura y Cambio Social en América Latina," *Boletin UNESCO*, July–December 1980, pp. 16–28.

Gorman, G.E. and L. Shaw, "Improving Information Flows in Current Development Research: A Western European Perspective," *International Social Science Journal*, 30: 4 (1978), pp. 929–934.

Gotleib, Allen E., "The Impact of Technology on the Development of Contemporary International Law," *Recueil des Cours*, Collected Courses of The Hague Academy of International Law, 1 (1980), pp. 277–284.

Gould, Peter and Jeffrey Johnson, "The Content and Structure of International Television Flows," *Communication*, 5 (1980), pp. 43–63.

Gouldner, Alvin W., *Dialectic of Ideology and Technology* (New York: Macmillan, 1976).

Guback, Thomas and Tapio Varis (in collaboration with José G. Canton, Heriberto Nuraro, Gloria Rojas, and Boonrak Booyaketmala), *Transnational Communication and Cultural Industries*, Reports and Papers on Mass Communication No. 92 (Paris: UNESCO, 1982).

Gudykunst, William B., ed., *Intercultural Communication Theory: Current Perspectives* (Beverly Hills, CA: Sage Publications, 1983).

Haas, Ernst and John Gerard Ruggie, "What Message in the Medium of Information Systems?" *International Studies Quarterly*, 26: 2 (1982), pp. 190–219.

Habermas, Jürgen, *Communication and the Evolution of Society* (Boston: MA: Beacon Press, 1979).

Hachten, William A., *World News Prism* (Ames, IA: Iowa State University Press, 1981).

Hall, Edward T., *Beyond Culture* (Garden City, NY: Doubleday, 1977).

Halloran, James D., "Warring Schools on Complementary Perspectives? A Case for Critical Eclecticism," Centre for Mass Communication Research, University of Leicester, 1983.

Halloran, James D. and Virginia Nightingale, "Young TV Viewers and Their Images of Foreigners: A Summary and Interpretation of a Four Nation Study," Centre for Mass Communication Research, University of Leicester, 1983.

Hamelink, Cees J., *Cultural Autonomy in Global Communication* (White Plains, NY: Longman, 1983).

Hamelink, Cees J., *Finance and Information: A Study of Converging Interest* (Norwood, NJ: Ablex Publishing Corporation, 1983).

Hancock, Allen, *Communication Planning for Development: An Operational Framework* (Paris: UNESCO, 1981).

Harasim, Linda, ed., *Global Networks: Computers and International Communication* (Cambridge, MA: MIT Press, 1993)

Harley, William G., *Creative Compromise: The MacBride Commission* (Lanham, MD: University Press of America, 1993).

Hirschleifer, Joseph, "Where Are We in the Theory of Information?" *American Economic Review*, 63: 2 (May 1973), pp. 31–39.

Hoffman, Arthur S., ed., *International Communication and the New Diplomacy* (Bloomington, IN: University of Indiana Press, 1968).

Hoso-Bunka Foundation, *Symposium 2 on Public Role and Systems of Broadcasting: Summary Report* (Tokyo: Hoso-Bunka Foundation, 1981).

Hovic, Tord and Turid Heilberg, "Center–Periphery Tourism and Self-Reliance," *International Social Scene Journal*, 32: 75 (January 1980), pp. 75–105.

Hudson, Heather, *Telecommunications and Development* (Norwood, NJ: Ablex Publishing Corporation, 1983).

Huntington, Samuel, "The Clash of Civilizations," *Foreign Affairs* 72 (Summer 1993). pp. 22–49.

Independent Commission on International Issues (Brandt Commission), *North–South: A Programme for Survival* (Cambridge, MA: MIT Press, 1980).

International Association for Mass Communication Research, *Aspects of the Mass Media Declaration of UNESCO*, Occasional Papers, University of Leicester, 1989.

International Association for Mass Communication Research, *New Structures of International Communication? The Role of Research* (Main Papers from the 1980 Caracas Conference) (Leicester, IAMCR, 1982).

International Association for Mass Communication Research and UNESCO, "Communication in the Eighties: The Nature of the Problem and Some Proposals for an International Research Strategy," report prepared by Annabelle Sreberny-Mohammadi on the IAMCR/UNESCO Consultation Meeting of July 1982 (Leicester: IAMCR, January 1983).

International Commission for the Study of Communication Problems, *Many Voices, One World* (London: Kogan Page, 1980).

International Organization of Journalists, *Clashes of Ideas on Modern Media* (Prague: International Organization of Journalists, 1975).

Jandt, Fred E., ed., *Conflict Resolution Through Communication* (New York: Harper and Row, 1973).

Janis, Irving L., *Victims of Groupthink* (Boston, MA: Houghton Mifflin Company, 1972).

Jansky, Donald and Michel Jerichim, *Communication Satellites in the Geostationary Orbit* (Dedham, MA: Artech House, 1983).

Kamalipour, Yahya R., ed., *The U.S. Media and the Middle East Image and Perception* (Westport CT: Greenwood Publishing Group, 1995).

Kamalipour, Yahya R. and Hamid Mowlana, eds, *Mass Media in the Middle East: A Comprehensive Handbook* (Westport, CT: Greenwood Publishing Group, 1994).

Katz, Elihu and George Wedell, *Broadcasting in the Third World* (Cambridge, MA: Harvard University Press, 1977).

Kelman, Herbert C., ed., *International Behavior: A Socio-psychological Analysis* (New York: Holt, Rinehart and Winston, 1965).

Keune, Reinhard, ed., "The New International Information and Communication Order," *Viertel Jahres Berichte Probleme der Entwicklungslander* (special issue), 85 (September 1981). Bonn: Friedrich-Ebert-Stiftung.

Kirschenmann, Peter Paul, *Information and Reflection: On Some Problems of Cybernetics and How Contemporary Dialectical Materialism Copes With Them* (Dordrecht: D. Reidel Publishing, 1970).

Khomeini, Ruhollah, *Islam and Revolution: Writings and Declarations of Imam Khomeini*, trans. H. Algar (Berkeley, CA: Mizan Press, 1981).

Klineberg, Otto, *The Human Dimension in International Relations* (New York: Holt, Reinhart and Winston, 1964).

Lamberton, D.M., *Economics of Information and Knowledge* (London: Penguin Books, 1971).

Larson, James F., *Television's Window on the World: International Affairs Coverage on the U.S. Networks* (Norwood, NJ: Ablex Publishing Corporation, 1983).

Lasswell, Harold, *World Politics and Personal Insecurity* (New York: World Publishing, 1935).

Lasswell, Harold, Daniel Lerner, and Hans Speier, eds, *Propaganda and Communication in World History* (Honolulu: University of Hawaii Press, 1980). Add Vol. III.

Lawrence, John Shelton and Bernard Timberg, eds, *Fair Use and Free Inquiry: Copyright Law and the New Media* (Norwood, NJ: Ablex Publishing Corporation, 1980).

Lee, Chin-Chuan, *Media Imperialism Reconsidered: The Homogenizing of Television Culture* (Beverly Hills, CA, and London: Sage Publications, 1980).

Lehman, Maxwell and Burke Thomas, eds, *Communication Technologies and Information Flow* (Elmsford, NY: Pergamon Press, 1980).

Lenin, V.I., *What Is to Be Done?* (Moscow: Progress Publishers, 1947).

Lent, John A., ed., *A Different Road Taken: The State of Critical Communication Research* (Boulder, CO: Westview Press, 1996).

Lent, John A., *Third World Mass Media: Issues, Theory and Research* (Williamsburg, VA: College of William and Mary, Publications No. 9, 1979).

Lerner, Daniel, *The Passing of Traditional Society* (Glencoe, IL: Free Press, 1958).

Lerner, Daniel and Wilbur Schramm, eds, *Communication and Change in the Developing Countries* (Honolulu: University of Hawaii Press, 1967).

Lewin, Leonard, ed., *Telecommunications in the United States: Trends and Policies* (Dedham, MA: Artech House, 1981).

Lindahl, Rutger, *Broadcasting Across Borders: A Study on the Role of Propaganda in External Broadcasts* (Göteborg: C.W.K. Gleerup, 1978).

Lippmann, Walter, *Public Opinion* (New York: Free Press, 1922).

Lorimer, Rowland, "Multinationals in Book Publishing: Culture Homogenized," *Media Information Australia*, 39 (August 1983), pp. 35–41.

McAnany, Emile G., *Communications in the Rural Third World* (New York: Praeger, 1980).

McCavitt, William E., *Broadcasting Around the World* (Blue Ridge Summit, PA: Tale Books, 1981).

McChesney, Robert W., *Telecommunications, Mass Media, and Democracy: The Battle for the Control of U.S. Broadcasting, 1928–1935* (New York: Oxford University Press, 1993).

McClelland, Charles A., *Theory and the International System* (New York: Macmillan, 1966).

McClelland, David C., *The Achieving Society* (Princeton, NJ: Van Nostrand, 1961).

Machlup, Fritz, *Knowledge: Its Creation, Distribution and Economic Significance* (Princeton, NJ: Princeton University Press, 1980).

McLuhan, Marshall, *Understanding Media* (New York: McGraw-Hill, 1964).

McPhail, Thomas L., *Electronic Colonialism* (Beverly Hills, CA: Sage Publications, 1981).

Malek, Abbas, *New Media and Foreign Relations: A Multifaceted Perspective* (Norwood, NJ: Ablex Publishing Corporation, 1996).

Mankekar, D.R., *One-Way Flow: Neo-Colonialism Via News Media* (New Delhi: Clarion Books, 1978).

Mansell, Robin, *The New Telecommunications: A Political Economy of Network Evolution* (London: Sage Publications, 1993).

Martin, John L. and Anjugrover Chaudhary, eds, *Comparative Mass Media Systems* (White Plains, NY: Longman, 1983.

Martin-Barbero, J., *Communication, Culture and Hegemony: From the Media to the Mediations*, trans. Elizabeth Fox and Robert White (London: Sage Publications, 1993).

Masuda, Youeji, *Information Society as Post-Industrial Society* (Tokyo: Institute for Information Society, 1980).

Mattelart, Armand, *Mapping World Communication* (Minneapolis, MN: University of Minnesota Press, 1993).

Mattelart, Armand, *Mass Media, Ideologies and the Revolutionary Movement* (Atlantic Highlands, NJ: Humanities Press, 1980).

Mattelart, Armand, *Multinational Corporations and the Control of Culture* (Brighton: Harvester Press, 1979).

Merrill, John C., *The Elite Press: Great Newspapers of the World* (New York: Pitman Publishing Corporation, 1968).

Merrill, John C., ed., *Global Journalism: A Survey of the World's Mass Media* (New York: Longman, 1983).

Merritt, Richard L., ed., *Communication in International Politics* (Urbana, IL: University of Illinois Press, 1972).

Moemeka, Andrew A., ed., *Communicating for Development: A New Pan-Disciplinary Perspective* (Albany, NY: State University of New York Press, 1994).

Moemeka, Andrew A., ed., *Development [Social Change] Communication: Building Understanding and Creating Participation* (New York: McGraw-Hill College Custom Services, 1993).

Mosco, Vincent, *Pushbutton Fantasies: Critical Perspectives on Videotex and Information Technology* (Norwood, NJ: Ablex Publishing Corporation, 1982).

Mosco, Vincent and Janet Wasko, eds, *Changing Patterns of Communications Control* Vol. 2 of The Critical Communications Review (Norwood, NJ: Ablex Publishing Corporation, 1983).

Mowlana, Hamid, "The Communication Dimension of International Studies in the United States: A Quantitative Assessment," *International Journal of Communication Research* (University of Cologne), 1: 1 (Winter 1974), pp. 3–22.

Mowlana, Hamid, "Communication Ecology and the Changing International Order," in Hyeon-Dew Kang, ed., *Changing International Order in North-East Asia and Communications Policies* (Seoul: NANAM Publishing House, 1992), pp. 111–118.

Mowlana, Hamid, "Communication for Political Change: The Iranian Revolution," in George Gerbner and Marsha Siefert, eds, *World Communications: A Handbook* (White Plains, NY: Longman, 1984).

Mowlana, Hamid, "Communication Policy and Planning: An Integrative Approach," *Telematics and Informatics*, 9: 2 (Spring 1992), pp. 113–122.

Mowlana, Hamid, "Cross-National Comparison of Economic Journalism: A Study of Mass Media and Economic Development," *Gazette*, XIII: 4 (1967), pp. 363–378.

Mowlana, Hamid, *Global Communication in Transition: The End of Diversity?* (Thousand Oaks, CA: Sage Publications, 1996).

Mowlana, Hamid, "Information Hunger and Knowledge Affluence: How to Bridge the Gap," *Development: Journal of the Society for International Development*, 3 (1993), pp. 23–26.

Mowlana, Hamid, *International Communication: A Selected Bibliography* (Dubuque, IA: Kendall/Hunt Publishing, 1971.

Mowlana, Hamid, "International Communication Research in the 21st Century: From Functionalism to Post Modernism and Beyond," in Cees J. Hamelink and Olga Linne, eds, *Mass Communication Research: On Problems and Policies* (Norwood, NJ: Ablex Publishing Corporation, 1994), pp. 353–368.

Mowlana, Hamid (with Medhi Mohsenian RAD), "International Flow of Japanese Programs: The 'OSHIN' Phenomenon," *Keio Communication Review*, 14 (1992), pp. 51–68.

Mowlana, Hamid, ed., *International Flow of News: An Annotated Bibliography* (Paris: UNESCO, 1983).

Mowlana, Hamid, "The Islamization of Iranian Television," *Inter Media*, 17: 5 (October–November 1989), pp. 35–39.

Mowlana, Hamid, "Mass Media and Culture: Toward an Integrated Theory," in William B. Gudykunst, ed., *Intercultural Communication Theory: Current Perspectives* (Beverly Hills, CA: Sage Publications, 1983), pp. 149–170.

Mowlana, Hamid, "Mass Media Systems and Communication Behaviour," in Michael Adams, ed., *The Middle East: A Handbook* (New York: Facts On File Press, 1988).

Mowlana, Hamid, "The Multinational Corporation and the Diffusion of Technology." In Abdul A. Said and Luiz R. Simmons, eds, *The New Sovereigns: Multinational Corporations as World Powers* (Englewood Cliffs, NJ: Prentice Hall, 1975), pp. 77–90.

Mowlana, Hamid, "Muslims and Genocide in the Balkans," *Peace Review*, 6: 3 (Fall 1994), pp. 373–381.

Mowlana, Hamid, "The New Global Order and Cultural Ecology," *Media, Culture, & Society*, 15: 1 (1993), pp. 9–27.

Mowlana, Hamid, "On the New World Information Order and UNESCO," *Review of U.S.*

*Participation in UNESCO*, hearings and markups before the Subcommittees on International Operations and on Human Rights and International Organizations of the Committee on Foreign Affairs, US House of Representatives, Ninety-Seventh Congress, March 10, July 9, and July 16, 1981 (Washington, DC: US Government Printing Office, 1982).

Mowlana, Hamid, "A Paradigm for Comparative Mass Media Analysis," in Heinz-Dietrich Fischer and John C. Merrill, eds, *International and Intercultural Communication* (New York: Hastings House, 1976), pp. 474–484.

Mowlana, Hamid, "A Paradigm for Source Analysis in Events Data Research: Mass Media and the Problems of Validity," *International Interactions*, 2: 1 (Summer 1975), pp. 33–44.

Mowlana, Hamid, "Political and Social Implications of Communications Satellite Applications in Developed and Developing Countries," in Joseph N. Pelton and Marcellus S. Snow, eds, *Economics and Policy Problems in Satellite Communications* (New York: Praeger, 1977), pp. 124–142.

Mowlana, Hamid, "Technology versus Tradition: Communication in the Iranian Revolution," *Journal of Communication*, 29: 3 (Summer 1979), pp. 107–112.

Mowlana, Hamid, "Toward a NWICO for the Twenty-First Century?" *Journal of International Affairs*, 47: 1 (Summer 1993), pp. 59–72.

Mowlana, Hamid, "Toward a Theory of Communication Systems: A Developmental Approach," *Gazette* XVII: 1/2 (1971), pp. 17–28.

Mowlana, Hamid, "Trends in Middle Eastern Societies," in George Gerbner, ed., *Mass Media Policies in Changing Cultures* (New York: John Wiley, 1977), pp. 73–82.

Mowlana, Hamid, "Trends in Research on International Communication in the United States," *Gazette* XIX: 2 (1973), pp. 79–90.

Mowlana, Hamid, "Who Covers America?" *Journal of Communication*, 25: 3 (Summer 1975), pp. 86–91.

Mowlana, Hamid and Nanette Levinson, *Telecommunications and International Relations: An East–West Perspective* (Washington, DC: International Communication Program/School of International Service, The American University, 1991).

Mowlana, Hamid and Gerald W. McLaughlin, "Some Variables Interacting with media Exposure Among Foreign Students," *Sociology and Social Research*, 53: 4 (July 1969), pp. 511–522.

Mowlana, Hamid and Ann Elizabeth Robinson, "Ethnic Mobilizations and Communication Theory," in Abdul A. Said and Luiz R. Simmons, eds, *Ethnicity in an International Context* (New Brunswick, NJ: Transaction Books, 1976), pp. 48–63.

Mowlana, Hamid and Ginger Smith, "Tourism as International Relations: Linkages Between Telecommunications Technology and Transnational Banking," in Donald E. Hawkins, J.R. Ritchie, Frank Go, and Douglas Frechtling, eds, *World Travel and Tourism Review: Indicators, Trends and Forecasts*, Vol. I (CAB International, 1991), pp. 215–218.

Mowlana, Hamid and Ginger Smith, "Tourism in a Global Context: The Case of Frequent Traveler Programs," *Journal of Travel Research*, 12 (Winter 1992), pp. 20–27.

Mowlana, Hamid and Ginger Smith, "Tourism, Telecommunications and Transnational Banking: A Framework for Policy Analysis," *Tourism Management*, II: 4 (1990), pp. 85–106.

Mowlana, Hamid and Laurie J. Wilson, *The Passing of Modernity: Communication and the Transformation of Society* (White Plains, NY: Longman, 1990).

Mowlana, Hamid, George Gerbner and Herbert Schiller, eds, *Triumph of the Image: The Media's War in the Persian Gulf – A Global Perspective* (Boulder, CO: Westview Press, 1992).

Mutahhari, Mortaza, *Fundamentals of Islamic Thought: God, Man and the Universe*, trans. A. Campbell (Berkeley, CA: Mizan Press, 1985).

Mutahhari, Mortaza, *Social and Historical Changes: An Islamic Perspective* (Berkeley, CA: Mizan Press, 1986).

Nair, Basskaran, *Mass Media and the Transnational Corporation* (Singapore: Singapore University Press, 1980).

Nakamura, H., *Ways of Thinking of Eastern Peoples* (Honolulu: East-West Center Press, 1964).

National Aeronautics and Space Administration, *A Forecast of Space Technology: 1980–2000* (Washington, DC: US Government Printing Office, 1976).

National Telecommunications and Information Administration, "Long-Range Goals in International Telecommunication and Information: An Outline for the United States Policy," report to the Congress of the United States, US Department of Commerce, Washington, DC, February 1983.

National Telecommunications and Information Administration, "Present and Projected Business Utilization of International Telecommunications," Washington, DC: US Department of Commerce, September 1981.

Neustadt, Richard, *The Birth of Electronic Publishing: Legal and Economic Issues in Telephone, Cable and Over-the-Air Teletex and Videotex* (White Plains, NY: Knowledge Industry Publications, 1982).

Ngwainmbi, Emmanuel K., *Communication Efficiency and Rural Development in Africa* (Lanham, MD: University Press of America, 1994).

Nnaemeka, Tony and Jim Richstad, "Structured Relations and Foreign News Flow in the Pacific Region," *Gazette*, 26: 4 (1980), pp. 235–257.

Nordenstreng, Kaarle, *The Mass Media Declaration of UNESCO* (Norwood, NJ: Ablex Publishing Corporation, 1983).

Nordenstreng, Kaarle and Herbert L. Schiller, eds, *Beyond National Sovereignty: International Communication in the 1990s* (Norwood, NJ: Ablex Publishing Corporation, 1993).

Nordenstreng, Kaarle and Herbert I. Schiller, eds, *National Sovereignty and International Communication* (Norwood, NJ: Ablex Publishing Corporation, 1979).

Nordenstreng, Kaarle and Tapio Varis, *Television Traffic: A One-Way Street?* Reports and Papers on Mass Communication No. 70 (Paris: UNESCO, 1974).

Novotny, Eric J., "Transborder Data Flow Regulation: Technical Issues of Legal Concern," *Computer Law Journal*, 3: 2 (Winter 1981), pp. 105–124.

Novotny, Eric J., "Transborder Data Flows and International Law: A Framework for Policy-Oriented Inquiry," *Stanford Journal of International Law*, 16 (Summer 1980), pp. 141–180.

Nye, Joseph S., Jr, *Bound to Lead: The Changing Nature of American Power* (New York: Basic Books, 1990).

Nye, Joseph S., Jr, "Soft Power," *Foreign Policy*, 80 (1990), pp. 153–171.

Ouedraogo, J.P.G., "Regional Needs and Utilization of Remote Sensing in West and Central Africa," paper read at the United Nations International Seminar on Remote Sensing Applications and Satellite Communications for Education and Development, Toulouse, April 21–25, 1981.

Pasquali, Antonio, *Comprendar la Communicación* (Caracas: Monte Avila Editors, 1978).

Pavlic, Breda and Cees J. Hamelink, "Interrelationship Between the New International Economic Order and a New International/World Information Communication Order" (Report prepared for UNESCO), Research Centre for Cooperation with Developing Countries, Ljubljana, 1982.

Pearce, Douglas G. and Richard W. Butler, eds, *Tourism Research: Critiques and Challenges* (New York: Routledge, 1993).

Pelton, Joseph N., *Global Talk* (Boston, MA: A.W. Sijthoff, 1981).

Pelton, Joseph N. and Marcellus S. Snow, eds, *Economics and Policy Problems in Satellite Communications* (New York: Praeger, 1977).

Ploman, Edward W., "The International Flow of Information: Legal Aspects," in Friedrich-Ebert-Stiftung, *Mass Media Annual: Television News in a North–South Perspective* (Bonn: Friedrich-Ebert-Stiftung, 1981).

Ploman, Edward, *International Law Governing Communications and Information: A Collection of Basic Documents* (Westport, CT: Greenwood Press, 1982).

Pool, Ithiel de Sola, *Forecasting the Telephone: A Retrospective Technology Assessment* (Norwood, NJ: Ablex Publishing Corporation, 1983).

Pool, Ithiel de Sola and Richard Jay Solomon, "Intellectual Property and Transborder Data Flows," *Stanford Journal of International Law*, 16 (Summer 1980), pp. 113–139.

Porat, Marc, *The Information Economy* (Washington, DC: US Office of Telecommunications, 1977).

Preston, William, Jr, Edward Herman and Herbert I. Schiller, *Hope and Folly: The United States and UNESCO, 1945–1985* (Minneapolis, MN: University of Minnesota Press, 1989).

Prosser, Michael, *Intercommunication Among the Nations and Peoples* (New York: Harper and Row, 1973).

Pye, Lucian W., ed., *Communication and Political Development* (Princeton, NJ: Princeton University Press, 1963).

Quester, George H., *The International Politics of Television* (Lexington, MA: Lexington Press, 1990).

Rappaport, Anatol, *Strategy and Conscience* (New York: Schocken Books, 1964).

Raskin, A.H., "Report on News Coverage of Belgrade UNESCO Conference," The National News Council, New York, 1981.

Reijnen, Gisjsbertha C., *Utilization of Outer Space and International Law* (Amsterdam: Elsevier Scientific Publishing, 1981).

Reyes Matta, Fernando, "El Encandilamiento Informativo de América Latina," *La Circulación de Noticias en América Latina* (Mexico: Federación Latinoamericana de Periodistas, 1978), pp. 115–139.

Reyes Matta, Fernando, "Las Agencias de Noticias en el Nuevo Orden Internacional de la Información," Memorias de la Semana Internacional de la Comunicación, 18–20 August 1980, *Cuadernos de Comunicación Social* (Bogotá: Universidad Pontificia Javeriana, 1981), pp. 211–237.

Rheingold, Howard, *The Virtual Community: Homesteading on the Electronic Frontier* (Reading, MA: Addison-Wesley Press, 1993).

Richstad, Jim and Michael H. Anderson, eds, *Crisis in the International News: Politics and Prospects* (New York: Columbia University Press, 1981).

Righter, Rosemary, *Whose News? Politics, the Press and the Third World* (London: Burnett Books, 1978).

Roach, Colleen, ed., *Communication and Culture in War and Peace* (London and New Delhi: Sage Publications, 1993).

Roach, Colleen, "Mexican and U.S. News Coverage of the IPDC at Acapulco," *Journal of Communication*, 32: 3 (Summer 1982), pp. 71–85.

Robertson, Roland, *Globalization: Social Theory and Global Culture* (London: Sage Publications, 1994).

Robinson, Gertrude Jach, *News Agencies and World News in Canada and the United States and Yugoslavia: Methods and Data* (Fribourg: University Press of Fribourg, 1981).

Rogers, Everett M. and Livia Antola, "Television Flows in Latin America," paper read at the Conference on Flow of Messages, Flow of Media in the Americas, Stanford University, Stanford, CA, December 9–10, 1982.

Rogers, Everett M. and F. Floyd Shoemaker, *Communication of Innovations: A Cross-Cultural Approach* (New York: Free Press, 1971).

Roncagliolo, Rafael, "Flow of News and Freedom of the Press," *The Democratic Journalist*, March 1979, pp. 7–11.

Roncagliolo, Rafael and Norene Janus, "Publicidad Transnacional, Medios de Comunicación y Educación en Los Paises en Desarrollo" (Transnational Advertising, Communications Media, and Education in the Developing Countries), *Perspectives*, X: 1 (1980), p. 32.

Rosenblum, Mort, *Coups and Earthquakes: Reporting the World for America* (New York: Harper and Row, 1979).

Rosengren, Karl E., "Bias in News: Methods and Concepts," in Cleveland Wilhoit, ed., *Mass Communication Review Yearbook 1* (Beverly Hills, CA: Sage Publications, 1980), pp. 249–264.

Rosengren, Karl E., "Communication Research: One Paradigm, or Four?" in E.M. Rogers and F. Balle, eds, *Mass Communication Research in the United States and Europe* (Norwood, NJ: Ablex Publishing Corporation, 1983), pp. 14–20.

Rosengren, Karl E., "Four Types of Tables," *Journal of Communication*, 27: 1 (Winter 1977), pp. 67–75.

Sabins, Floyd F., *Remote Sensing: Principles and Interpretation* (San Francisco: W.H. Freeman, 1978).

Said, Edward W., *Covering Islam: How the Media and the Experts Determine How We See the Rest of the World* (New York: Pantheon, 1981).

Said, Edward W., *Orientalism* (New York: Vintage Books, 1978).

Santoro, Eduardo, "La Información Sobre Latinoamérica en Una Semana de Prensa en Caracas," *Comunicación y Cambio Social*, Colección Intiyán, Second Edition (Quito: CIESPAL, 1981), pp. 323–343.

Saunders, Robert J., Jeremy J. Warford and Bjorn Wellenius, *Telecommunications and Economic Development* (Baltimore, MD: Johns Hopkins University Press, 1983).

Schelling, Thomas C., *The Strategy of Conflict* (New York: Oxford University Press, 1963).

Schiller, Daniel, *Telematics and Government* (Norwood, NJ: Ablex Publishing Corporation, 1982).

Schiller, Herbert I., *Communication and Cultural Domination* (White Plains, NY: International Arts and Sciences Press, 1976).

Schiller, Herbert I., *Culture, Inc.: The Corporate Takeover of Public Expression* (New York: Oxford University Press, 1989).

Schiller, Herbert I., *Information Inequality: The Deepening Social Crisis in America* (New York: Routledge, 1996).

Schiller, Herbert I., *Mass Communication and American Empire*, updated 2nd edn (Boulder, CO: Westview Press, 1992).

Schiller, Herbert I., *The Mind Managers* (Boston, MA: Beacon Press, 1973).

Schiller, Herbert I., *Who Knows: Information in the Age of the Fortune 500* (Norwood, NJ: Ablex Publishing Corporation, 1981).

Schnitman, Jorge A., *Film Industries in Latin America: Dependency and Development* (Norwood, NJ: Ablex Publishing Corporation, 1983).

Schramm, Wilbur, *Mass Media and National Development* (Stanford, CA: Stanford University Press, 1964).

Schramm, Wilbur and L. Erwin Atwood, *Circulation of News in the Third World: A Study of Asia* (Hong Kong: Chinese University Press, 1981).

Scrales, Christopher, *Copyright* (Cambridge: Cambridge University Press, 1980).

Shari'ati, Ali, *Marxism and Other Western Fallacies* (Berkeley, CA: Mizan Press, 1980).

Singer, J. David, ed., *Quantitative International Politics* (New York: Free Press, 1968).

Singer, Marshall R. *Weak States in a World of Power* (New York: Free Press, 1972).

Singh, Indu B., ed., *Telecommunications in the Year 2000: National and International Perspectives* (Norwood, NJ: Ablex Publishing Corporation, 1983).

Smith, Anthony, *The Age of Behemoths: The Globalization of Mass Media* (New York: Priority Press, 1991).

Smith, Anthony, *The Geopolitics of Information: How Western Culture Dominates the World* (New York: Oxford University Press, 1980).

Smith, Datus C., *The Economics of Book Publishing in Developing Countries* (Paris: UNESCO, 1977).

Smith, Esselli M., "The Cultural Costs of Tourism," *Cultural Survival Quarterly*, 6: 7 (Summer 1982), pp. 7–12.

Smith, Ginger, "Tourism, Telecommunications, and Transnational Banking: A Study in International Interactions," doctoral dissertation, School of International Service, The American University, 1992.

Smythe, Dallas W. *Dependency Road: Communications, Capitalism, Consciousness, and Canada* (Norwood, NJ: Ablex Publishing Corporation, 1981).

Splichal, Slavko, Andrew Calabrese, and Colin Sparks, eds, *Information Society and Civil*

*Society: Contemporary Perspectives on the Changing World Order* (West Lafayette, IN: Perdue University Press, 1994).

Stanger, Ross, *Psychological Aspects of International Conflict* (Belmont, CA: Brooks/Cole Publishing, 1967).

Stevenson, Robert L. and Donald Lewis Shaw, eds, *Foreign News and the World Information Order* (Ames, IA: University of Iowa Press, 1984).

Straus, Richard, ed., *Communication and International Trade: A Symposium* (Washington, DC: United States National Committee of the International Institute of Communication, 1982).

Szalai, Alexander (with Margaret Croke and Associates), *The United Nations and the News Media* (New York: United States Institute for Training and Research [UNITAR], 1972).

Szecsko, Tamas, "The Grammar of Global Communication," *Intermedia*, 10: 2 (March 1982), pp. 24–26.

Szecsko, Tamas, *Recent Studies (on Radio and Television) 1976–77* (Budapest: Mass Communication Research Centre, 1978).

Szecsko, Tamas and Elihu Katz, *Mass Media and Social Change* (London: Sage Publications, 1981).

Tan, Alexis, *Mass Communications in the Third World* (Norwood, NJ: Ablex Publishing Corporation, 1983).

Taubert, Sigfred and Peter Weidhaas, *The Book Trade of the World* (Munich: K.G. Saur, 1981).

Tehranian, Majid, *Technologies of Power* (Norwood, NJ: Ablex Publishing Corporation, 1990).

Tehranian, Majid, Farhad Hakimzadeh, and Marcello L. Vidale, eds, *Communication Policy for National Development: A Comparative Perspective* (London: Routledge and Kegan Paul, 1977).

Terestyeni, Tamas, "Geopolitical Regions in the News," *JEF-KEP: The Quarterly of the Mass Communication Research Centre, Budapest* (Special Edition, August 1982), pp. 128–144.

Trezise, James, James G. Stovall, and Hamid Mowlana, *Watergate: A Crisis for the World – A Survey of British and French Press Reaction Toward an American Political Crisis* (Oxford: Pergamon Press, 1980).

Tunstall, Jeremy, *The Media are American* (New York: Columbia University Press, 1977).

Ugboajah, Frank, "Oramedia' or Traditional Media as Effective Communication Options for Rural Development in Africa," *Communicatio Socialis* (Aachen), 15: 3 (September 1982), pp. 211–221.

Uka Uche, Luke, ed., *North–South Information Culture* (Lagos and London: Longman, 1995).

Ume-Nwagbo, Ebele N., "Foreign News Flow in Africa: A Content Analytical Study on a Regional Basis," *Gazette*, 29 (1982).

UNESCO, "Consultation of Experts on Means of Communication and the Nature of Human Communication," Vienna, 1980 (SS. 80/CS. 9/12; SS. 81/WS/7).

UNESCO, "Consultative Meeting of Specialists and Representatives of Intergovernmental and Non-governmental Organizations Active in the Field of Communication," Paris, 1981 (CC.81fWS/27).

UNESCO, *Cultures: Dialogue Between the Peoples of the World*, "An Introduction to Cultural Policies" (Special Issue), Paris, 1983.

UNESCO, *Domination or Sharing? Endogenous Development and the Transfer of Knowledge* Paris, 1981.

UNESCO, *Draft Medium-Term Plan (1984–1989)*, General Conference, Fourth Extraordinary Session, Paris, 1982 (4XC/4).

UNESCO, *Educational Documentation and Information*, Bulletin of the International Bureau of Education No. 215, Paris, 1980.

UNESCO, "Intergovernmental Council of the International Programme for the Development of Communication," Second Session, Acapulco, 18–25 January 1982, *Final Report*, Paris.

UNESCO, "Intergovernmental Council of the International Programme for the Development of Communication (IPDC)," Third Session, Paris, 13–20 December 1982.

UNESCO, "International Commission for the Study of Communication Problems: Final Report," Paris, 1980.

UNESCO, *List of Documents and Publications in the Field of Mass Communication 1981*, Paris: 1982 (COM/82fWS/15).

UNESCO, "Meeting of the Coordinating Committee: News Agencies Pool of Non-aligned Countries," 6th, New Delhi, 1981 (MC/1371/81).

UNESCO, *Moving Toward Change* (Some Thoughts on the New International Order), Paris, 1976.

UNESCO, *The Multinational Exchange of Educational Audio-Visual Material*, Paris, 1980.

UNESCO, Reports and Papers on Mass Communication (series), Paris, UNESCO:

*The Right to Communicate: A Status Report*, No. 94 (1981).

*News Dependence*, No. 93 (1980).

*Transnational Communication and Mass Media Industries*, No. 92 (1980).

*The Site Experience*, No. 91 (1980).

*Community Communications: The Role of Community Media in Development*, No. 90 (1979)

*The SACI/EXTERN Project in Brazil: An Analytical Case Study*, No. 89 (1979).

*Rural Journalism in Africa*, No. 88 (1979).

*Communication in the Community*, No. 87 (1979).

*Mass Media: Codes of Ethics and Councils*, No. 86 (1979).

*News Values and Principles of Cross-Cultural Communication*, No. 85 (1979)

*Mass Media: The Image, Role and Special Condition of Women*, no. 84 (1979).

*National Communication Policy Councils*, No. 83 (1979).

*The Book in Multilingual Countries*, No. 82 (1978).

*External Radio Broadcasting and International Understanding*, No. 81 (1977).

*Media Studies in Education*, No. 80 (1977)

*The Economics of Book Publishing in Developing Countries*, No. 79 (1977).

*Planning for Satellite Broadcasting*, No. 78 (1976).

*Cross-Cultural Broadcasting*, No. 77 (1976).

*Towards Realistic Communication Policies*, No. 76 (1976).

*Technology and Access Communications Media*, No. 75 (1975).

*National Communication Systems: Some Policy Issues and Options*, No. 74 (1975).

*Training for Mass Communication*, No. 72 (1975).

*Promoting the Reading Habit*, No. 73 (1975).

*Television Traffic – A One-Way Street*, No. 70 (1974).

*Mass Media in an African Context*, No. 69 (1973).

*The Practice of Mass Communication: Some Lessons from Research*, No. 65 (1972).

*Mass Media in a Violent World*, No. 63 (1971).

*Mass Media in Society: The Need of Research*, No. 59 (1970).

UNESCO, *Statistical Yearbook*, Paris, 1981.

UNESCO, *World Communication Report* (Paris: Unesco Press, 1989).

UNESCO, *World Communication Report* (Paris: Unesco Press, 1992).

United Nations, *The Impact of Multinational Corporations on Development and International Relations* (New York: United Nations, 1974).

United Nations, "Preparation of an International Convention on Principles Governing the Use by States of Artificial Earth Satellites for Direct Television Broadcasting," General Assembly Resolution 2727 (XXVI), Annex, A/37/646, New York, 1982.

United Nations, *World Media Handbook* (New York: United Nations, 1995).

United Nations Centre on Transnational Corporations (UNCTC), *Transnational Corporations in World Development, Reexamined*, 1978, E/C. 10/38, Sales number 78, Annex 1.

United Nations Centre on Transnational Corporations (UNCTC), "Transnational Corporations and Transborder Data Flow: An Overview," paper presented at the Seventh session of UN Economic and Social Council Commission on Transnational Corporations, Geneva, August 31–September 14, 1981.

US Congress, House of Representatives, "International Information Flow: Forging a New Framework," Washington, DC: US Government Printing Office, 1980.

US Congress, House of Representatives, Committee on Government Operations, Subcommittee of Government Information and Individual Rights, "Hearings on International Broadcasting: Direct Broadcast Satellite" (Washington, DC: US Government Printing Office, 1981).

US Congress, House of Representatives, Subcommittees on International Operations and on Human Rights and International Organizations of the Committee on Foreign Affairs, "Review of the US: Participation in UNESCO" (Washington, DC: US Government Printing Office, 1982).

US Congress, Senate, Committee on Commerce, Science and Transportation. "International Telecommunications Act of 1982" (Washington, DC: US Government Printing Office, 1982).

US Department of Commerce, International Trade Administration, *An Assessment of U.S. Competitiveness in High Technology Industries* (Washington, DC, 1983).

US Department of State, *International Aspects of Communication and Information* (Washington, DC, 1982).

Van Dinh, Tran, *Independence, Liberation, Revolution: An Approach to the Understanding of the Third World* (Norwood, NJ: Ablex Publishing Corporation, 1983).

Waldrop, M. Mitchell, "Imaging the Earth (1): The First Decade of Landsat," *Science*, 215: 4540 (March 1982), pp. 1600–1603.

Waldrop, M. Mitchell, "What Price Privatizing Landsat?" *Science*, 219: 4585 (February 1983), pp. 752–754.

Wallerstein, Immanuel, *The Modern World-System*, Vols I and II. (New York: Academic Press, 1974 and 1980).

Weaver, David H., *Videotex Journalism: Teletext, Viewdata, and the News* (Hillsdale, NJ: Lawrence Erlbaum Associates, 1983).

White, Ralph K., *Nobody Wanted War* (Garden City, NY: Doubleday, 1970).

Wiener, Norbert, *The Human Use of Human Beings: Cybernetics and Society* (New York: Avon Books, 1967).

William, Raymond, *Television: Technology and Cultural Form* (London: Fontana/Collins, 1974).

Wilson, Laurie J. and Ibrahim Al-Muhanna, "The Political Economy of Information: Transborder Data Flows," *Journal of Peace Research*, 22: 4 (1985), pp. 289–301.

Woodward, Kathleen, *The Myths of Information: Technology and Post Industrial Culture* (Madison, WI: Coda Press, 1980).

Woolfe, Roger, *Videotex: The New Television/Telephone Information Services* (London: Heyden, 1980).

Yonah, Alexander, *The Role of Communications in the Middle East Conflict* (New York: Praeger, 1973).

# Index